Taking Blender to the Next Level

Implement advanced workflows such as geometry nodes, simulations, and motion tracking for Blender production pipelines

Ruan Lotter

BIRMINGHAM—MUMBAI

Taking Blender to the Next Level

Copyright © 2022 Packt Publishing

Group Product Manager: Rohit Rajkumar
Publishing Product Manager: Vaideeshwari Muralikrishnan
Senior Editor: Keagan Carneiro
Content Development Editor: Abhishek Jadhav
Technical Editor: Shubham Sharma
Copy Editor: Safis Editing
Project Coordinator: Rashika Ba
Proofreader: Safis Editing
Indexer: Rekha Nair
Production Designer: Aparna Bhagat
Marketing Coordinator: Elizabeth Varghese

First published: May 2022

Production reference: 1290422

Published by Packt Publishing Ltd.
Livery Place
35 Livery Street
Birmingham
B3 2PB, UK.

ISBN 978-1-80323-356-7

www.packt.com

I would like to take a moment to thank everyone who supported me during the writing process of this book. I want to dedicate this book to my mother, Ronel, who is the number one reason I'm doing what I'm doing today. She bought my first computer when I was about 8 years old and she always allowed me to spend my younger days tinkering at the computer, day and night, which changed my life forever! Thanks Mom, I love you lots! I also want to thank everyone who has motivated me constantly and given me the confidence that I can do this! And a huge thanks to all the Blender developers for creating this amazing free application! You are the best!

Ruan Lotter

Contributors

About the author

Ruan Lotter is a 3D generalist and visual effects (VFX) artist specializing in motion graphics, compositing, 3D tracking, and 3D simulations. He currently works as a VFX artist and compositor in the advertising industry and also teaches multiple 3D and VFX-related classes online. He also created the YouTube channel, TunnelvizionTV where he shares tutorials on multiple creative topics.

About the reviewer

Everton Velho is a Brazilian 3D artist focused on Environment Art for games. He is passionate about games, music, movies, and cats. He graduated in Information Technology and Animation Design, combining creativity with the technical aspects.

Table of Contents

2

Creating a Motion Graphics Scene Using Geometry Nodes

3

Organic Modeling P1: Creating a Mushroom

4

Organic Modeling P2: Creating the Landscape around the Mushroom

5

PBR Materials: Texturing our Mushroom Scene

6

3D Scanning and Photogrammetry: Creating Your Own 3D Scans

7
Modeling an Alien Cartoon Character

8
Rigging and Animating Your 3D Cartoon Character

Part 2: Let's Do Some Physics

9
Rigid Body Simulation: Destroying a Statue Using Physics

10

Dynamic Cloth Simulations

11

Creating Dynamic Hair Using Particles

Part 3: Match Moving and Compositing

12

Matching Blender's Camera Movement to Live Action Footage

13

Compositing the Alien Cartoon Character onto the Live Action Footage

14

The Final Render

Index

Other Books You May Enjoy

Preface

If you're ready to start exploring the more advanced workflows and processes in Blender to create intricate 3D models, then Taking Blender to the Next Level is for you.

This book focuses on a few different VFX-related workflows such as geometry nodes, organic modeling, 3D camera tracking, photogrammetry, sculpting, compositing, and physics simulations. You'll learn how to use geometry nodes to create dynamic motion graphic scenes as well as perform 3D scanning of real-world objects using photogrammetry. You'll also find out how to model, rig, and animate your own 3D characters from scratch. Next, you'll progress to using simulations to break objects apart and then use cloth and hair simulations to add realism to your 3D creations. Finally, you'll go over the final render settings and export your 3D animation masterpiece as a video.

By the end of this Blender book, you'll be able to model your own 3D characters, objects, and landscapes; rig, animate, and texture your characters; 3D track live-action footage; and composite your 3D characters into live-action scenes.

Who this book is for

This Blender 3D book is for 3D modelers, texture artists, character animators, technical animators, match-moving artists, compositors and anyone interested in learning about advanced concepts in Blender. Motion graphics artists will also benefit from this book. Readers are expected to have a very basic understanding of 3D concepts and the Blender UI.

What this book covers

Chapter 1, Using Geometry Nodes to Create Dynamic Scenes, focuses on creating interesting and dynamic scenes.

Chapter 2, Creating a Motion Graphics Scene Using Geometry Nodes, uses Geometry Nodes to create a motion graphics scene that you can easily modify using different nodes.

Chapter 3, Organic Modeling P1: Creating a Mushroom, focuses on modeling an organic Mushroom, using tools such as Sculpting, Proportional Editing, and Lattice.

Chapter 4, Organic Modeling P2: Creating the Landscape around the Mushroom, deals with creating the landscape and grass around the mushroom using tools such as Proportional Editing and Geometry Nodes.

Chapter 5, PBR Materials: Texturing our Mushroom Scene, teaches you how to add color to our scene using the Shader Editor node system to create realistic and customizable materials.

Chapter 6, 3D Scanning and Photogrammetry: Creating Your Own 3D Scans, deals with creating 3D scans of almost any object using a camera, Meshroom, and Blender.

Chapter 7, Modeling an Alien Cartoon Character, teaches you how to create a cartoon character from scratch using your own reference images.

Chapter 8, Rigging and Animating Your 3D Cartoon Character, helps you understand how to rig your character using the Rigify add-on as well as animate a walk cycle.

Chapter 9, Rigid Body Simulation: Destroying a Statue Using Physics, teaches you how to destroy a statue dynamically using Cell Fracture and Rigid Body Simulations.

Chapter 10, Dynamic Cloth Simulations, assists in creating clothing for your characters using cloth simulations that interact with physics and forces.

Chapter 11, Creating Hair Using Particles, helps in creating hair for your character using particles, that interact with physics and forces, while also adding custom hair materials to create amazing-looking hair styles.

Chapter 12, Matching Blender's Camera Movement to Live Action Footage, helps you understand how to import footage and track the real-world camera to create a virtual camera that matches the real-world camera's movement.

Chapter 13, Compositing the Alien Cartoon Character onto the Live Action Footage, deals with compositing our cartoon character into the live-action footage and using the compositing nodes to enhance the look of our final shot.

Chapter 14, The Final Render, focusses on rendering the final animation to an image sequence and converting the image sequence into an MP4 that you can share easily.

To get the most out of this book

You only need a copy of Blender 2.93.x to follow along – a basic understanding of Blender is recommended but not mandatory.

Software/hardware covered in the book	Operating system requirements
Blender 2.93.x `https://www.blender.org/download/lts/2-93/`	Windows, macOS, or Linux
Meshroom 2021	Windows or Linux

For *Chapter 6, 3D Scanning and Photogrammetry: Creating Your Own 3D Scans*, you will need a free copy of Meshroom 2021 which is only available on Windows and Linux.

All the projects in this book have been created and built on Blender 2.93.x. The projects should work perfectly fine with Blender 3.x versions too. There may obviously be slight changes going forward as they develop Blender 3, but most of the changes they usually do are minor and should not break any workflows. However, the Geometry nodes chapters will work strictly on versions 2.93.x, since these nodes are updated with every version change. Version 2.93 has Long Term Support (LTS) till 2023 and you can download it from here. `https://www.blender.org/download/lts/2-93/`

If you are using the digital version of this book, we advise you to type the code yourself or access the code from the book's GitHub repository (a link is available in the next section). Doing so will help you avoid any potential errors related to the copying and pasting of code.

Download the example files

You can download the example files for this book from GitHub at `https://github.com/PacktPublishing/Taking-Blender-to-the-Next-Level`. If there's an update to the code, it will be updated in the GitHub repository.

We also have other code bundles from our rich catalog of books and videos available at `https://github.com/PacktPublishing/`. Check them out!

Download the color images

We also provide a PDF file that has color images of the screenshots and diagrams used in this book. You can download it here: `https://static.packt-cdn.com/downloads/9781803233567_ColorImages.pdf`.

Conventions used

There are a number of text conventions used throughout this book.

`Code in text`: Indicates code words in text, database table names, folder names, filenames, file extensions, pathnames, dummy URLs, user input, and Twitter handles. Here is an example: "You can also name your texture here – let's call it `MyTexture`."

Bold: Indicates a new term, an important word, or words that you see onscreen. For instance, words in menus or dialog boxes appear in **bold**. Here is an example: "Click on **File** and select **New | General**."

> **Tips or important notes**
> Appear like this.

Get in touch

Feedback from our readers is always welcome.

General feedback: If you have questions about any aspect of this book, email us at customercare@packtpub.com and mention the book title in the subject of your message.

Errata: Although we have taken every care to ensure the accuracy of our content, mistakes do happen. If you have found a mistake in this book, we would be grateful if you would report this to us. Please visit www.packtpub.com/support/errata and fill in the form.

Piracy: If you come across any illegal copies of our works in any form on the internet, we would be grateful if you would provide us with the location address or website name. Please contact us at copyright@packt.com with a link to the material.

If you are interested in becoming an author: If there is a topic that you have expertise in and you are interested in either writing or contributing to a book, please visit authors.packtpub.com.

Share Your Thoughts

Once you've read *Taking Blender to the Next Level*, we'd love to hear your thoughts! Scan the QR code below to go straight to the Amazon review page for this book and share your feedback.

https://www.amazon.in/review/create-review/error?asin=1803233567&

Your review is important to us and the tech community and will help us make sure we're delivering excellent quality content.

Part 1: Modeling, Materials, and Animation Workflows

In the first part of this book, we will be looking at some advanced ways to create geometry such as using Geometry Nodes, Sculpting, 3D Scanning and organic 3D modeling. We will also be focusing on creating advanced materials to make your scenes look amazing!

We will cover the following chapters in this section:

- *Chapter 1, Using Geometry Nodes to Create Dynamic Scenes*
- *Chapter 2, Creating a Motion Graphics Scene Using Geometry Nodes*
- *Chapter 3, Organic Modeling P1: Creating a Mushroom*
- *Chapter 4, Organic Modeling P2: Creating the Landscape around the Mushroom*
- *Chapter 5, PBR Materials: Texturing our Mushroom Scene*
- *Chapter 6, 3D Scanning and Photogrammetry: Creating Your Own 3D Scans*
- *Chapter 7, Modeling an Alien Cartoon Character*
- *Chapter 8, Rigging and Animating Your 3D Cartoon Character*

1
Using Geometry Nodes to Create Dynamic Scenes

Geometry Nodes is one of the latest additions to the ever-evolving world of Blender and is one extremely powerful tool. It allows you to create and change an object's geometry in more complex ways than regular modifiers, and it allows you to create complex scenes quickly and in non-destructive ways, meaning you can always go back and tweak some of the parameters, making it extremely dynamic and versatile. Welcome to the exciting world of Geometry Nodes!

One thing to note is that Geometry Nodes is still being developed extensively by the developers of Blender, which means that new nodes will be added, and more workflow options will be available to you, making it one of the most exciting new features to come to the Blender toolset.

In this chapter, you will learn how to use some of the most popular nodes, and you will get a feel of what you can do using Geometry Nodes. You will learn how to distribute objects on points, using Math nodes to calculate attributes such as the distance between objects, as well as how to modify certain attributes such as scale, position, and rotation. Additionally, you will learn how to randomize certain attributes, which is important when creating dynamic motion graphics scenes.

This chapter will give you a good, but basic, understanding of Geometry Nodes, and later in this book, we will make use of other methods that will build on this chapter.

In this chapter, we're going to cover the following main topics:

- Introduction to Geometry Nodes in Blender
- Creating and manipulating geometry using nodes
- Using textures to control attributes
- Animating with Math nodes

> **Technical Requirements**
>
> All the projects in this book have been created and built on Blender 2.93.x. The projects should work perfectly fine with Blender 3.x versions too. There may obviously be slight changes going forward as they develop Blender 3, but most of the changes they usually do are minor and should not break any workflows. However, the Geometry nodes chapters will work strictly on versions 2.93.x, since these nodes are updated with every version change. Version 2.93 has Long Term Support (LTS) till 2023 and you can download it from here. `https://www.blender.org/download/lts/2-93/`
>
> All the projects of this book have been uploaded on Github here: `https://github.com/PacktPublishing/Taking-Blender-to-the-Next-Level`

Introduction to Geometry Nodes in Blender

In this section, we will be looking at the Geometry Nodes workspace and how to apply the Geometry Nodes modifier to our base mesh. Additionally, we will take a quick look at the different nodes that are currently available in Blender. You will learn how to distribute an instance object across points on another object. Additionally, we will make use of some of the most used nodes such as the **Point Instance** node and the **Subdivide** node. You will also learn what attributes are and how you can use them to change the way your instance objects are displayed. Finally, we will use nodes to randomize different attributes of our instance objects such as the position, rotation, and scale.

The Geometry Nodes workspace

Geometry Nodes functions as a basic modifier, but it also has its own workspace and editor. If you look at the top of the Blender interface, you should see a tab called **Geometry Nodes**. Additionally, you can change any window in Blender to the Geometry Nodes workspace by clicking on the drop-down menu in the upper-left corner of the window and selecting **Geometry Node Editor** from the list of available workspaces. This means you always have control over how you work:

Figure 1.1 – The Geometry Node Editor

If you look at the workspace, you will see the 3D Viewport window in the upper-right corner, the Spreadsheet window in the upper-left corner, and the Geometry Nodes window at the bottom. Currently, there is a total of 63 nodes in Blender version 2.93.2, but this number will quickly grow in later versions of Blender:

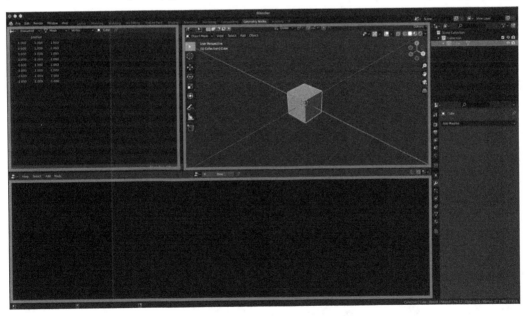

Figure 1.2 – The Geometry Nodes workspace

One area that Blender has been lacking in for a while now is in the creation of MoGraph dynamically; Geometry Nodes changes that completely by turning Blender into a powerful **MoGraph**-making machine! The reason why Geometry Nodes is perfect for MoGraph is that you can quickly manipulate many objects at once and because of its non-destructive nature. Additionally, you can introduce textures to drive movement or even use other modifiers in conjunction with Geometry Nodes.

Another great use for Geometry Nodes is for scattering objects quickly and easily. In previous versions of Blender, we had to make use of a particle or hair system to scatter objects across geometry, and that only gave us a certain amount of control. However, with Geometry Nodes, we have complete control to customize our node tree exactly the way we want.

You can even expose some of the parameters and values directly in the **Modifier** panel, making it very easy to customize your Geometry Nodes creations or giving you the ability to build custom node setups to share with others.

Geometry Nodes

As mentioned earlier, there are currently 63 available nodes to use (including the Frame and Reroute nodes), as shown in the following screenshot. This number will likely increase with later versions:

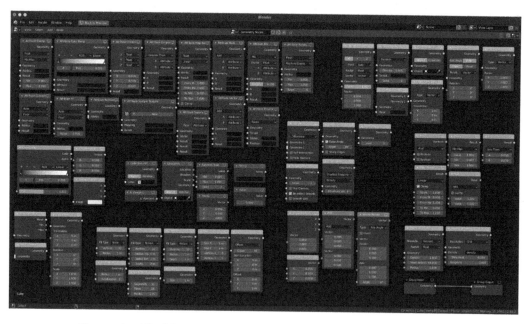

Figure 1.3 – All of the Geometry Nodes currently available in Blender 2.93.2

If you have used the Compositing or Shading workspaces before, then you should be familiar with using nodes. However, don't fear if this is your first time using nodes. It can be very daunting at first, but we will look at the process step by step, and in no time, you will be able to create amazing and dynamic scenes using Geometry Nodes. In the next section, we will create our first, very basic node setup, and see it in action!

Creating and manipulating geometry using nodes

In this section, we will be creating our very first basic scene using Geometry Nodes. You will learn how to add the Geometry Nodes modifier to your base mesh and how to instance an object onto each vertex of your base mesh. We will look at some of the nodes that you can use to manipulate these instances such as **Position, Scale**, and **Rotation**. Additionally, you will learn how to randomize certain attributes, and we will also take a look at the different types of attributes and how they are used.

Let's begin by creating a new Blender project.

Creating the base mesh

Let's begin by creating our base mesh. For this example, we will be creating a plane object and applying the Geometry Nodes modifier to it. Then, we will use this plane object to distribute instances of another object across it:

1. Click on **File** and select **New | General**.
2. Delete everything in your scene by pressing *A* and then pressing *X*. Click on **Delete** to confirm. You now should have a blank new scene. Now feel free to save your project!
3. Create a plane by pressing *Shift + A* and selecting **Mesh | Plane**.

    Now, let's scale our plane.

4. Select the plane, press *S*, then *10*, and then *Enter*. This will scale your plane to a size of 10 m x 10 m. It's always good practice to select **Apply your scale** whenever you modify the scale of an object in Blender, especially if you will be adding any modifiers to that mesh.

5. To do this, select the plane, press *Ctrl + A*, and then select **Scale** from the drop-down menu. This will apply the scale factor and reset the object's scale to **1**:

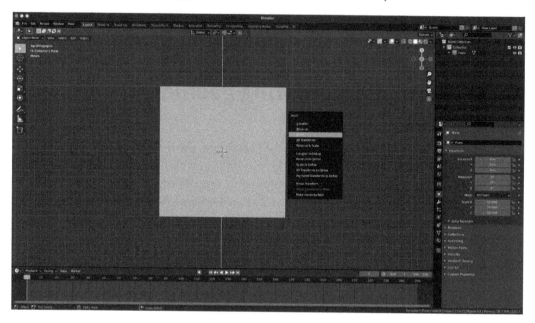

Figure 1.4 – Applying the scale to your plane

6. You can view the scale factor by selecting your plane and pressing the *N* shortcut to open the side menu. In the Item tab, underneath Transform, you will see the **Scale** factor, which should currently be **X: 1.000/Y: 1.000/Z: 1.000**:

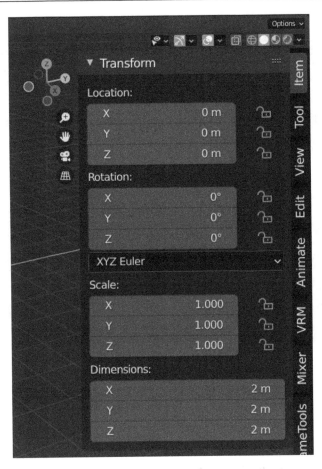

Figure 1.5 – The scale of the plane set to 1/1/1

Creating a new Geometry Nodes modifier

Now, let's open the Geometry Nodes workspace by clicking on the tab at the top of the **Geometry Nodes** interface. You will now see the Geometry Nodes workspace split into three main views: the 3D Viewport window (in the upper-right corner), the **Spreadsheet** window (in the upper-left corner), and the **Geometry Node Editor** window at the bottom. Perform the following steps:

1.   To create our first Geometry Nodes system, let's click on our plane to select it.

2. Click on the **NEW** button at the top of the Geometry Node Editor:

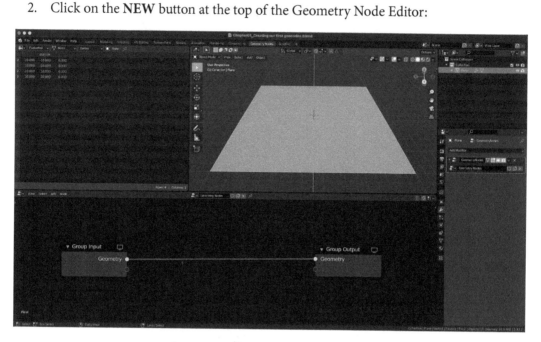

Figure 1.6 – The Geometry Node Editor

Congratulations! You have created your first Geometry Nodes setup! You will see two nodes that have been added automatically: the **Group Input** node and the **Group Output** node.

It's important to note that your data will always flow from the **Group Input** node on the left-hand side to the **Group Output** node on the right-hand side. Everything between these two nodes will modify our geometry.

Creating our instance object

Before we start adding any nodes to our node setup, we need something to use as our instance object. So, let's create a mesh that we can use:

1. With your mouse pointer over the 3D Viewport window (in the upper-right corner), press *Shift* + *A* and select **Mesh | Icosphere**.

2. Select the Icosphere instance in the 3D Viewport window, press *G*, and then press *X* to move it along the *X* axis away from the plane.

In the next section, we will use this Icosphere node as an instance object.

Creating our first nodes

Let's begin adding some nodes! In this section, we will look at how you can add new nodes to the node tree and how to distribute your instance object across your base mesh:

1. Click on the plane object in the 3D Viewport window to select it.

   With your Icosphere instance out of the way and your plane selected, you should now see two nodes in the Geometry Node Editor. If you don't see any nodes, make sure that the **Geometry Nodes** modifier is selected or has been highlighted in the modifiers panel on the right-hand side:

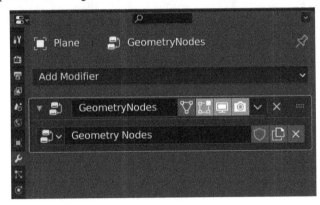

Figure 1.7 – The Geometry Nodes modifier

2. With your mouse pointer over the Geometry Node Editor window, press *Shift + A* to access the **Node Add** menu.

3. Hover over the **Point** category and click on **Point Instance** to create your first node.

4. Click anywhere to place your node.

5. Now, let's drag our new node onto the line that connects the **Group Input** node and the **Group Output** node.

6. Additionally, you can zoom in and out by scrolling the mouse wheel and pan by holding down the mouse wheel.

7. Move your **Point Instance** node closer to the **Group Output** node as we will be adding new nodes, mainly between the **Group Input** node and the **Point Instance** node, in this example:

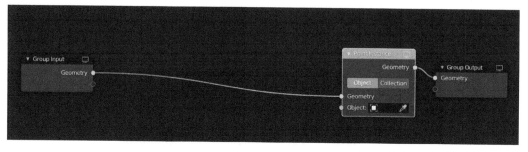

Figure 1.8 – Your node tree should now look like this

Nodes that change attributes should almost always be placed before the **Point Instance** node, as the points are not referenced after this node.

Specifying the instance object

Note that your plane object has disappeared in the 3D Viewport window! The reason for this is that we have not yet specified an instance object for our **Point Instance** node.

Let's do this now:

1. Click on the **Object** drop-down menu on the **Point Instance** node to select the Icosphere mesh object that we created from the list earlier:

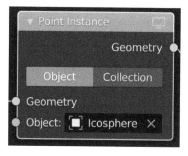

Figure 1.9 – The Point Instance node

2. You can also click on the eyedropper icon and select the Icosphere object that way.

Now, let's take a look at what has happened in the 3D Viewport window:

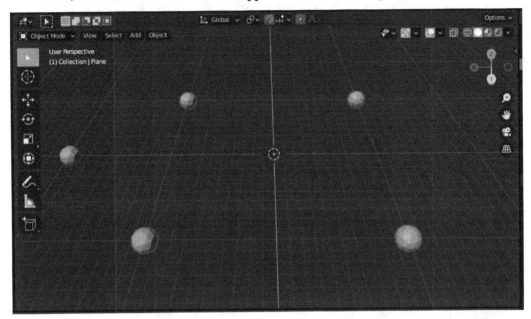

Figure 1.10 – Instances are placed on each vertex of the plane

As you can see, we now have four Icosphere instances. Ignore the original Icosphere instance that we moved off to the side – you can even hide it if you want. The reason we see four Icosphere instances is that our plane has four vertices. It's creating an instance on each vertex. Let's increase the number of vertices by subdividing our plane. We can do this right inside the Geometry Node Editor as there is a **Subdivide** node that we can use.

The Subdivide node

The **Subdivide** node will increase the number of points or vertices on our base mesh. Let's examine how we can use it in our scene:

1. Press *Shift + A* to access the **Add** menu, point to the **Mesh** category, and click on the **Subdivide** node.

2. Move the node and place it on the line just right of the **Group Input** node:

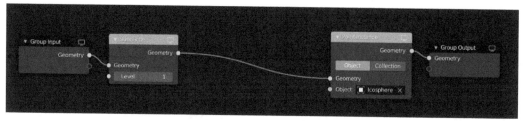

Figure 1.11 – Your node tree should now look like this

Notice that you now have nine Icospheres in your scene. The reason for this is that our plane now has nine vertices because of the **Level 1 Subdivide** node.

3. Change the subdivision **Level** value to 3. Now you should see a total of 81 Icospheres because we have increased the number of vertices on our plane to 81:

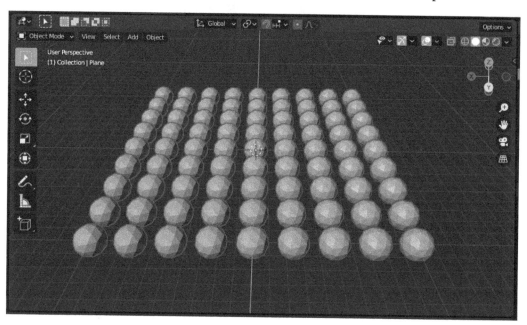

Figure 1.12 – Increasing the number of vertices will increase the number of instance objects

The Point Scale node

Now, let's change the scale of our Icospheres – there is a node for that, too! Let's add a **Point Scale** node:

1. Press *Shift + A* and select **Point | Point Scale**.

2. Slot it in right after our **Subdivide** node:

Figure 1.13 – Your node tree should now look like this

Additionally, you can search for nodes without needing to know where to find them. When you press *Shift + A* to bring up the nodes menu, click on the **Search** option at the top and type in the name of the node you are looking for.

Notice that on the **Point Scale** node, you have access to three different numbers: *X, Y,* and *Z*. This is called a **vector** as it's a set of three numbers. Change one of the numbers by clicking on it and dragging sideways. You will see how the scale of your Icospheres changes according to the axis you scale on. Let's change the **Type** setting from **Vector** to **Float**.

3. Click on the drop-down menu next to **Type** and select **Float** from the list. Now you only have one number to change, which will scale your Icospheres uniformly.

4. Click and drag the **Factor** value to adjust the size of the instance. For now, set it to any size you like.

We have now set the scale of our instance objects using the **Point Scale** node. In the next section, we will look at the different types of attributes available in Geometry Nodes.

Different types of attributes

Let's take a moment to look at the different types of attributes and data types that you will see:

*   **Integer**: An integer is a number that can be written without a fractional component.

*   **Float**: A float is a floating-point number, which means it is a number that has a decimal place.

- **Vector**: A vector is a set of three float numbers and is mostly used to calculate a position in world space.

- **Boolean**: A Boolean only has two values and can be used for something that's either `true` or `false`.

- **Attribute**: This is a text field to input an attribute name.

The most commonly used attributes are **Position, Scale**, and **Rotation** (these are all vector-based as they consist of three numbers, which each correspond to the three axes of *X*, *Y*, and *Z*). However, there are also a few others that we will look at in later chapters.

The Point Rotate node

Let's look at how we can rotate our objects. To do this, we will need a new node called **Point Rotate**. Let's add it to our tree:

1. Press *Shift + A* and select **Point | Point Rotate** (or you can use the search function).

2. Add this node to the right-hand side of the **Point Scale** node:

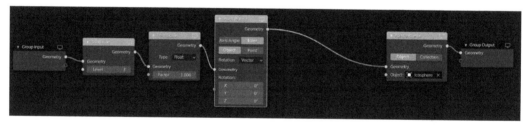

Figure 1.14 – Your node tree should now look like this

You will see that the **Point Rotate** node uses a **Vector** data type because you can rotate using the different *X*, *Y*, and *Z* axes.

Click and drag the values next to the different axes to see how your Icospheres rotate in your scene. Please note that the difference between **Object** and **Point** is that **Object** will rotate every point in the local space of the object, while **Point** will rotate every point in its local space as specified by its Rotation attribute.

The Point Translate node

Next, let's take a look at how to change the position of our objects. For this, we need the **Point Translate** node. Let's add it now after our **Point Rotate** node:

1. Press *Shift + A* and select **Point | Point Translate** or use the search function. Again, you will see that it uses a vector as we can translate in either *X*, *Y*, or *Z*.

2. Drag the values next to **X**, **Y**, and **Z** to see all of your Icospheres moving along that axis:

Figure 1.15 – Your node tree now looks like this

The Attribute Randomize node

Our scene still looks very uniform and a bit boring; however, Geometry Nodes allows you to easily randomize your attributes! Let's see how we can randomize the **Scale** attribute of our Icospheres. For this, we will need a node called **Attribute Randomize**.

Let's add it now:

1. Press *Shift + A* and select **Attribute | Attribute Randomize** to add the node.
2. Place it on the right-hand side of the **Point Translate** node:

Figure 1.16 – The Attribute Randomize node

This node is slightly more complex, as we can choose which attribute it will randomize and how it will influence the current attribute values.

Let's examine how we can randomize the **Scale** attribute.

Randomizing the Scale attribute

We can use the **Attribute Randomize** node to randomize different attributes. Let's see how we can randomize the *Scale* attribute of our instance objects:

1. Click on the empty box next to **Attribute**. You will see a list of available attributes that we can use.

2. Select **Scale** from the list. Instantly, you will see that all of your Icospheres now have different sizes! Additionally, you can type in the attribute name in the empty box. However, note that the attribute names are case sensitive, so be aware of this when typing in an attribute name rather than selecting it from the drop-down list.

3. The **Min** and **Max** float numbers determine the range of randomness. Change these numbers to see how they affect your scene. (**Tip**: Hold *Shift* while dragging these values to have more accurate control.)

    The default data type value is set to **Float**, which means we use one number for all three axes, which will result in a uniform scale.

4. Change this to **Vector** by clicking on the drop-down list at the top of the node and selecting **Vector**:

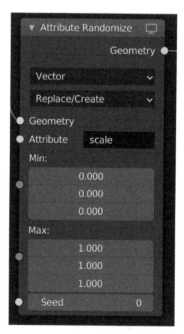

Figure 1.17 – The Attribute Randomize node

Now we have much more control over how our instances will be scaled. We can adjust the minimum and maximum values for all three *X*, *Y*, and *Z* axes.

5. Adjust the three values under **Min** and **Max** to see how this affects your scene and how the scaling is no longer uniform by adjusting these values:

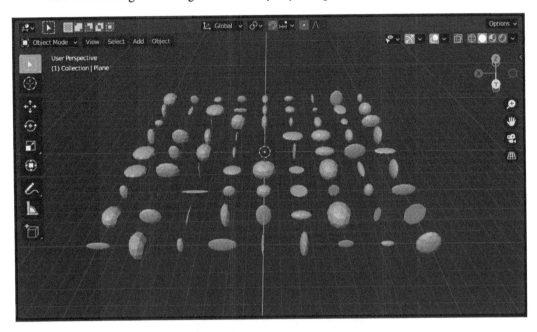

Figure 1.18 – The 3D Viewport window showing non-uniform scaling because of the vector

6. This might be the desired effect you are going for, but let's change the data type back to **Float** so that we're scaling our instance uniformly.

7. Set the **Min** value to 0 and the **Max** value to 1. Notice that some of the Icospheres are not being displayed or might be very tiny. This is because we're using the **Replace/Create** operator, which means we're choosing a value between 0 and 1 and replacing the current **Scale** attribute with this new number. Note this value can be 0, which will result in some Icospheres with a scale of 0, making them *disappear*.

8. Change the operator setting from **Replace/Create** to **Add**.

    Now we are adding our random value to the current **Scale** attribute, which will not result in Icospheres with a scale of 0. Other operators you can use are **Multiply** and **Subtract**, which work in a similar way to the **Add** operator.

Randomizing the Position attribute

Let's randomize the position of our Icospheres!

This time, we're going to duplicate our **Attribute Randomize** node and reuse it for the **Position** attribute:

1. Click the current **Attribute Randomize** node to select it.
2. Press *Shift + D* to create a duplicate copy.
3. Drag the new copy to the right-hand side of the current **Attribute Randomize** node:

Figure 1.19 – The Attribute Randomize node

Let's configure the node as follows:

1. Change the data type to **Vector**. The reason for this is that we want to randomize the X, Y, and Z positions for each instance.
2. Set the **Operator** setting to **Add**.

3. Select the **position** attribute from the **Attribute** drop-down box, or you can simply type position into the box. Please note that attribute names are case sensitive:

Figure 1.20 – Your node tree should now look like this

4. Set your **Min** value to -10 and **Max** value to 10. This will randomize our Icospheres' positions from -10, -10, and -10 to 10, 10, and 10 in world space:

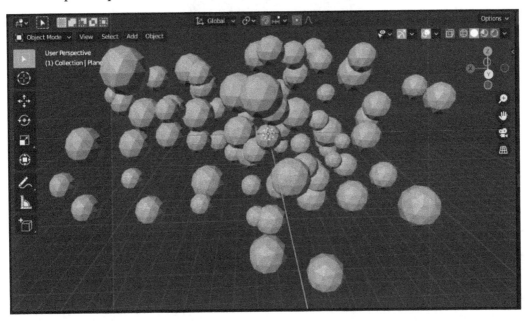

Figure 1.21 – The 3D Viewport window showing the randomized positions

Randomizing the Rotation attribute

Let's randomize the rotation of our Icospheres. For this, we will again duplicate our **Attribute Randomize** node and place it on the right-hand side of the *position* **Attribute Randomize** node:

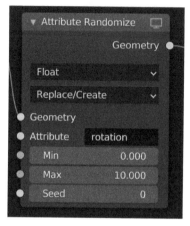

Figure 1.22 – The Attribute Randomize node

Let's configure this node as follows:

1. Change the data type to **Float**. The reason we're using a float is that we want to use one value to rotate our instance in all axes. You can use a vector to have exact control over how we rotate. However, for this example, we're going to use a float.

2. Change the **Operator** setting to **Replace/Create**.

3. Change the **Attribute** setting to **rotation**:

Figure 1.23 – Your node tree and scene should now look like this

4. Set the **Min** value to 0 and the **Max** value to 10:

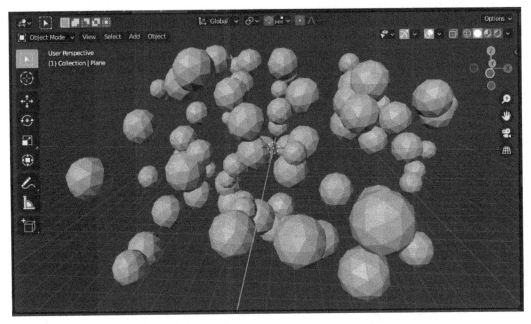

Figure 1.24 – The 3D Viewport window showing randomized rotations

Changing the instance object

It's very easy to change your instance object into something else. Let's do that now.

Start by creating a new instance object in our scene. For this, we will be adding a **Suzanne** object:

1. With your mouse pointer over the 3D Viewport window, press *Shift + A* and select **Mesh | Monkey**.

2. Move the **Suzanne** mesh to the side of our scene by pressing *G* and then pressing *X*.

3. Click on one of the Icospheres to view your Geometry Nodes.

4. Click on the **Point Instance** node to select it.

5. Click on the **Icosphere** item next to **Object** and select **Suzanne** from the drop-down list:

Figure 1.25 – The Point Instance node

Now, let's take a look at what happened in the 3D Viewport window:

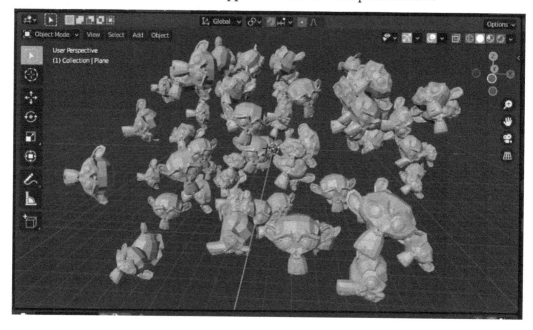

Figure 1.26 – Updated instances in the 3D Viewport window

Muting nodes

You can also mute or deactivate certain nodes to see exactly what they do. This is good practice for troubleshooting your node tree. To do this, highlight the node or nodes you want to mute and press the *M* shortcut.

Now, let's mute our three **Attribute Randomize** nodes:

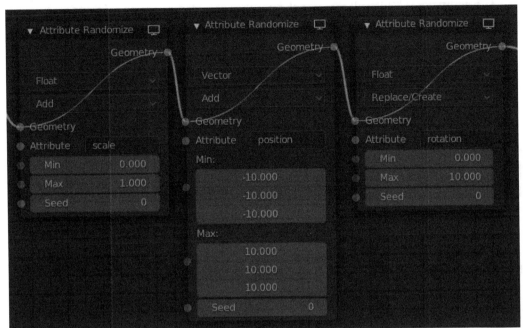

Figure 1.27 – Muting nodes by selecting them and pressing M

Observe how your scene will update instantly! You can unmute/reactivate these nodes again by selecting them all and pressing *M* again.

Congratulations! You have now created your first basic scene using Geometry Nodes. Please save your project now, as we will continue to work on it during the next section.

Using textures to control attributes

In this section, we will be using textures to manipulate attributes to create interesting and more complex scenes. You will learn how to use the **Attribute Sample Texture** node to change specific attributes using a texture map.

Let's begin by making some changes to the scene that we saved in the previous section:

1. First, let's delete all three of our **Attribute Randomize** nodes. You can highlight them all at once and press *X* to delete them. However, remember to reconnect the line between the **Point Translate** node and the **Point Instance** node. Additionally, you can also use the *Ctrl + X* shortcut when deleting nodes while keeping the connection in place.

2. Next, let's increase our level of subdivisions to 5 by adjusting the **Level** value on the Subdivide node. This will increase the number of instances we have in our scene.

3. Also, decrease the **Point Scale** factor to 0.2 to decrease the size of our **Suzanne** instances:

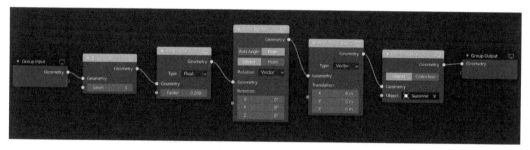

Figure 1.28 – Your node tree and scene should now look like this

Now, let's take a look at what happened in the 3D Viewport window:

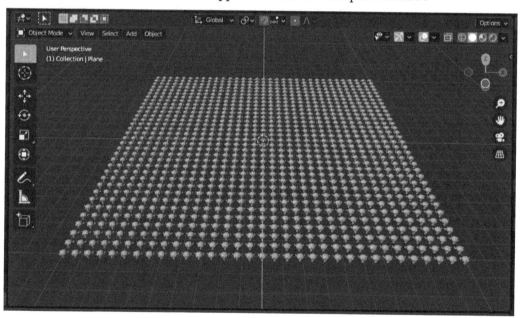

Figure 1.29 – The 3D Viewport window showing the updated scene

The Attribute Sample Texture node

Now it's time to introduce a new node called the **Attribute Sample Texture** node. This node is used to sample a texture and apply the results to an attribute such as *Rotation, Scale or Position*:

1. Add a new **Attribute Sample Texture** node to your node tree between the **Point Translate** node and the **Point Instance** node:

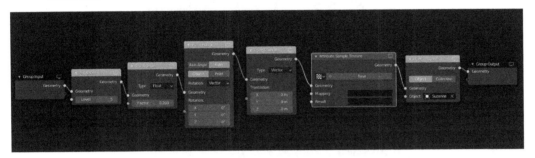

Figure 1.30 – The node tree

1. Click on **New** on the **Attribute Sample Texture** node to create a blank texture.

2. You can also name your texture here – let's call it MyTexture.

3. Click on the **Show texture in texture tab** icon on this node to open the new texture in the texture side menu:

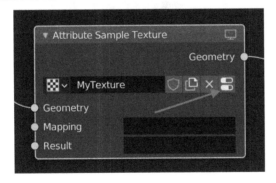

Figure 1.31 – The Attribute Sample Texture node

Your texture will now be displayed in the side menu:

Figure 1.32 – The texture side menu

4. Let's change the texture type by clicking on the drop-down list that is currently showing **Image or Movie**. For now, change this to a **Wood** texture:

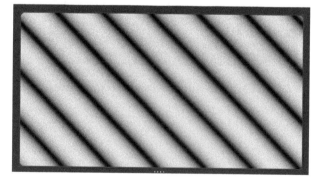

Figure 1.33 – The Wood texture

Nothing will happen yet as we still need to configure our new node. Let's do that next.

Back in the Geometry Node Editor, let's take a look at the **Attribute Sample Texture** node. It has two attribute slots that we can use. The **Mapping** attribute is used to determine where and how the texture is evaluated.

5. Click on the empty box next to **Mapping** and select **UVMap** from the list of attributes.

6. The **Result** setting can be any attribute we want to affect using the texture. So, let's choose **scale**. You can either select it from the drop-down list or type the word scale, in lowercase, and then press *Enter*:

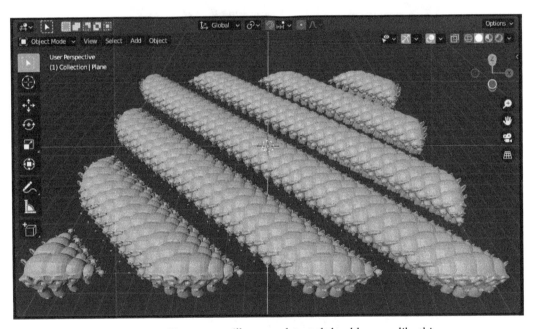

Figure 1.34 – Your scene will now update and should appear like this

Notice that our instance's scale has been updated and matches our wood texture. Where we have *black pixels*, the scale factor will be set to 0. And where we have *white pixels*, we will have a scale factor of 1. Feel free to experiment with other texture types to see how it affects your scene.

You can even load your own custom image texture by choosing **Image or Movie** as the **Type** setting and then clicking on **Open** to load your image:

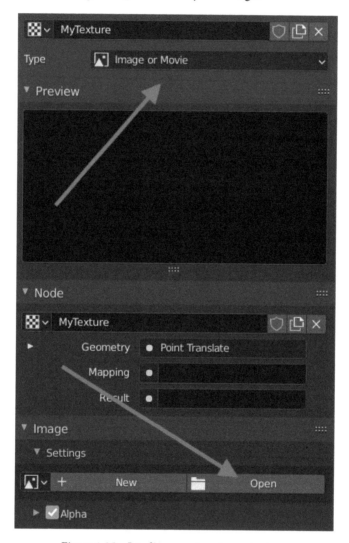

Figure 1.35 – Loading a custom image texture

Try loading a grayscale image to see how it affects the scale of your instances. The following example uses a grayscale image of the Blender logo:

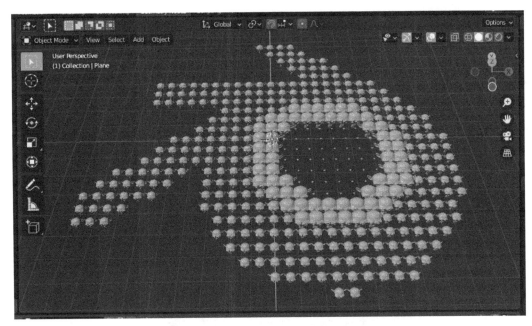

Figure 1.36 – Here is an example of using a grayscale Blender logo

For this example, I've moved the **Point Scale** node after the **Attribute Sample Texture** node and lowered the value to 0.4. The reason for placing the node here is that our **Attribute Sample Texture** node is changing our *scale* attribute. Therefore, any node before the **Attribute Sample Texture** node will not have any effect on the scale attribute. Remember that the data is flowing from left to right:

Figure 1.37 – This is what your node tree should look like to get this effect

By now, you should have a basic understanding of what Geometry Nodes is and how it can be used to create amazing patterns or scenes.

In the next section, we will look at how to add keyframes and animation to our Geometry Nodes using basic math.

Animating with Math nodes

In this section, we look at how to create interesting animations using Math nodes and other objects in your scene. We will create a basic scaling animation by using the distance value between two objects in our scene and modify the scaling attribute using some easy math. So, let's get started!

For this section, you can start with a new Blender project:

1. Delete all of the default objects by pressing *A* and then pressing *X* to confirm the deletion.

2. Create a plane object by pressing *Shift* + *A* and selecting **Mesh | Plane**.

3. Using the pop-up **Add Plane** dialog box in the lower-left corner of the 3D Viewport window, set the **Size** setting of the plane to 10 m. Click anywhere in the viewport to confirm these parameters:

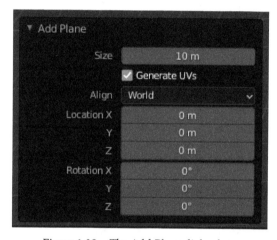

Figure 1.38 – The Add Plane dialog box

4. With the plane selected, click on the **Geometry Nodes** tab at the top of the interface.

5. Click on the **New** button to create a new Geometry Nodes modifier on the plane. You should now see the Geometry Node Editor with two default nodes, **Group Input** and **Group Output**.

6. Let's create our instance mesh. With your mouse pointer hovering over the 3D Viewport window, press *Shift + A* and select **Mesh | Torus**.

7. Scale down the torus by 50% by pressing *S* and then pressing *0.5*.

8. Move the torus out of view by pressing *G* then pressing *X*. Move the mouse until it's away from our plane object.

9. Most importantly, we need to apply the scale of this torus; otherwise, we might run into some interesting surprises later. With the torus selected, press *Ctrl + A* and click on **Scale**. Now, let's jump back into our node tree!

10. Select the plane to enable the Geometry Nodes view. Remember, if you still can't see the nodes, ensure that the **Geometry Nodes** modifier is highlighted if you have other modifiers in this object.

    Now, let's add our first nodes.

11. For node number one, we will create a **Subdivide** node. Slot it in just after the **Group Input** node.

12. Additionally, we need a **Point Instance** node to instance our mesh. Slot it right before the **Group Output** node.

13. Set your **Subdivide** node **Level** to 3.

14. Select your new **Torus** object from the drop-down list of the **Point Instance** node:

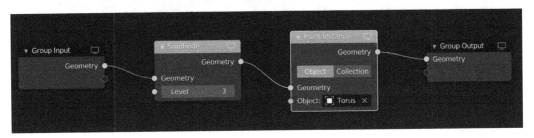

Figure 1.39 – Your node tree should now look like this

Note that you have lots of tori in your scene. Yup, I also didn't know that the plural of a torus is tori until now!

Now, let's create a new *cube* object in our scene that we will use to calculate some math later on:

1. Hover over the 3D Viewport window, press *Shift* + *A*, and select **Mesh | Cube**.

2. Move the cube to the edge of our torus instances by pressing *G* and then pressing *X*:

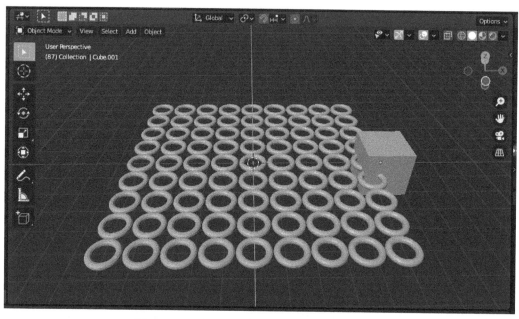

Figure 1.40 – Your scene should now look like this

3. Back in our node tree, click on one of the torus instances to view the node tree if it's not visible.

4. Add a new node, called the **Object Info** node, by pressing *Shift* + *A* and selecting **Input | Object Info** or using the search function. We are not going to connect this node to our other nodes at this moment – just place it directly beneath the **Subdivide** node. We are going to use this node to calculate the distance between our tori and the cube object.

5. On this **Object Info** node, click on the **Object** drop-down list and select the **Cube** object from the list. You can also use the eyedropper tool.

6. Then, click on the **Relative** button. This will calculate the current information of the cube and not just the original data:

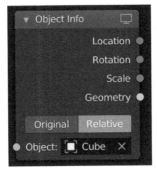

Figure 1.41 – The Object Info node

Great! You should now have enough instance objects in the scene. In the next section, we will use basic math to calculate the distance between the cube object and each of the instance objects.

The Attribute Vector Math node

Now, let's create our first Math node – the **Attribute Vector Math** node. There are a few Math nodes available, but for this specific example, we need to use the **Attribute Vector Math** node because of its **Distance** operator:

1. Press *Shift + A* and select **Attribute | Attribute Vector Math**.

2. Slot it in right after the **Subdivide** node:

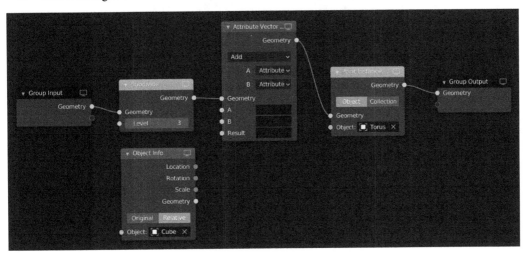

Figure 1.42 – Your node tree should now look like this

Notice that the **Object Info** node is not yet connected.

> **Important Note**
>
> One thing to bear in mind is that any node that uses an attribute is calculating that attribute for each instance in every frame.

Now, let's take a moment to look at the **Attribute Vector Math** node and how we will use it. We want to calculate the *distance* between our Cube object and *every* Torus instance object. We already have the position value of each Torus instance saved in the *position* attribute, and with our **Object Info** node (connected to our cube object), we also have the relative position of the cube. Let's see how we can calculate the distance.

3. First, let's change the operation of our **Attribute Vector Math** node from **Add** to **Distance** by clicking on the top drop-down menu on the node and selecting **Distance** from the many different operations available.

4. Then, change **B** from **Attribute** to **Vector**. The reason we're using a vector here is that the cube's position will be a type of vector for each axis:

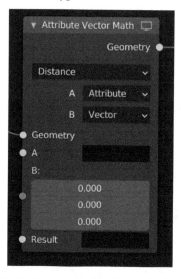

Figure 1.43 – Your node should now look like this

5. For attribute **A**, we want to use our torus positions. To do this, click on the empty box next to **A** and select **position** from the list or enter the word `position` and press *Enter*.

6. For attribute **B**, we want to use our cube's position, so let's connect our **Object Info** node's **Location** to the **Attribute Vector Math** node's **B** input.

    Now we need to save the result of this operation to an attribute. Here, we can create our new attribute by entering a new attribute name that's not in use, but an easier option would be to simply overwrite the current scale attribute with our new result. Let's do that next.

7. Click on the empty box next to **Result** and select **scale** from the list. If you don't see the **scale** attribute in the list, you can type in the word `scale` and press *Enter*:

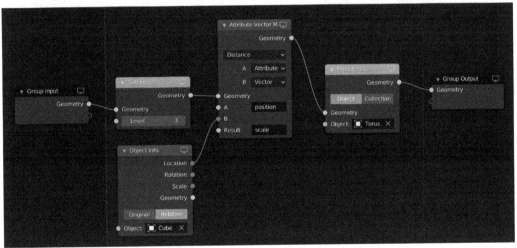

Figure 1.44 – Your node tree should now look like this

8. Looking at the 3D Viewport window, you will see that the scale of the instance objects has changed. Instances closer to the cube have a smaller scale, while instances further away from the cube have a bigger scale value. Please refer to the following screenshot:

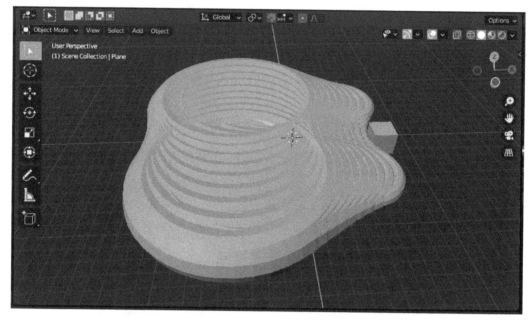

Figure 1.45 – You will see something interesting happening in the 3D Viewport window

As you can see in the 3D Viewport window, our scale factor is currently too big. We can use some more basic math to change that:

1. Add a new **Attribute Math** node and slot it in after the **Attribute Vector Math** node. Note these are different nodes – one uses vectors and the other uses float data types.

    We want to make our *scale* factor smaller, so let's use the divide operation to do this. We will perform a simple calculation to make our scale factor smaller:

    scale / value = smaller scale

2. Change the operation at the top of this node from **Add** to **Divide**. Leave **A** as **Attribute**, but let's change **B** to **Float**. This will give us access to change this value manually.

3. For **Attribute A**, select **scale** from the drop-down menu, or you can enter it manually and press *Enter* to confirm.

    For the **Result** setting, we can overwrite an existing attribute. In this example, let's overwrite the **scale** attribute. To do this, click on the empty box next to **Result** and select **scale** from the list. Again, you can enter this manually and press *Enter* to confirm.

    Your tori will disappear from the 3D Viewport window because we are now *dividing by 0*, resulting in their new scale being *0*.

4. Let's change our **B** value by clicking and dragging the **Float** value to the right-hand side – find a number that gives you good results. I chose 10.

    Let's examine our node tree:

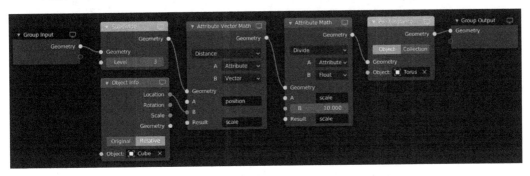

Figure 1.46 – Your node tree should now look like this

First, we are subdividing our plane into three levels. Then, we calculate the distance between our cube object and every torus in our scene by using the **Attribute Vector Math** node. We then save this distance value into our existing scale attribute, overwriting the current value. Following this, we divide our new scale attribute by **10** (the float we entered manually), resulting in a smaller scale factor.

Now, let's move our cube around the scene to see the effect in action.

5. Select your cube in the 3D Viewport window and press *G*. Then, press *Shift + Z*. This key combination will limit your cube's movement to the *X* and *Y* axes, excluding the *Z* axis. As you can see, you have created a cool-looking scaling animation. The closer the cube gets to a torus, the smaller the torus will become.

6.   Experiment by adding some position keyframes to your cube and see what you can create:

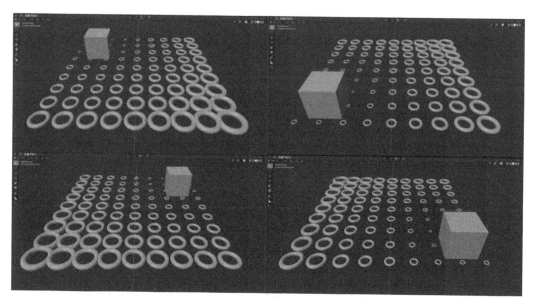

Figure 1.47 – Your first Geometry Nodes scene that animates dynamically

Using this method, you can easily create interesting and dynamic motion graphics scenes inside of Blender. Experiment with this technique and try to affect the rotation or position of your instance objects rather than their scale. Have fun creating interesting animations!

Summary

Congratulations! You should now have a basic understanding of how to create different Geometry Nodes and how to use them to change certain attributes to create dynamic effects. Now, let's use what we have learned to create something more interesting.

In the next chapter, we will create a motion graphics scene using all of the techniques we've learned so far. Additionally, we will look at how to apply materials to our instance objects!

2
Creating a Motion Graphics Scene Using Geometry Nodes

In this chapter, we're going to build an exciting motion graphics scene using mainly Geometry Nodes and some other modifiers. You will learn how to use multiple Math nodes to manipulate attributes, and we're also going to create our own attributes. Additionally, you will learn how to output certain values back into the modifiers panel. This is so you can make adjustments to your creation quickly and easily without going into the Geometry Node Editor. Let's get started.

In this chapter, we'll cover the following main topics:

- Creating a more interesting instance object
- Using an empty object to calculate the proximity between each instance
- Using proximity data to modify any attribute value

- Exposing certain values in the modifier stack by using inputs
- Adding keyframes to animate our scene
- Adding materials to our scene

Creating our base mesh and instance object

In this section, we will create our base mesh and also spend some time modeling a basic but more interesting instance object and distributing it across our base mesh using the nodes that we've looked at in *Chapter 1, Using Geometry Nodes to Create Dynamic Scenes*.

Let's start by creating a plane object, which we will use as our base mesh.

Creating the base mesh

Follow these steps to create the base mesh and apply its scale:

1. Create a new Blender project.
2. Delete all the objects in the scene by pressing *A* and then pressing *X* to confirm the deletion.
3. Click on the **Geometry Nodes** tab to enter its workspace.

   Let's begin by creating our plane – this will be the area where our objects will appear. Let's make the plane 10 m x 10 m.

4. Create a plane by pressing *Shift + A*, and then select **Mesh | Plane**.
5. Scale the plane by pressing *S* and then pressing *10*. Click anywhere to confirm the scale.
6. It's always good practice to apply the scale of your mesh. Let's do that now. With the plane selected, press *Ctrl + A* and then select **Scale**.

Creating the instance object

Before we start creating our nodes, let's create our instance object. This will be the main object that we will be using to construct the MoGraph scene. This object can also be modified later, so don't spend too much time on it:

1. Create a cube object by pressing *Shift + A* and selecting **Mesh | Cube**.
2. Move it away from our plane object by pressing *G*, then *X*, and dragging the mouse.

   Let's change the cube slightly so that we have something a bit more interesting.

3. With the cube still selected, press *Tab* to enter **Edit Mode**. Make sure you are in **Face Selection mode (3)** and then select the top and bottom faces of the cube:

Figure 2.1 – Selecting the top and bottom faces

4. With both the top and bottom faces selected, press *I* to create an inset:

Figure 2.2 – Inset at the top and bottom faces

Next, we're going to extrude both these faces at the same time by using their normals.

5. With both of these faces still selected, press *Alt + E* and select **Extrude Faces Along Normals**:

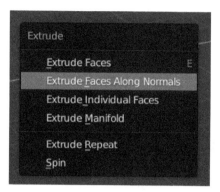

Figure 2.3 – Extrude Faces Along Normals will extrude in the direction of the normals

6. Drag your mouse to create an inward extrusion, as follows:

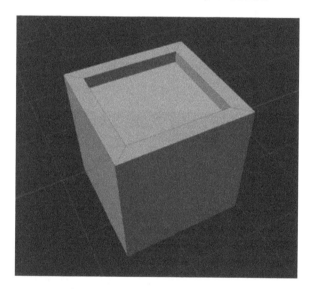

Figure 2.4 – Inward extrusion of both the top and the bottom faces

7. Press *Tab* to exit **Edit Mode.**

Let's add a Subdivision Surface modifier to our plane object to give ourselves more vertices. Later in this section, we will be distributing our cube instances onto each of these vertices.

8. With the plane selected, click on the **Modifiers** tab to the right-hand side, and click on **Add Modifier**. Then, select **Subdivision Surface** from the list. Let's configure it as follows.

9. Click on **Simple** and set the **Levels Viewport** and **Render** values to **3**:

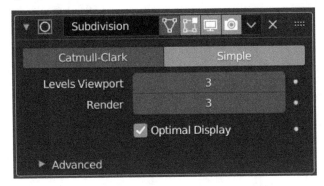

Figure 2.5 – Adding a Subdivision Surface modifier

Adding a Subdivision Surface modifier will give us more vertices. This means that more instances of our cube object will be distributed across our base mesh.

Distributing the instance object across our base mesh

Now it's time to distribute our instance object across our base mesh using some basic nodes. Let's do that now:

1. Select the plane again, and click on **NEW** in the Geometry Node Editor to create the modifier.

2. Let's create our first node – a **Point Instance** node. This is so that we can bring our cube into our scene. Press *Shift + A*, select **Point | Point Instance**, and place it just before the **Group Output** node.

3. Click on the **Object** drop-down box, and select the **Cube** instance object:

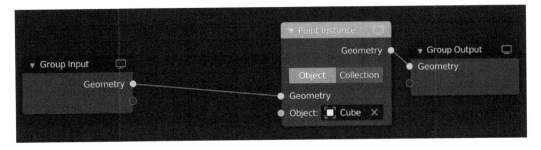

Figure 2.6 – Your node system should look like this

Your scene should now update, and you will see multiple cube instances where our plane was. Note that each instance is placed on a vertex of our plane object. The more vertices, the more instances you will have:

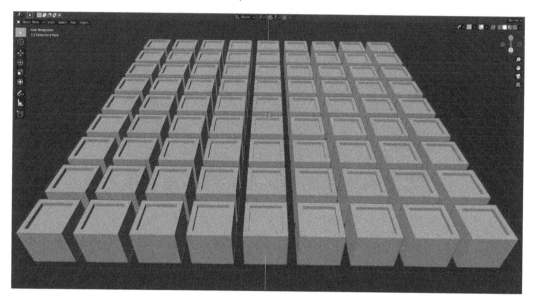

Figure 2.7 – Your scene should now look like this

In the next section, you will learn how to calculate proximity data between an empty object and the position of each instance object. Then, this data can be used to create interesting effects.

Using an empty object to calculate proximity data

Let's take a moment to discuss the next few steps. The idea is to calculate the proximity between an empty object in our scene and each of the cube instances. We can then use this proximity data to modify each cube's rotation or any other attribute. For this, we will also be using the **VertexWeightProximity** modifier to calculate the proximity and then save it into a vertex group that we will create.

You will discover that there are many different ways to do interesting things using Geometry Nodes, so never feel that you need to do it a certain way. If you can calculate the data that you need, you are on the right track. Experiment and practice!

Calculating the proximity

In this section, we will be creating an empty object and using it to calculate proximity data:

1. Let's start by creating an empty object in our scene. Press *Shift + A* and select
    Empty | Sphere. You can choose any shape you want.

2. Scale the empty object by pressing *S* and moving the mouse until it's a
    comfortable size.

3. Move the empty object to the edge of the cube instances. With the empty object
    selected, press *G*, then *X*, and drag the mouse:

Figure 2.8 – Notice the position of the empty object

Next, let's add a **VertexWeightProximity** modifier to our plane object.

4. Click on one of the cube instances to select our *hidden* plane.

5. In the **Modifier** panel, click on **Add Modifier** and select **VertexWeightProximity** from the list under the **Modify** column:

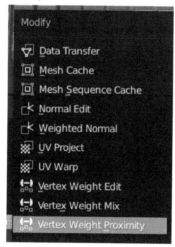

Figure 2.9 – Adding the Vertex Weight Proximity modifier to your plane object

6. Make sure this modifier is between our **Subdivision** modifier and the **Geometry Nodes** modifier, as our modifiers are applied from the top down. If we place it below the **Geometry Nodes** modifier, we won't be able to use the data within the Geometry Node Editor window. You can drag the modifier using the handle on the right-hand side to rearrange the modifier stack:

Figure 2.10 – Rearranging the modifier stack

Next, we need to create a new vertex group on the plane so that we can configure this modifier.

Before we do this, let's disable the viewport display of the *Geometry Nodes* modifier. The reason for this is that we need to see our plane to create the vertex group.

7. Click on the **Viewport Display** icon on **Geometry Nodes modifier** to disable it. Now, you will be able to see the plane object again in the viewport:

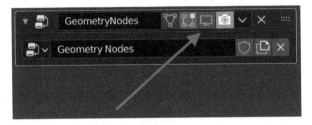

Figure 2.11 – Disabling the Geometry Nodes modifier

8. Select the plane in the 3D Viewport window and click on the **Object Data Properties** tab. Then, click on the + icon under **Vertex Groups**:

Figure 2.12 – Creating a new vertex group

9. Rename the vertex group by double-clicking on its name – call it Plane.

10. Mouse over the 3D Viewport window and press *Tab* to enter **Edit Mode**.

11. Ensure you are in **Vertex select** mode by pressing the *1* shortcut key.

12. Press *A* to select all the vertices of the plane, and then click on the **Assign** button in the **Vertex Groups** window:

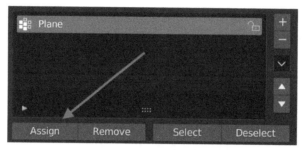

Figure 2.13 – Pressing Assign to add the vertices to the group

13. Hover over the 3D Viewport window and press *Tab* to exit **Edit Mode**.

14. Now, let's configure our **VertexWeightProximity** modifier. With the plane object still selected, click on the **Modifier** tab to see the modifiers.

15. You will see two empty boxes in the **VertexWeightProximity** modifier. Click on the box next to **Vertex Group** and select **Plane** from the list. This is the vertex group we have just created.

16. Click on the box next to **Target Object** and select the **Empty** object. Change **Proximity Mode** from **Object** to **Geometry**. This will ensure that we are using the plane geometry and not just the entire object:

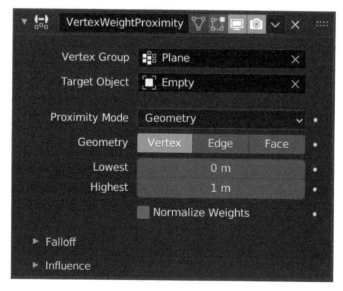

Figure 2.14 – The VertexWeightProximity modifier

17. Hover your mouse over the 3D Viewport and click on the drop-down list in the upper-left corner. Then, select **Weight Paint** from the list:

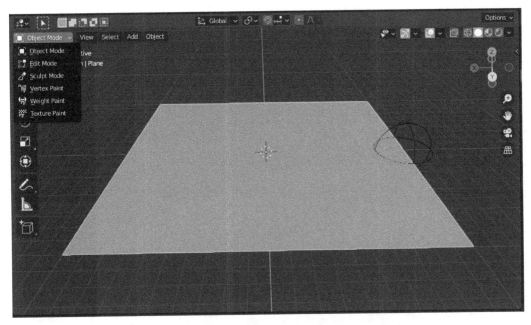

Figure 2.15 – Changing the mode to Weight Paint

Now you will be able to see the weight and how the position of the empty object affects it.

Using the default settings, you will see something similar to the following screenshot. Remember that **Red** is displaying a value of **1**, and **Blue** is displaying a value of **0**:

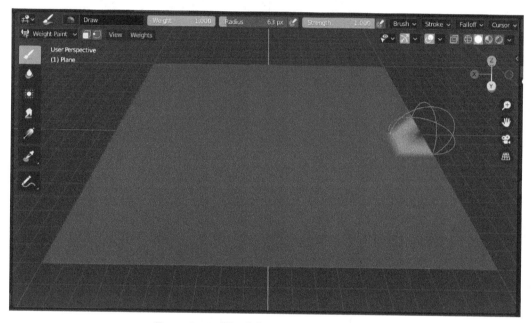

Figure 2.16 – The default Weight Paint effect

Let's invert this by having **Red** closest to our **Empty** object and **Blue** furthest away.

18. In the **VertexWeightProximity** modifier, change the **Lowest** value to **10 m** and the **Highest** value to **2 m**. This should invert our colors:

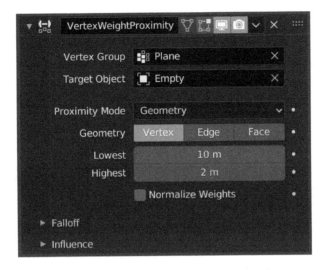

Figure 2.17 – Configuring the VertexWeightProximity modifier

Looking at the 3D Viewport window, you will see that the weight paint colors have been inverted. The area closest to the Empty object is showing *red*, which has a weight paint value of 1, while the area furthest away from the empty object is showing *blue*, which has a weight paint value of 0, as shown in the following screenshot:

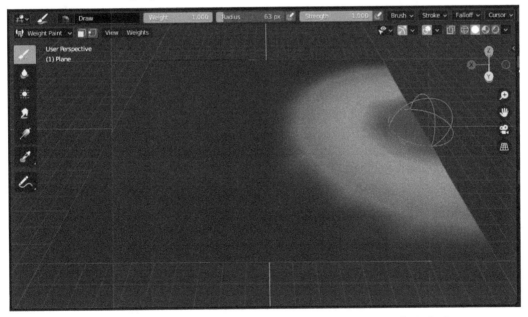

Figure 2.18 – The inverted colors are now correct: 1 is closer to empty and 0 is further away

Now your weight paint should look similar to the preceding screenshot. If you want, you can move the empty object around to see how the weight paint values update. Move your empty object back to this position – on the edge of the plane.

19. In the 3D Viewport window, let's change back to **Object Mode** by clicking on the drop-down menu in the upper-left corner again and selecting **Object Mode**.

20. Enable the **Geometry Nodes** modifier in the viewport by clicking on the viewport display icon next to the modifier again:

Figure 2.19 – Enabling the Geometry Nodes modifier

You should now see your cube instances in the viewport.

21. Click on one of the cube instances to select the plane.

Let's go back to the Geometry Node Editor window and start adding our next nodes. If you don't see the nodes in the node editor, make sure that the **Geometry Nodes** modifier has been selected in the **Modifier** stack.

Using the proximity data to modify the attributes

In this section, we will be using the proximity data to modify the Rotation attribute of our instance objects. We will make use of the data that's being captured by the **VertexWeightProximity** modifier using the vertex group called **Plane**. This value will be different for each cube instance because it calculates the distance from the empty object to each vertex on the plane object.

With this data, we can influence each of our instance objects slightly differently. In this section, we will use this value to change the rotation attribute of each cube instance. Let's examine how we can do this.

Adding our nodes

Let's begin by adding our next node:

1. Press *Shift + A*, select **Attribute | Attribute Combine XYZ**, and slot it in right after the **Group Input** node:

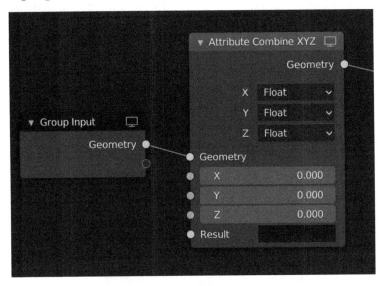

Figure 2.20 – The Attribute Combine XYZ node

The **Attribute Combine XYZ** node combines three values into one vector attribute as the result. For the three values, we can either use a float value or another attribute.

The idea is to make use of the vertex group proximity data that is in the vertex group called **Plane**. We're going to take this proximity value and use it to drive the Z-axis rotation of our instance objects. We're only going to rotate our cubes in the Z axis and not the X axis and Y axis.

Let's explore how we can do this.

2. For the X value, leave it as **Float** (we will be using a value of **0** because we're not changing this X rotation value).

3. For the Y value, leave it as **Float** as well (we will also be using a value of **0** because we don't want to rotate in the Y axis).

4.   Change the **Z** value to **Attribute**. Here, we will make use of the proximity data.

5.   In the empty box next to **Z**, type in the name of the vertex group that we have created, `Plane`, and press *Enter*. Additionally, you can select it from the list. These attributes are case sensitive, so make sure you are using the correct case.

Now we need to save these three results (**0, 0, Plane**) into an **Attribute** node. We can either create a new attribute or overwrite an existing attribute. Let's overwrite the **rotation** attribute of our instance objects with these new values.

6.   Enter `rotation` into the empty box next to **Result**, and press *Enter*:

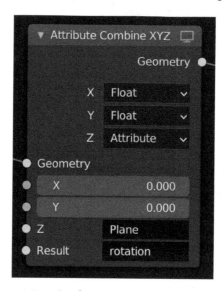

Figure 2.21 – Configuring Attribute Combine XYZ

You will notice that your scene in the 3D Viewport window has been updated. The cube instances closest to the empty object should have a Z rotation value that is higher than the cubes further away from the empty object.

7.   Go ahead and move the **Empty** object around in the 3D Viewport window – see how it affects the cubes. Cool, right? If you want to move the empty object along the Z axis only, click on the **Empty** object in the viewport to select it. Press *G*, and then press *Shift + Z*. This will enable you to move the empty object along the X and Y axes only:

Figure 2.22 – Cubes closer to the empty object should now have a higher Z rotation value

Let's see how we can increase the amount of Z rotation each cube instance will have. To do this, we're going to use an **Attribute Math** node to increase or decrease the rotation amount.

8.   Let's add an **Attribute Math** node. Press *Shift + A* and select **Attribute | Attribute Math**. Place it before the **Attribute Combine XYZ** node:

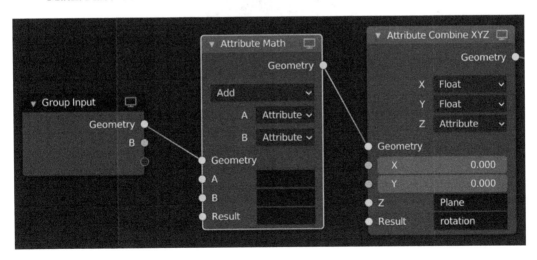

Figure 2.23 – Adding the Attribute Math node before the Attribute Combine XYZ node

With the **Attribute Math** node, we can do some simple as well as very complex math calculations. For this example, we're going to perform a simple multiply operation to increase the Z-axis rotation by a certain amount. To do this, we will be increasing the proximity value that we are using to rotate our instances.

9. In the **Attribute Math** node, change the operation to **Multiply**. Leave **A** as **Attribute**, and change **B** to **Float**.

10. Click on the empty box next to **A** and select **Plane** from the list. This is our proximity value.

11. For the **Result** setting, choose **Plane** as well.

Here, we're taking our proximity value (which is saved in the **Plane** attribute) and multiplying it with a float number that we can control. Then, we are saving this new result back into the plane or proximity attribute and overwriting the previous value:

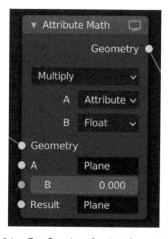

Figure 2.24 – Configuring the Attribute Math node

12. Adjust the **B** value on the **Math** node by clicking on the **0.000** value and dragging it to the right and left. Notice how the rotation of the cube instances updates in the 3D Viewport window. For now, let's set this value to 2.

13. Connect the dot on the left-hand side of this **B** value on the **Attribute Math** node to the available slot on the **Group Input** node. This will expose the value in the modifier panel so that you can easily make adjustments:

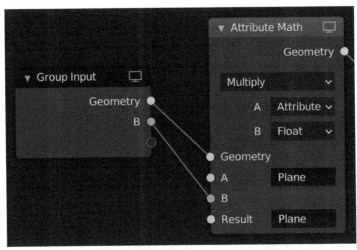

Figure 2.25 – Connecting the B value to the Group Input node to expose the value in the modifier stack

Now we have successfully used the proximity data between the empty object and each instance object to affect the Z-axis rotation of our instance objects.

In the next section, we will expose some custom values to easily make adjustments directly from the modifiers panel.

Naming the input value

Let's see how we can give more meaningful names to our input values. You can build quite complex input values, so naming them keeps things organized.

With your mouse hovering over the **Node** editor, press *N* to bring out the side menu on the right-hand side:

1. Double-click on the **B Inputs** name and rename it to `Rotation Amount`:

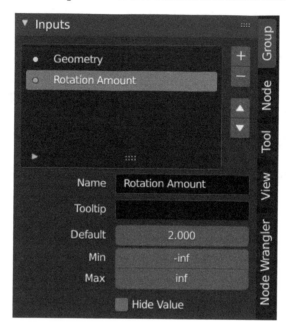

Figure 2.26 – Renaming the input value

2. Now, let's take a look at the **Modifiers** tab again. Notice that inside the **Geometry Nodes** modifier, you now have **Rotation Amount**, which can be adjusted without going into the Geometry Node Editor:

Figure 2.27 – Adjusting the Rotation Amount value in the modifiers panel

Now, let's add some movement to our scene to make things a bit more interesting.

Animating our scene

In this section, we will be animating our empty object by creating basic keyframes over time. Then, we will create a new input value/parameter to easily adjust the overall scale of our instance objects right from the modifier stack.

Adding keyframes

Let's add some keyframes to our empty object to create an animation. For this, let's go back to the layout window:

1. Click on the **Layout** tab at the top of the interface.

2. Select the empty object and move it to the right-hand side so that it's not affecting any of the cube instances. Press *G*, then *X*, and drag it toward the right-hand side:

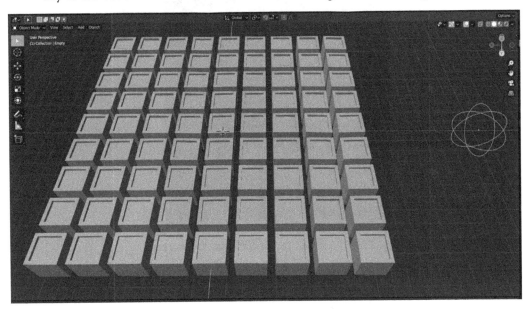

Figure 2.28 – Moving the empty object away from the cubes

3. With the empty object selected, make sure you are on **frame 1** by looking at the **Timeline** section at the bottom.

4. Press *I* and select **Location** from the drop-down menu to insert a **Location** keyframe:

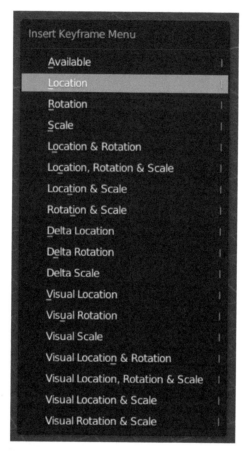

Figure 2.29 – Pressing I to insert a Location keyframe

5. Go to frame number **250** by scrubbing the timeline at the bottom of the interface.

6. With the empty object selected, press *G* and then *X*. Move the empty object over to the left-hand side of the cube instances so that no cubes are rotated.

7. Press *I* and insert another **Location** keyframe:

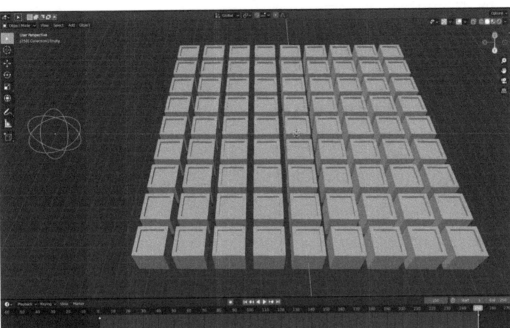

Figure 2.30 – Creating a second keyframe in the empty object

8. Play the animation back by pressing the *Spacebar*.

Adjusting the overall scale of the instance objects

We can create another input parameter to adjust the scale of our instance objects easily from the modifier panel:

1. Go back to the **Geometry Nodes** workspace by clicking on the tab at the top of the interface. Now, let's add one more node. Remember to select one of the cubes to see the nodes.

2. Add a **Point Scale** node by pressing *Shift + A*, selecting **Point | Point Scale**, and connecting it between the **Group Input** node and the **Attribute Math** node.

3. Change the **Type** setting to **Float**. The reason we're using **Float** is that we want to scale the cube uniformly using only one value.

4. Connect the **Factor** value to the **Group Input** node to expose this value in the modifier stack:

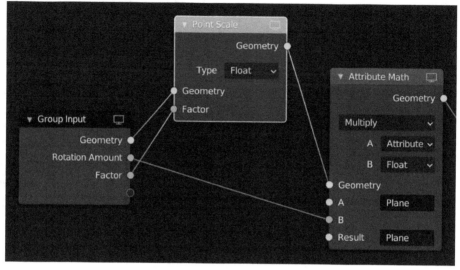

Figure 2.31 – Adding the Point Scale node before the Attribute Math node

5. Press *N* to bring up the side menu; double-click on the **Factor** input name, and let's rename it to Cube Size. You can call it anything you like.

6. You can also set a **Min** value and a **Max** value to limit the input value:

Figure 2.32 – Renaming the Factor input name

Great! Now we have exposed a custom value to easily change the cube size directly from the modifiers panel:

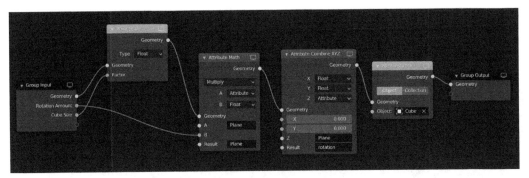

Figure 2.33 – Your node tree should now look like this

7. Let's take a look at the modifier panel again. Check that we can now change the **Cube Size** value right here in the modifier panel! Let's change it to a value of `0.500`.

8. Also, adjust the **Subdivision** levels to 4 to increase the number of cube instances:

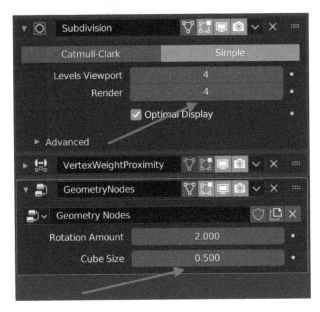

Figure 2.34 – Changing the Cube Size setting

Pay attention to how your scene has changed. The cube instances have increased because we added more vertices to our plane, and we've also adjusted the size of our cubes.

9. Press *Spacebar* to view your animation; as you will see, it looks slightly more dramatic now:

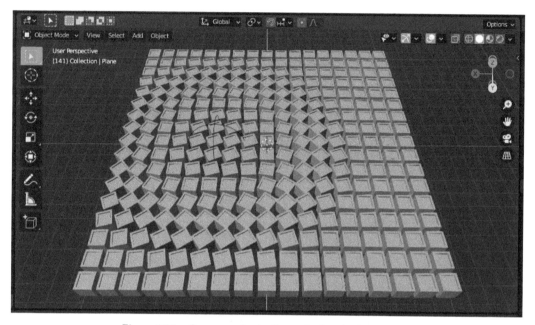

Figure 2.35 – Our scene is starting to look quite interesting

You should now have a good understanding of how powerful proximity data can be. You can create some amazing-looking animations by simply making use of simple math and an object's proximity. Add a few interesting keyframes, and you have a masterpiece!

Well done! In the next section, you will learn how to add some color to your creation.

Adding color using materials

In this section, we will be adding materials to our objects to make our scene more interesting! You will learn how to use the Shading workspace to assign random colors to our instance objects by using basic shading nodes and a color ramp.

To add materials to our Geometry Nodes scene, we need to apply the material to our instance object. In this case, it's the cube that we have created and moved over to the side of our scene:

1. Click on the **cube** to select it, and open the Shading workspace by clicking on the **Shading** tab at the top of the interface.

2.   With the cube instance still selected, click on **New** to create a new material:

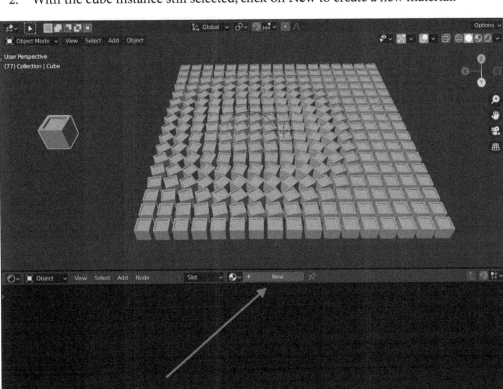

Figure 2.36 – Selecting the instance object and creating a new material

By default, you will see two nodes: the **Material Output** node and a **Principled BSDF** shader node. Let's create a new node called the **Object Info** node.

3.   Hover your mouse over the **Shader Editor** window and press *Shift + A* to bring up the **Add** menu. You can either search for this node by using the search function and typing in `Object Info`, or you can browse to the node. You can find this node underneath the **Input** category.

4.   Move the **Object Info** node to the left-hand side of the **Principled BSDF** node.

5. Connect the **Random** value to the **Base Color** input, as follows:

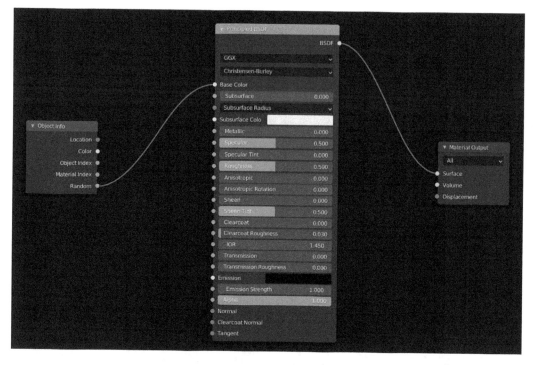

Figure 2.37 – Creating an Object Info node and connecting it to the Principled BSDF node

6. You will see that your scene has been updated with some random shades of gray! If you don't see any material changes, make sure you are in **Viewport Shading** mode by enabling it in the upper-right corner of the 3D Viewport window:

Figure 2.38 – Enabling Viewport Shading to see your materials in the 3D Viewport window

Let's make our random colors a bit more interesting. An easy way to do this is by adding a **ColorRamp** node. Let's do that now.

7. Press *Shift + A* and search for ColorRamp. You can find it under the **Converter** category.

8. Let's slot this node in between the **Object Info** node and the **Principled BSDF** node:

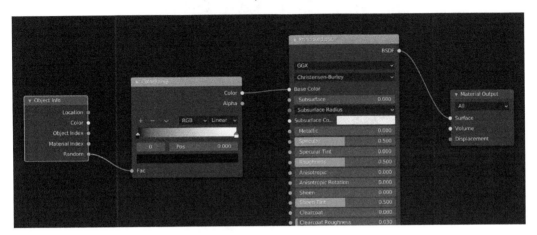

Figure 2.39 – Creating a ColorRamp node

Now we can configure our **ColorRamp** node to generate more colors. To do this, let's add another **Color Stop** to our **ColorRamp** node.

9. Click on the + symbol to add another stop.

10. Now, let's change the colors a bit. You can click on the triangle of the color stop to adjust the color. Click on the first one. Then, click on the black color strip and adjust this to blue.

11. Make the middle color stop green and the last color stop black. Additionally, you can drag these color stops around to adjust the ramp. Experiment with different color combinations until you are happy with the results:

Figure 2.40 – Configuring the ColorRamp node

Notice how the instance objects in your scene have random colors. Feel free to experiment with the **ColorRamp** node to create interesting color variations:

Figure 2.41 – Your scene looks far more interesting with some color

12. Press *Spacebar* to play through your animation!

Congratulations! You have created your first MoGraph animation using Geometry Nodes! Geometry Nodes is expanding and evolving with each Blender release, so be sure to check out the Blender documentation (`https://docs.blender.org/manual/en/latest/modeling/geometry_nodes/index.html`) from time to time to check which new nodes are available.

Summary

You should now have a basic understanding of how some of the nodes work and what you can create with Geometry Nodes. Additionally, you can make use of data from other modifiers such as the **VertexWeightProximity** modifier to calculate proximity. We've also looked at various ways to make use of the Math nodes to modify the different attribute values.

Experiment with all the different nodes and see what you can create! Have fun with Geometry Nodes!

In the next chapter, we will be looking at organic modeling. We will be creating a nature scene that focuses on a mushroom as our main object. Additionally, we will make use of Geometry Nodes to determine how you can use it in your day-to-day modeling projects.

3

Organic Modeling P1: Creating a Mushroom

In this chapter, we will be creating a mushroom! We will focus on creating organic shapes while keeping our topology optimized. We will first create the base mesh using basic modeling tools. Then we will make use of the Multires modifier to add geometry to our model. We will then use sculpting brushes to add finer details. We will then use a lattice object to easily shape our mushroom, and finally, we will look at how to UV unwrap our mesh and how to bake textures from a high-poly mesh onto a low-poly mesh.

UV mapping is the process of placing a 2D image on a 3D model's surface. The letters U and V indicate the axes of the 2D texture because X, Y, and Z are already used for the axes of the 3D model in the world space. Let's get started.

The main topics that we will cover in this chapter are as follows:

- Creating our base mesh for the mushroom
- UV unwrapping our model
- Adding a Multires modifier to increase the level of geometry in our mesh
- Adding finer details using sculpting brushes
- Using a lattice to organically shape our model

- Creating a low-poly and high-poly mesh
- Baking a normal map from the high-poly object

Creating our base mesh for the mushroom

In this section, we will begin creating our base mesh for our mushroom model. Organic modeling can be tricky sometimes, but if we start with basic geometry and slowly add more details, the process can be a lot easier. We will also focus on creating good geometry, which can be challenging to achieve when creating organic models, but following this process will allow you to create good topology and amazing organic models. Let's begin with our base mesh.

Using primitive objects to create our base mesh

We are going to use a basic primitive mesh to create our base model. Let's do this now:

1. Create a new Blender project.
2. Delete all objects in the scene by pressing *A* to select all the objects, and then pressing *X* to **confirm** the delete.
3. To add a cylinder mesh, press *Shift + A* and select **Mesh | Cylinder**.

   Let's now move our cylinder so that it's positioned on top of the floor grid of our scene.
4. Let's change our view to **Front View** by pressing Numpad *1*. You can also click the y axis gimbal in the corner of the 3D Viewport to change to the front view.
5. Click the cylinder to select it and press *G* and then *Z* to move the cylinder along the z axis.
6. Now, hold *Ctrl* while moving the mouse to enable snapping. Position the cylinder so that the base is on the grid.

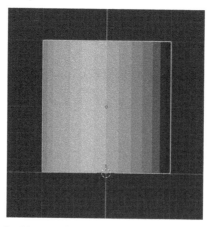

Figure 3.1 – Positioning the cylinder so that the base is on the grid

7. With the cylinder still selected, press *Tab* to enter **Edit Mode**.

8. Press *3* to activate **Face selection**.

9. Click the top face of the cylinder to select that face.

10. Now, press *G* and then *Z* and move this face upward to create a shape as shown in *Figure 3.2*. Left-click the mouse to confirm its position.

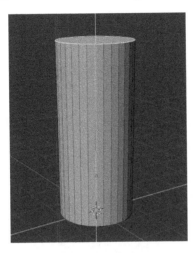

Figure 3.2 – Moving the top face upward to create a shape like this

11. Now, press *Tab* again to exit **Edit Mode**.

12. With the cylinder still selected in **Object Mode**, press *S* and then *Shift + Z* to scale only in the y and x axes. Move the mouse to make the cylinder thinner.

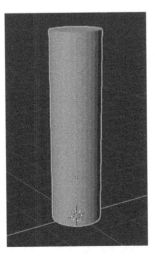

Figure 3.3 – Scaling the cylinder to make it slightly thinner

13. Let's continue modifying our base mesh. With the cylinder selected, press *Tab* to enter **Edit Mode**.

14. Ensure you are in **Face Selection** mode by pressing *3*.

15. Click the top face of your cylinder to select it.

16. Now, press *E* to extrude the face but press *Esc* immediately to position the new face on top of the current face.

17. Press *S* to scale this face and move your mouse until you get a shape as shown in *Figure 3.4*:

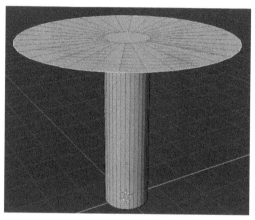

Figure 3.4 – Extruding and scaling the top face to create this shape

18. With the top faces still selected, press *E* to extrude. Move your mouse slowly until you have a shape as shown in the following figure:

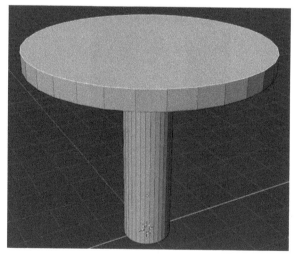

Figure 3.5 – Extruding the top faces

19. With the top face still selected, press *S* to scale and make it slightly smaller.

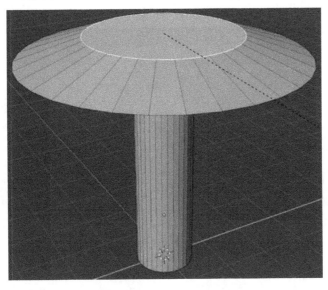

Figure 3.6 – Scaling the top face

20. With this top face still selected, press *E* again to extrude.

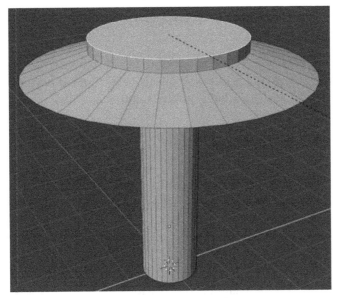

Figure 3.7 – Extruding the top face again

21. Scale this top face by pressing *S* and moving your mouse until you have something similar to the following figure. Click anywhere in the 3D Viewport to confirm.

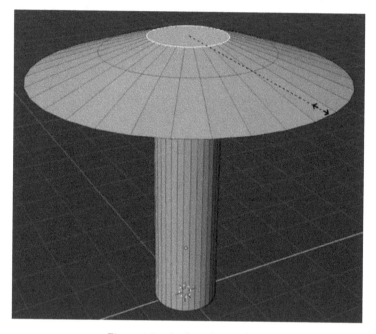

Figure 3.8 – Scaling the top face

22. Press *Tab* to exit **Edit Mode**.

23. It's always good practice to apply the scale of your object – let's do that now. With your model selected, press *Ctrl + A* and select **Scale** from the pop-up menu. This will set your object's scale to **1.000 / 1.000 / 1.000**.

Optimizing our topology

Next, we need to subdivide our mesh to optimize our base topology. The idea is to create faces that are closer to squares rather than rectangles, which will give us a much better topology when sculpting later in this chapter. Let's see how we can do this by using the Loop Cut tool as well as Grid Fill:

1. With our object selected, press *Tab* to enter **Edit Mode**.

2. Let's start by adding some loop cuts around the stem of our mushroom. Hover your mouse pointer over the stem and press *Ctrl + R* to create a loop cut. Left-click to confirm the loop cut and press *Esc* as we need to increase the number of loop cuts.

3. In the bottom-left corner of the 3D Viewport, expand the **Loop Cut and Slide** dialog box by clicking the arrow to the left of **Loop Cut and Slide**.

4. Increase the **Number of Cuts** option to 3 0, or until the faces on the mushroom stem look like little squares.

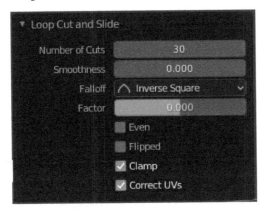

Figure 3.9 – Increasing the number of cuts to 30

5. Left-click in the 3D Viewport to confirm the loop cuts.

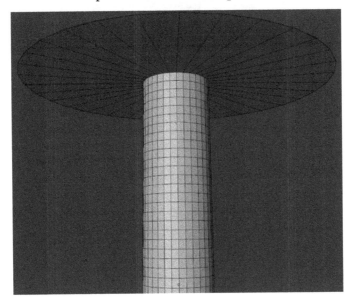

Figure 3.10 – Adding loop cuts to create square faces

6. Next, let's do the same to the underside of the mushroom. Hover your mouse pointer over the underside of the mushroom and press *Ctrl + R* to create a loop cut.

7. Left-click to confirm the loop cut and press *Esc* as we need to increase the number of loop cuts again.

> **Tip: Loop Cuts Using the Mouse Wheel**
>
> You can also use the mouse wheel to increase or decrease the number of loop cuts.

8. Using the **Loop Cut and Slide** dialog box in the corner of the 3D Viewport, increase the number of loop cuts to around 7 or until you have square faces. Left-click the viewport to confirm the loop cuts.

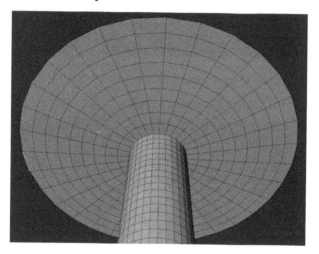

Figure 3.11 – Adding loop cuts to the underside of the mushroom

Let's do the same to the top side of our mushroom.

9. Add two loop cuts to the inner and outer faces of the top of the mushroom. I used three loop cuts on the outer faces and three loop cuts on the inner faces:

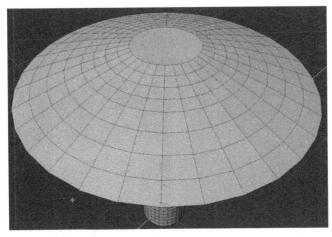

Figure 3.12 – Adding more loop cuts at the top of our mushroom

Next, we need to fix the top and bottom faces of our mushroom as they are currently **N-Gons**, meaning they have more than four edges. We need to delete these faces before we can create square or quad faces.

10. Click the top face to select it and press *X* to bring up the **Delete** dialog box.

11. Click **Faces** to delete the top face.

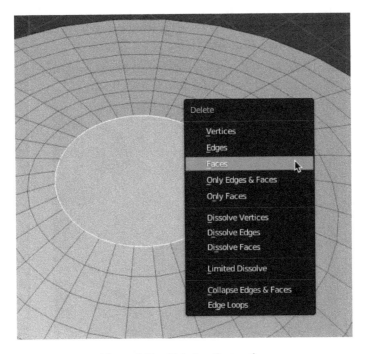

Figure 3.13 – Deleting the top face

12. Delete the bottom face of your mushroom as well – Select the bottom face, press *X* and click **Faces** to confirm.

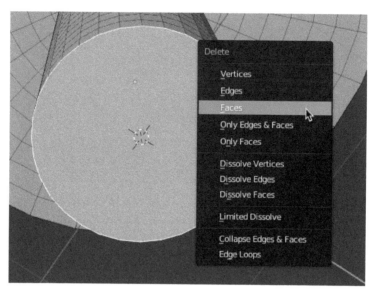

Figure 3.14 – Deleting the bottom face

13. Next, we're going to create new geometry where we have deleted these top and bottom faces. First, we need to select the edge loop around this missing face. Press *2* to enable **Edge Select** mode.

14. Hold *Alt* and left-click one of the edges along the bottom edge to select the edge loop. You can also double-click the edge to select the loop.

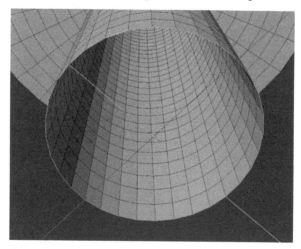

Figure 3.15 – Alt-clicking one edge to select the edge loop

15. With this edge loop selected, click the **Face** drop-down menu in the 3D Viewport and select **Grid Fill** from the dropdown:

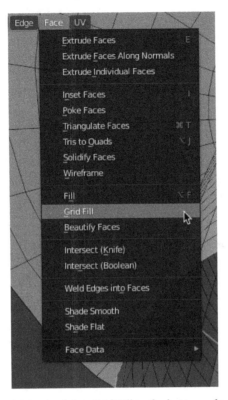

Figure 3.16 – Applying Grid Fill to the bottom edge loop

16. The **Grid Fill** dialog box will appear in the lower-left corner of the 3D Viewport. You can adjust how many faces you want here – I went with a setting of **Span** – 8 and **Offset** – 0. You can adjust these settings until you are happy with the results.

Figure 3.17 – Grid Fill dialog box

17. See how your mesh updates in the 3D Viewport as you change the **Grid Fill** parameters.

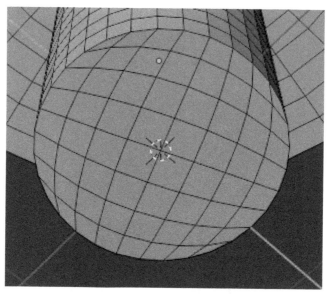

Figure 3.18 – Creating a Grid Fill at the bottom of our mushroom

18. Now, let's do the same at the top of our mushroom. Hold the *Alt* key and left-click the edge loop where we have deleted the top face. You can also double-click on the edge to select the edge loop.

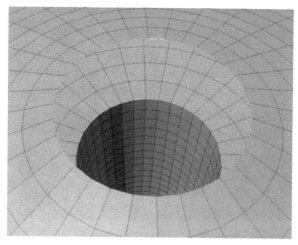

Figure 3.19 – Selecting the top edge loop by holding the Alt key and clicking on the edge

19. With the top edge loop selected, click the **Face** drop-down menu in the 3D Viewport and select **Grid Fill** from the dropdown.

For **Grid Fill**, I used the same settings: **Span** – 8 and **Offset** – 0.

Click anywhere in the 3D Viewport to apply the changes.

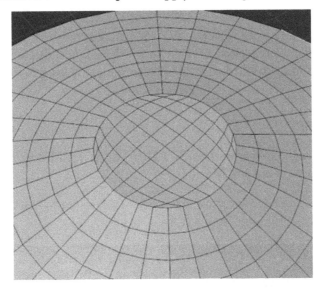

Figure 3.20 – Creating a Grid Fill at the top

20. Press *Tab* to exit **Edit Mode**.

Our base mesh for our mushroom model is now complete. In the next section, we will be UV unwrapping our model.

UV unwrapping our model

In this section, we will be looking at how to UV unwrap our base mesh. A UV Map is the flat representation of the surface of our 3D model. This process of creating a UV Map is called **UV unwrapping**. Think of this as taking your 3D mesh and unfolding it flat onto a surface; this will allow us to map a 2D image or texture onto our 3D model when adding materials in *Chapter 5, PBR Materials: Texturing our Mushroom Scene*. Let's do this now.

The UV Editing workspace

The UV Editing workspace has been configured and optimized for UV-related work. Let's see how we can use it:

1. Click the mesh to select it in the 3D Viewport and click the **UV Editing** tab at the top of the interface to enter the **UV Editing** workspace.

2. The UV Editing workspace will open and you will see your mesh on the right and your UV Map on the left. Let's make sure that we're in **Edge Select** mode by hovering your mouse over the right 3D Viewport and pressing *2* to enable **Edge Select** mode.

Adding seams

Next, we're going to mark the **seams** of our UV Map. This will tell Blender where we would like to have seams in our UV Map:

1. Let's select the outer edge of the top part of our mushroom. While holding the *Alt* key, click one of the edges to select the edge loop.

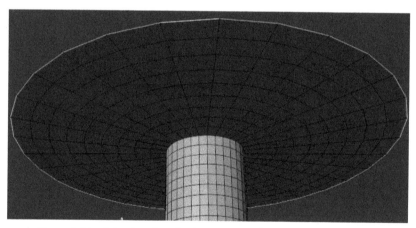

Figure 3.21 – Selecting the edge loop around the top part of our mesh

2. Right-click in the 3D Viewport and select **Mark Seam** from the drop-down menu to mark these edges as a seam. You will see that the edges will turn red.

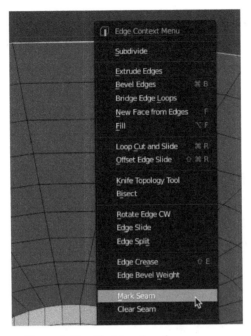

Figure 3.22 – Marking the edges as seams

Let's now add another seam at the bottom of our mesh.

3. Select all the edges around the bottom of the stem. *Alt* + click might not work here because of **Grid Fill**, but you can hold down *Shift* while clicking the edges to select multiple edges. You can also click one edge, and then hold down the *Ctrl* key and click another edge to select all the edges between these two edges.

4. With these edges selected, right-click the 3D Viewport and click **Mark Seam** from the drop-down menu. Note that you can also remove a seam by clicking **Clear Seam** from the drop-down menu.

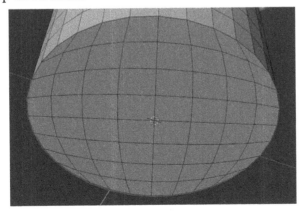

Figure 3.23 – Marking the bottom edge loop as a seam

Unwrapping the faces

We can add more seams, but let's first see how our model will unwrap with only these two seams:

1. To unwrap our faces, we need to be in **Face Select** mode. Hover your mouse pointer over the 3D Viewport and press *3* to enter **Face Select** mode.

2. Select all the faces by hovering the mouse pointer of the 3D Viewport and pressing *A*.

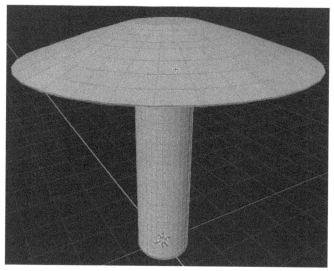

Figure 3.24 – Selecting all the faces by pressing the shortcut A

3. Right-click the 3D Viewport and select **UV Unwrap Faces | Unwrap**. This will unwrap all the selected faces.

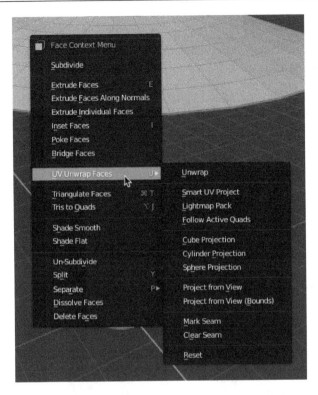

Figure 3.25 – Clicking UV Unwrap Faces | Unwrap to unwrap all selected faces

4. You will notice that a UV Map has been created in the UV Editor on the left. It's not bad, but you will notice that we don't have a nice unwrap for our mushroom stem.

Let's see how we can make this UV Map even better.

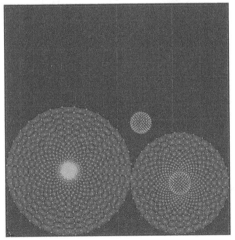

Figure 3.26 – The unwrapped UV Map will appear in the UV Editor

Adding more seams

We can always go back and add more seams to our mesh. This means we can try different seams and see how they unwrap:

1. Let's add another seam to our stem part. For this, we need to be in **Edge Select** mode. With your mouse pointer over the 3D Viewport, press *2* to enable **Edge Select** mode.

2. Let's select an edge from the top of the stem right to the bottom of the stem. You can either hold the *Shift* key while clicking the edges, or an easier way is to click the top edge to select it, and then hold the *Ctrl* key and click the bottom edge to select all the edges in-between. Try this now.

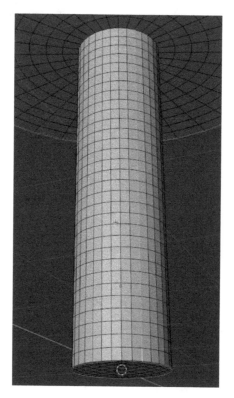

Figure 3.27 – Selecting edges from the top of the stem to the bottom of the stem

3. With these edges selected, right-click the 3D Viewport and select **Mark Seam** from the drop-down menu. This will mark the selected edges as seams.

Unwrapping the stem

Next, we're going to only unwrap the stem part of our mesh. To do this, we need to select all the faces around the stem. An easy way to do this is to change our view to a side view for easy selecting. Let's do this now:

1. With your mouse over the 3D Viewport, press *3* to enter **Face Select** mode.

2. Now, press *1* on the numpad to change to **Front view**.

3. Click and drag a box around the faces of the stem part just to select them. Note that we are only selecting the faces visible to us. We need to ensure that we are selecting all the faces around the stem.

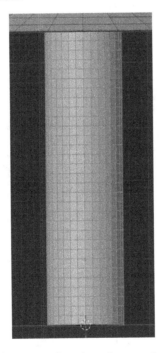

Figure 3.28 – In front view, dragging a box to select the visible faces

4. Press *3* and / or *9* on the numpad to view the right and left sides of the model and box select those faces too. Hold the *Shift* key while you select the new faces to keep the existing selection.

5. Once you have all the stem faces selected, rotate around your object to ensure that all the faces are selected.

6. Right-click the 3D Viewport and select **UV Unwrap Faces | Unwrap** to unwrap the stem section.

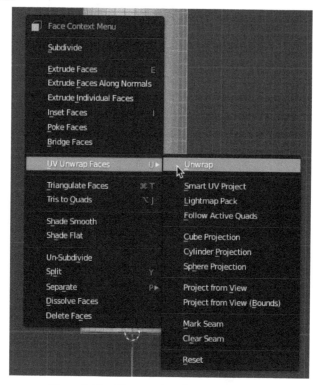

Figure 3.29 – Unwrapping the stem part only

7. Notice how the UV Map has changed in the UV Editor.

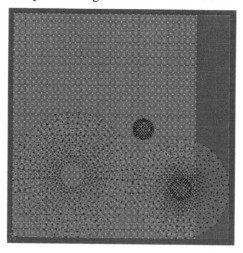

Figure 3.30 – The stem section is selected in the UV Editor

Optimizing the UV layout

Let's take a moment to see how we can optimize the layout of our UV Map in the UV Editor:

1. Hover your mouse pointer over the UV Editor and, with the stem faces still selected, press *G* and move this UV island away from the other UV islands so that we can have a better view of our UV Map.

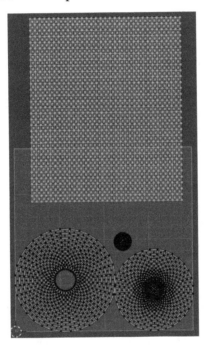

Figure 3.31 – Moving the stem UV island so that it's not overlapping any other UV islands

> **Note**
>
> A **UV island** is a set or group of faces that are connected in the UV space but also not connected to any other section of the UV Map, just like a real island. Always ensure that your UV islands are not overlapping any other UV islands. Overlapping UV islands will cause problems when adding Material assets to our mesh later.

2. Hover your mouse pointer over the **UV Editor** and press *A* to select all the UV islands.

3. With all the UV islands selected, click the **UV** drop-down menu at the top of the UV Editor and click **Average Island Scale**. This will average out the scale of the different UV islands. You may need to scale all the UV islands to fit into the UV layout.

4. With all the UV islands still selected, click the **UV** drop-down menu again and click **Pack Islands**. This will ensure that all the UV islands are within the UV space and that they do not overlap each other.

Feel free to manually move some of the UV islands around to use the UV space better. To select a UV island, hover your mouse pointer over a UV island and press *L* to select all the linked UVs. Then, press *G* to move that UV island to the desired location.

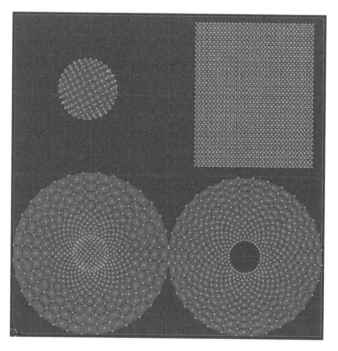

Figure 3.32 – Your UV Map should look similar to this

Congratulations! You have now UV unwrapped your base mesh successfully! In the next section, we will be looking at how we can use the Multires modifier to add more details to our mesh.

The multiresolution modifier

In this section, we will be looking at the **Multiresolution** (**Multires**) modifier and how it can be used to increase the geometry of our mesh. The reason we need to increase the amount of geometry is that we will be adding finer details to our mesh using sculpting brushes, but more on sculpting later in this chapter under the *Sculpting finer details onto our mushroom* section:

1. Let's go back to the main layout by clicking the **Layout** tab at the top of the interface.

2. With your object selected in the 3D Viewport, click the **Modifier Properties** field in the side panel to bring up the **Modifier Properties** panel.

3. Click **Add Modifier** and select **Multiresolution** under the **Generate** column.

Figure 3.33 – Adding a multiresolution modifier to our mesh

The multiresolution modifier shown in the following screenshot works similar to the **Subdivision Surface** modifier, but it allows us to set different subdivision levels for **Viewport**, **Sculpt**, and **Render**, which is exactly what we need.

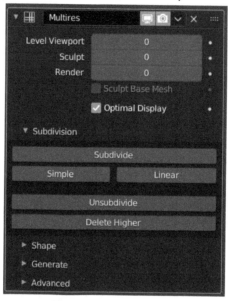

Figure 3.34 – The Multires modifier

4. Click the **Simple** button four times until you have **Level Viewport**, **Sculpt**, and **Render** resolutions of **4**.

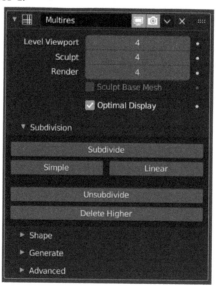

Figure 3.35 – Clicking Simple four times to increase the levels to 4

When working with the Multires modifier, it's important to keep note of the number of faces, edges, and vertices in your scene as this modifier can increase the level of geometry drastically. In the next section, we will look at how to easily keep an eye on this.

Statistics overlay

You can make use of the **Statistics** overlay in the 3D Viewport to display the number of faces, edges, and vertices in your scene. Let's do this now to see how much geometry we have:

1. At the top of the 3D Viewport, click the **Overlays** drop-down menu and then tick the box next to **Statistics**.

2. You will now see the **statistics** scene in the 3D Viewport – note the number of faces that have been added by the **Multires** modifier. Your face count might be different than mine – it all depends on your mesh and how many loop cuts you made.

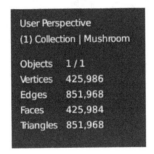

Figure 3.36 – Statistics showing the number of objects, vertices, edges, faces, and triangles in your scene

We now have enough extra geometry to start sculpting finer details onto our mesh. In the next section, we will be looking at the sculpting workspace and how we can use different sculpting brushes to add details to our mushroom. Remember to save your project now.

Sculpting finer details

In this section, we will be making use of different sculpting brushes to add finer details to our mushroom model.

Setting up the sculpting workspace

Let's start by making some minor changes to the sculpting workspace:

1. Click your model in the 3D Viewport to select it.

2. Click the **Sculpting** tab at the top of the interface to enter the sculpting workspace.

3. Let's disable **Fast Navigate** by clicking the **Options** dropdown at the top of the sculpting workspace and removing the tick from the box next to **Fast Navigate**. This will disable a low-resolution preview of the sculpt when orbiting around your model. This option can be enabled again if you are working with a complex sculpting model that causes the viewport to slow down.

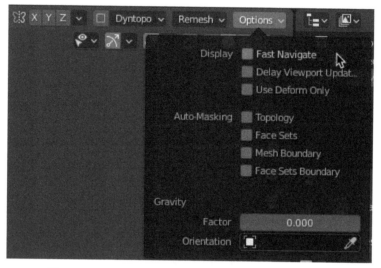

Figure 3.37 – Unticking Fast Navigate to view your sculpt
at a high resolution when orbiting the viewport

4. Next, let's expand the tools sidebar so that we can see the names of the sculpting brushes. Place your mouse cursor on the edge of the toolbar and click and drag to the right until you can see the brush names.

Figure 3.38 – Expanding the side toolbar to see the names of the sculpting brushes

Sculpting basics

Before we start adding finer details to our mushroom model, let's take a moment to look at the basics of sculpting. I will be using a default cube to demonstrate how the sculpting brushes work, but feel free to use your mushroom base mesh if you want. Remember to save your project now so that you can revert back to this saved state:

1. With **Draw Brush** selected, you will see the brush's **Radius** and **Strength** parameters at the top of the sculpting workspace.

Figure 3.39 – Brush radius and strength

2. **Radius** affects the size of your sculpting brush, and **Strength** will adjust the strength of your brush. The strength of the brush determines what effect it will have on the geometry. Think of this as the pressure you are applying with the brush when sculpting.

3. The two **PEN** icons next to **Radius** and **Strength** are the **Size Pressure** and **Strength Pressure** settings. These can be enabled to have your pen pressure affect either the **Radius** or **Strength** settings of the brush if you are using a stylus or tablet. I prefer to disable both, but feel free to experiment to see what works best for you.

> **Note**
> Each brush will have its own **Radius** and **Strength** settings, so changing this will only affect the selected brush.

4. You can also change the radius of the brush by using the shortcut key *F* and dragging the mouse pointer.

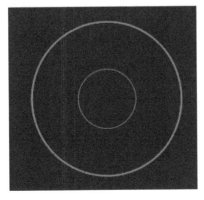

Figure 3.40 – Pressing F to adjust the radius of the brush

5. You can adjust the strength of your brush by using the shortcut *Shift + F* and dragging the mouse.

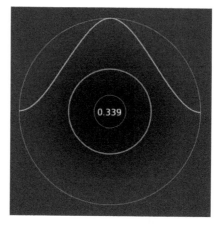

Figure 3.41 – Pressing Shift + F to adjust the strength of the brush

6. To start sculpting on your model, simply hold and left-click and drag across your model to create your first sculpt! Experiment with **Radius** and **Strength** to see how they affect the sculpt.

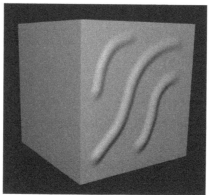

Figure 3.42 – Left-click and drag to sculpt on your model

7. You can also change the direction of your sculpting brush between **Add** or **Subtract**. Hold the *Ctrl* key while sculpting to invert the direction. You can also use the + and – buttons next to the **Radius** and **Strength** settings to set the direction of the brush. This parameter will also be saved per brush.

Figure 3.43 – You can change the direction of the brush from Add to Subtract

8. Let's try sculpting on the model while holding the *Ctrl* key – can you see the difference?

Figure 3.44 – Holding the Ctrl key while sculpting will invert the brush direction

9. You can also activate **Smooth Brush** by simply holding the *Shift* key while sculpting. This brush will smooth out your geometry. Note that holding *Shift* will make use of the smooth brush's strength settings as this parameter is saved per brush. To adjust the strength of the smooth brush, you need to select the smooth brush from the sidebar and adjust its strength. Try it now and see how it affects your mesh.

Figure 3.45 – Holding the Shift key while sculpting will smooth out your mesh

You should now have a basic understanding of how to use the sculpting brushes, how to adjust the brush size and strength, as well as how to switch the brush direction and use the smooth brush shortcut to quickly smooth out certain parts of your mesh. Play around with these parameters and practice a bit until you feel comfortable before moving on to the next section, where we will be adding details to our mushroom model. Have fun!

Sculpting finer details onto our mushroom

Now that you have a basic understanding of the sculpting workspace and how to use the sculpting brushes, let's add some finer details to the underside of our mushroom mesh:

1. Orbit your 3D Viewport so that you have a better view of the underside of the mushroom.

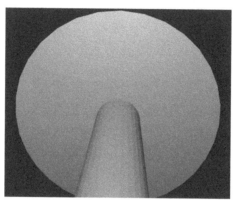

Figure 3.46 – Orbiting your viewport to see the underside of the mushroom

2. Click the **Draw** brush in the toolbar to select it.

3. Set your brush radius to 20 px and the strength of the brush to 0.400.

4. Now it's time to add our first sculpting stroke. Position the mouse pointer to the underside of the mushroom and click and drag outward toward the edge of the top part of the mushroom. Be sure to undo and try again until you are happy with the result.

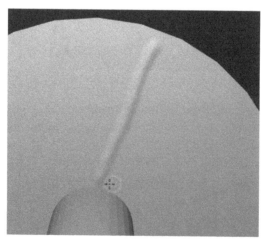

Figure 3.47 – Adding our first sculpting stroke

5. Now let's continue this process, orbiting around the underside of the mushroom, adding more strokes from the inside to the outer edge.

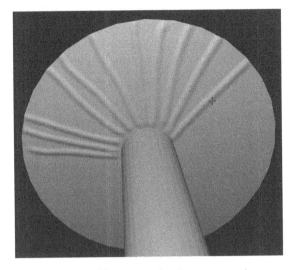

Figure 3.48 – Adding more details to our mushroom

6. Be sure to overlap your strokes until you have something that looks like the following figure:

Figure 3.49 – Overlapping your strokes to create something like this

7.   Let's smooth out the area where the stem meets the top part of the mushroom. I'm making use of **Draw Brush** as well as **Smooth Brush** by holding the *Shift* key while sculpting. **Draw Brush** is set to a radius of 8 7 px and a strength of 0 . 4 0 0. Feel free to experiment with different brush sizes and radii here.

Figure 3.50 – Smoothing out the part where the stem meets the top part of the mushroom

8.   Let's now add some organic-looking details to the stem part! Using **Draw Brush** with a radius of 3 9 px, start adding strokes from the top to the bottom of the stem. Hold the *Ctrl* key to invert your brush direction and experiment until you have something that looks nice. Make use of the **Smooth Brush** shortcut by holding the *Shift* key to smooth out the stem; be sure to adjust the **Smooth Brush** strength if you feel it's too powerful. See my example below:

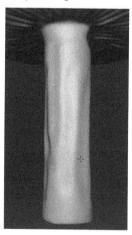

Figure 3.51 – Adding details to the stem by using the Draw and Smooth brushes

9.   Next, we're going to smooth out the top part of the mushroom. For this, let's orbit the viewport so we're looking down at our mushroom model. Click **Smooth Brush** to select it.

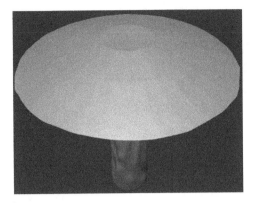

Figure 3.52 – Orbiting your viewport to see the top of the mushroom

10. Let's make our Smooth brush bigger by setting the radius to 148 px.

11. Next, let's enable a setting called **Front Faces Only** on our Smooth brush. This setting allows us to only affect the front-facing faces and not the back-facing faces. To enable this setting, click the **Brush** drop-down menu at the top of the interface and tick **Front Faces Only** at the bottom. If we don't enable this setting, we might affect the details we have sculpted under the top part of the mushroom. Experiment with this setting to see how it affects the sculpt.

Figure 3.53 – Enabling Front Faces only on the Smooth brush to only affect front-facing faces

12. Now, let's smooth out the top part by sculpting over it with the Smooth brush.

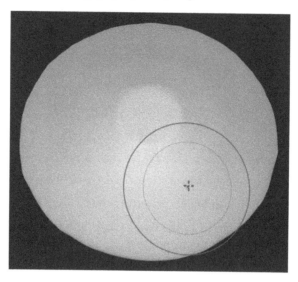

Figure 3.54 – Smoothing the top part of the mushroom until you can't see any geometry lines

13. Next, we're going to look at the Grab brush! This is a great brush for pushing and pulling your geometry to adjust the overall shape. Set the radius of the brush to 148 px and the strength to 0.400. Gently start pushing and pulling the sides of the stem to create something that looks more organic.

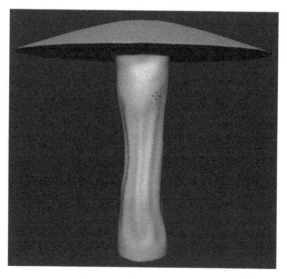

Figure 3.55 – Gently push and pull the sides of the stem to create a more organic shape

14. Let's make the bottom of the stem slightly bigger by using the Grab brush and pulling on the sides of the bottom of the stem outward. Orbit around the model to ensure you expand this from all sides until you have something that looks like the following figure:

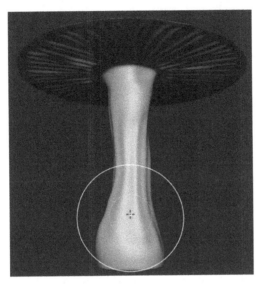

Figure 3.56 – Shaping the stem using the Grab brush

15. Next, we're going to give some shape to the top of the mushroom. Let's continue to use the Grab brush, but let's make its radius nice and big! I've set mine to 338 px. Place the cursor over to the side of the top part and gently pull down.

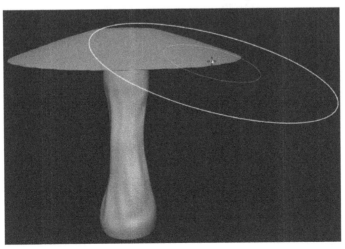

Figure 3.57 – Pulling down gently using the Grab brush

16. Continue orbiting around the model and pulling down on the top part. You can also pull the center of the top part upward if needed. Play around until you have something you like.

Figure 3.58 – Pulling down the top part to create a more organic shape

17. Now, let's add some finer details to the stem part. For this, we're going to use the Draw brush again. Set the radius to about 8 px so that it's quite tiny, and then add some random lines to the stem.

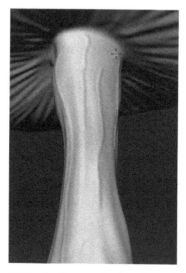

Figure 3.59 – Adding smaller details to the stem

18. We can smooth out these lines by switching to the Smooth brush. I'm using a radius of 88 px and a strength of 0.200. Gently smooth out the lines until you have something that you are happy with.

Figure 3.60 – Smoothing out the lines by using the Smooth brush

Congratulations! You have created your first sculpt. You should now have a basic understanding of how sculpting works in Blender. The best way to get better is to practice, practice, and then practice a bit more. Experiment with all the different brushes to see what they do and how they affect your mesh. Let's now save our project!

In the next section, we will be making use of a lattice object to easily change the overall shape of your model.

Using a lattice to shape your overall model

In this section, we will look at how we can use a lattice object and modifier to change the overall shape of the mushroom model. A lattice is great for adjusting the overall shape of something without having to edit the mesh or use sculpting brushes. Let's see how we can use it:

1. First, ensure that you are back in the **Layout** workspace by clicking the **Layout** tab at the top of the interface.

2. Let's now create a new lattice object by pressing *Shift + A* and selecting **Lattice** from the **Add** menu.

Figure 3.61 – Adding a lattice object from the Add menu

3. You will see a wireframe cube appear in the scene – this is the **Lattice** object. Let's position and scale it so it fits around our model. Click the lattice object to select it, and then move the lattice up by pressing *G* and then pressing *Z*.

4. Let's now scale the lattice by pressing *S* and dragging it with the mouse.

5. Orbit around the model to ensure that our mushroom fits inside the lattice object.

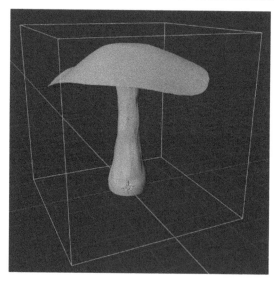

Figure 3.62 – Making sure your model fits completely inside the lattice object

6. Let's now configure our lattice object. With the lattice selected, click the **Object Data Properties** panel to access its properties.

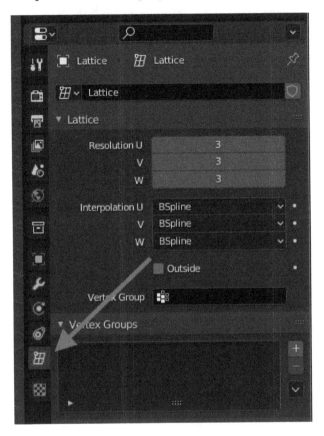

Figure 3.63 – Clicking the Object Data Properties panel to access the lattice properties

7. Set **Resolution** to: **U:3 V:3 W:3**. This will subdivide the lattice so that we have more points to use when adjusting the shape.

8. You will see the lattice updating in the 3D Viewport.

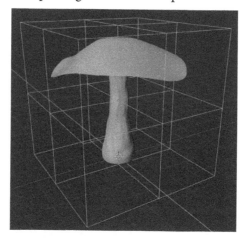

Figure 3.64 – The lattice now has more points

Now that we have created our lattice object, we also need to create a lattice modifier that will link or bind our lattice object to our model. In the next section, we will take a look at how to do this.

The Lattice modifier

We need to add a lattice modifier to our mushroom mesh so that it can be affected by the lattice object. Let's do that now:

1. Click the mushroom in the 3D Viewport to select it.

2. Click the **Modifier Properties** panel and add a **Lattice** modifier.

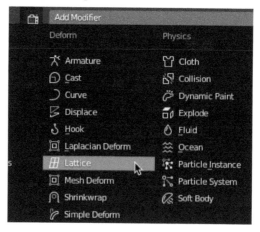

Figure 3.65 – Adding a Lattice modifier to our mushroom model

3. Make sure that the **Lattice** modifier is below the **Multires** modifier in the stack as the modifiers are applied from top to bottom.

4. Let's now configure the lattice modifier. Click the **Object** box inside the lattice modifier and select **Lattice** from the list. You can also use the eye dropper to pick it from the 3D Viewport.

Figure 3.66 – Selecting the Lattice object from the Object dropdown

Now that we have created the lattice modifier, we can start shaping our object by manipulating the lattice object. Let's see how we can do this in the next section.

Shaping your mesh using the lattice object

With our lattice object linked to our mushroom mesh via the lattice modifier, we can now make changes to the lattice object which, in turn, will affect our mushroom's shape. Let's do this now:

1. Click the **Lattice** object in the 3D Viewport to select it and press *Tab* to enter **Edit Mode**.

2. You will now see points on the lattice object. Click to select one of these points and, using the *G* key, move it around. See how it affects the shape of the mushroom.

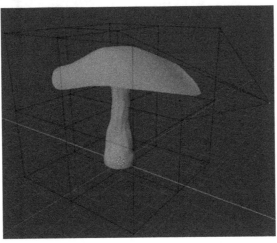

Figure 3.67 – Moving the points on the lattice object will affect the shape of the mushroom

3. Let's move the eight points on the bottom of the lattice outward to increase the radius of the bottom part of the stem. Click each point and use the G shortcut, followed by pressing *Shift* + *Z*, to move the points on the x and y axes.

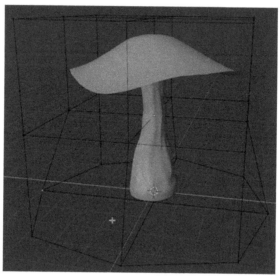

Figure 3.68 – Moving the bottom points outward to adjust the stem

4. Let's now make some adjustments to the top of our mesh by adjusting some of the lattice points at the top. Click the middle top point and move it upward by pressing G and then Z and moving the mouse.

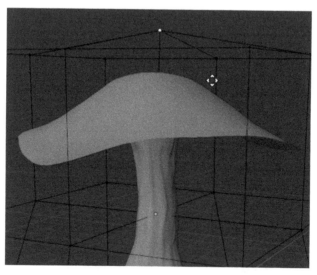

Figure 3.69 – Pulling the middle top point upward to adjust the top of the mushroom

5. Feel free to make more adjustments to the lattice object until you are happy with the overall shape. Once you are satisfied, press *Tab* to exit **Edit Mode**.

6. You can now also hide the lattice object from the 3D Viewport by selecting it and pressing *H* to hide. You can also use the **eye icon** in the outline to hide or unhide the lattice object, as shown in the following figure:

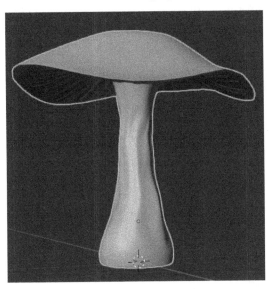

Figure 3.70 – Shaping our mushroom using a lattice

You should now have a better understanding of how you can use a lattice object to change the overall shape of your model easily without having to edit or add more sculpting details.

In the next section, we will be creating a low-poly and high-poly version of our mesh.

Creating a low-poly and high-poly mesh

In this section, we will be creating a low-poly and high-poly version of our mushroom model. Our current model has a very high-poly count and it's always good practice to decrease your poly count if possible, especially when working on video game assets, the reason being that high-poly counts will increase RAM usage and will also slow down your Blender project. It will also increase render times. High-poly meshes are also much more difficult to rig if needed. Let's see how we can do this.

Duplicating our models

Let's start by creating duplicate copies:

1. Ensure you are in the **Layout** workspace by clicking the **Layout** tab at the top of the interface.

2. Click on your mushroom model in the 3D Viewport to select it.

3. Let's take a moment to rename our mushroom in the outliner if you have not done so already. Double-click the object name in the **Outliner** window and rename it Mushroom.

Figure 3.71 – Renaming the mushroom object in the outliner

4. Let's create two new duplicate copies of our mushroom model. Click to select the model in the 3D Viewport and press the shortcut *Shift + D* to create a duplicate copy.

5. Press *Esc* to confirm the duplicate's position as we're not going to move it away from the current position.

6. Now, let's create one more duplicate. With the mushroom still selected, press *Shift + D* again followed by *Esc* to confirm its position. You should now have a total of three copies in the outliner.

7. Rename the first duplicate copy in the outliner to Mushroom_HP. This will be our **High-Poly** version.

8. Rename the second duplicate copy in the outliner to Mushroom_LP. This will be our **Low-Poly** version.

9. Hide the original mushroom model from the viewport and render it by clicking the **eye** and **camera** icons next to it in the outliner. We will keep this one as a backup.

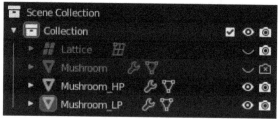

Figure 3.72 – Hiding the original "Mushroom" model from the viewport
and rendering it by clicking the eye and camera icons next to it.

Applying the modifiers

Next, we're going to apply the modifiers to both our high-poly and low-poly versions:

1. Click the **Mushroom_HP** high-poly version in the outliner to select it.

2. Click the **Modifier Properties** panel to view the modifier stack.

3. First, let's apply the **Lattice** modifier by clicking its drop-down menu and selecting **Apply** from the list.

4. Next, let's apply the **Multires** modifier. Leave the multires **levels** as **4 / 4 / 4** as this is our high-poly model. Click the drop-down menu of the **Multires** modifier and click **Apply**.

5. Now, for the low-poly version of our model, click the **Mushroom_LP** low-poly version in the outliner to select it.

6. Click the **Modifier Properties** panel to view the modifier stack.

7. First, let's apply the **Lattice** modifier by clicking its drop-down menu and selecting **Apply** from the list.

8. Next, let's apply the **Multires** modifier. For our low-poly model, we need to make some changes to the **Multires** modifier before we apply it. Change its **levels** to **1 / 4 / 4** as this is our low-poly model. Click the drop-down menu of the **Multires** modifier and then click **Apply**.

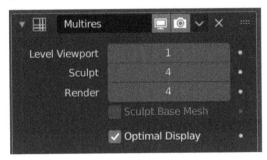

Figure 3.73 – Changing the low-poly version's Multires modifier
to a low resolution of 1 before applying it

You should now have low-poly and high-poly versions of your mushroom model. Let's see how they differ from one another.

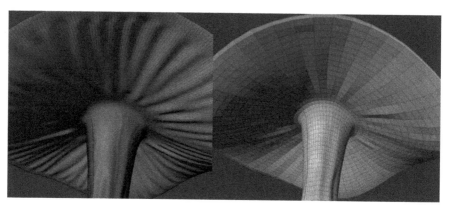

Figure 3.74 – High-poly and low-poly versions

9. Let's set both models to **Shade Smooth** so that we don't see the geometry lines. Click on the low-poly version in the outliner to select it, and then right-click the model in the 3D Viewport and select **Shade Smooth** from the drop-down menu.

10. Do this for the high-poly version as well. Click to select the high-poly version in the outliner, right-click the model in the 3D Viewport, and select **Shade Smooth** from the drop-down menu.

You should now have low-poly and high-poly versions of your mushroom model. In the next section, we're going to bake a normal map from the high-poly version so that we can apply that to our low-poly version later when we apply materials. Remember to save your project now!

Baking the normal map

In this section, we're going to bake a normal map from our high-poly mesh to our low-poly mesh. The reason why we're doing this is to add the finer details as a normal map to our low-poly mesh. This will result in a low-poly model that looks like a high-poly model because of the normal map. This is a great way to keep your poly count low without losing the finer details. Let's get started.

Creating the blank normal map image texture

We first need to create a blank image texture on our low-poly mesh. This image texture will become our normal map:

1. Click the **Mushroom_LP** low-poly mesh in the outliner to select it.

2. With the low-poly mesh selected, click the **Shading** tab at the top of the interface to enter the Shading workspace.

3. Click **New** to create a new material.

4. Let's create a new image texture by pressing *Shift + A* and then selecting **Texture | Image Texture**. You can also use the search function to search for Image Texture.

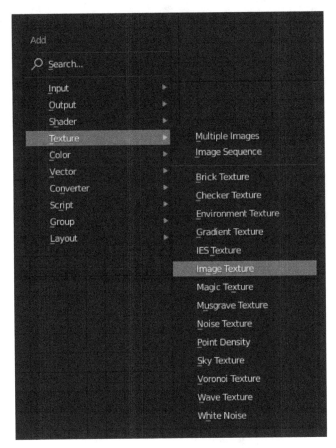

Figure 3.75 – Creating a blank image texture

5. Place this **Image Texture** node to the left of **Principled BSDF Shader**.

6. Click **New** on the **Image Texture** node to create a blank texture.

7. Let's rename the image texture to NormalMap.

8. Next, let's change the resolution of this texture to a 2K image. Set the **Width** and **Height** settings to 2048 px.

9. Untick the box next to **Alpha** as we do not need an alpha channel for our normal map.

10. Click **OK** to confirm.

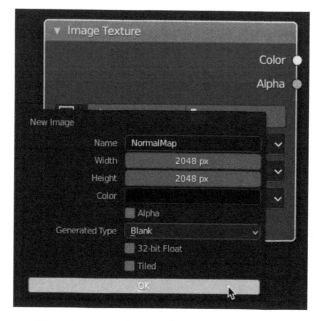

Figure 3.76 – Configuring the Image Texture node

11. Do not connect this node to any other nodes just yet; we first need to bake our normal map before we can use it.

12. Let's change the **Color Space** field of this image texture node to **Non-Color**. Click the **Color Space** drop-down menu and select **Non-Color** from the list.

Figure 3.77 – Setting Color Space to Non-Color

Now that you have created the blank normal map, we are ready to start the texture baking process. In the next section, we will bake the details from the high-poly mesh into this blank normal map image.

Baking from the high-poly mesh to the image texture

We are now ready to bake the normal map using our high-poly mesh. Let's do this now:

1. In the Shading workspace, make sure that the **Image Texture** node we created is **selected**. This is very important as the baking process will bake to the *selected* image texture node.

2. Click the **UV Editing** tab at the top of the interface to enter the UV Editing workspace.

3. By default, the UV Editing workspace will open in **Edit Mode**. Let's change it back to **Object Mode**. Hover your mouse pointer over the right window and press *Tab* to exit **Edit Mode**.

4. You should now see the blank **NormalMap** in the left window.

5. Next, we need to select the **High-Poly** mesh first and *Shift* select the **Low-Poly** mesh to bake to the active mesh. The active mesh is the last mesh you select. Let's do this now: Click the mesh in the 3D Viewport to select the **High-Poly** mesh first, and then hold the *Shift* key and click again to select the **Low-Poly** mesh. It's very important that you make sure to select the high-poly mesh *first* and the low-poly mesh second.

6. Click **Render Properties** in the **Properties** panel (the camera icon).

7. Change **Render Engine** to **Cycles** by clicking the drop-down menu next to **Render Engine**.

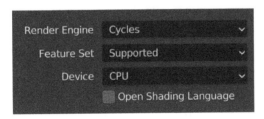

Figure 3.78 – We need to use the Cycles Render Engine to bake our normal map

8. Scroll down and expand the **Bake** section in the properties panel.

9. Change **Bake Type** to **Normal** by clicking the drop-down menu next to **Bake Type**.

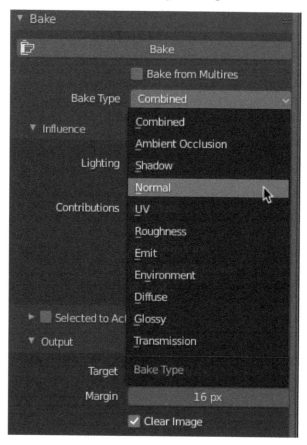

Figure 3.79 – Changing Bake Type to Normal

10. Tick the box next to **Selected to Active** and expand this section. This will enable us to bake from the selected mesh (the high-poly mesh) to the active mesh (the low-poly mesh).

11. Under **Selected to Active**, set **Extrusion** and **Max Ray Distance** to 0.1 m. These two settings help with matching the two objects by inflating the low-poly mesh slightly. I usually get good results with a 0.1 m setting for both options, but feel free to experiment if you don't get good results.

12. Finally, click the **Bake** button to start the baking process.

13. After a few moments, you will see your normal map in the UV Editor. Congratulations! You have baked your first normal map!

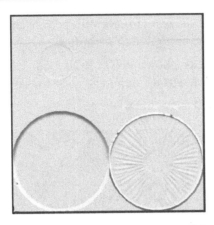

Figure 3.80 – The normal map will appear in the UV Editor following a successful bake

Saving the normal map texture

We need to save our normal map texture so that we can use it in *Chapter 5, PBR Materials: Texturing Our Mushroom Scene*, when we apply materials to our mushroom model. Let's see how we can save this texture:

1. Still in the **UV Editing** workspace, click **Image*** at the top of the UV Editor workspace and select **Save As** from the drop-down menu.

Figure 3.81 – Saving our normal map texture

2. Browse to a folder where you want to save your texture and let's give it a name by typing `NormalMap` at the bottom of this window.

3. Configure the file format as follows: **PNG / RGB / Color Depth: 8** and **Compression: 15%**. These settings should be good for saving our texture.

4. Click **Save As Image** to save our image texture.

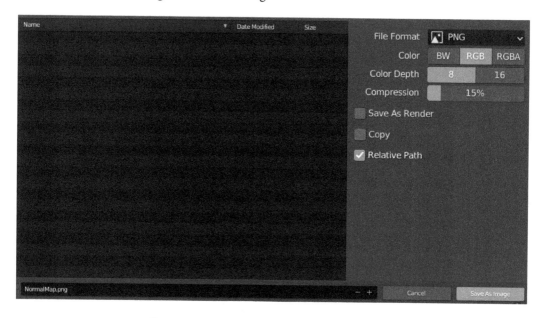

Figure 3.82 – Saving the normal map for later use

Congratulations! You have now completed the modeling process of the mushroom model.

Summary

You should now have a good understanding of how to go about creating organic models and how to UV unwrap them. You have also learned how to use the Multires modifier to create extra geometry for sculpting. We also looked at how you can use a lattice to easily deform objects without editing their geometry. We also looked at how you can create low-poly and high-poly versions of your mesh, as well as baking the high-poly details to a normal map that we will use in *Chapter 5, PBR Materials: Texturing Our Mushroom Scene*, when creating materials.

In the next chapter, we will focus on creating the landscape around our mushroom model and we will also be adding grass using geometry nodes.

4

Organic Modeling P2: Creating the Landscape around the Mushroom

In this chapter, we will create an organic-looking landscape with grass. You will learn how to make use of Proportional Editing to create an organic-looking landscape. Then we will create individual grass blades by using basic primitives and editing tools. You will then learn how to use Geometry Nodes to scatter these grass blades across the landscape using weight painting to control the density of the grass. Let's get started.

The main topics we'll cover in this chapter are as follows:

- Creating an organic-looking landscape using Proportional Editing
- Creating individual grass blades
- Scattering the grass blade objects using Geometry Nodes

Creating the landscape

In this section, we will create the landscape around our mushroom. For the landscape, we will be using a plane primitive and Proportional Editing. Let's do this now:

1. Click the **Layout** tab at the top of the interface to change to the Layout workspace.

2. Create a new Plane primitive by pressing *Shift + A* and select **Mesh | Plane**.

3. With the plane selected, press *S* and then type 10 to scale it to **10 m**.

4. Apply the scale by pressing *Ctrl + A* and selecting **Scale** from the drop-down menu.

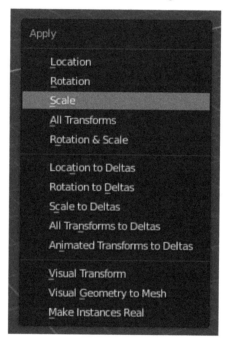

Figure 4.1 – Applying the scale to our plane object

5. Next, we need to subdivide our plane so we have enough geometry to create our landscape. With the plane selected, press *Tab* to enter **Edit Mode**.

6. Press *3* to activate **Face Select** mode.

7. Click on the plane's **Face** to select it.

8. Right-click on this **Face** to bring up the **Face** context menu and select **Subdivide** from the dropdown.

9. Expand the **Subdivide** panel in the bottom left of the 3D Viewport and change **Number of Cuts** to 50 to increase the number of faces on the plane.

10. Click anywhere in the 3D Viewport to apply these changes.

11. Next, we're going to make use of **Proportional Editing** to lift some parts of our plane to create an organic-looking landscape. Enable **Proportional Editing** by clicking the icon at the top of the 3D Viewport or by pressing the shortcut key *O*.

Figure 4.2 – Enable Proportional Editing using the icon or shortcut key O

12. Press *1* to activate **Vertex Select** mode.

13. Click and drag in the 3D Viewport to select only a small number of vertices on the plane object.

14. Press *G* and then press *Z* to move these vertices up.

15. Press *PageUp* and *PageDown* to adjust the size of the Proportional Editing circle. This will increase or decrease the area of vertices that will be affected by the move tool.

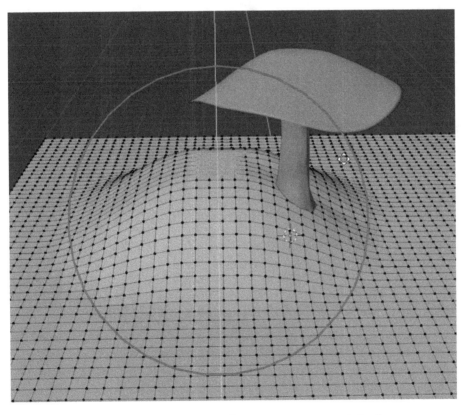

Figure 4.3 – Using Proportional Editing to create an organic landscape

16. Continue with this method to pull and push vertices upward as well as down, until you have something that you like.

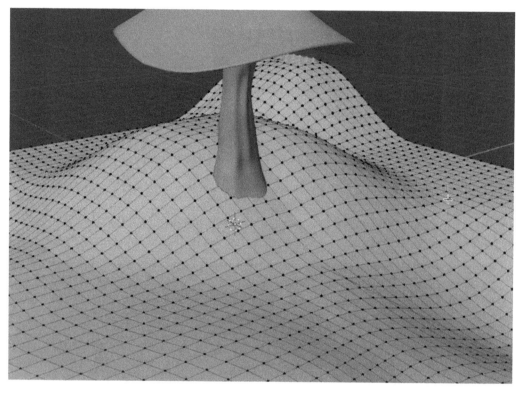

Figure 4.4 – Pushing and pulling vertices until you have something like this

17. Once you are happy with the landscape, press *Tab* to exit **Edit Mode**.

18. Let's rename our Plane object to `Group` or `Landscape`. Double-click the Plane object in the **Outliner** and give it a name.

In the next section, we will be adding some grass to our landscape by using simple plane objects and Geometry Nodes. Please save your project now.

Adding grass using Geometry Nodes

Let's add some grass to our Landscape object. To do this, we will be creating some basic grass objects by using simple plane primitives and then we will make use of Geometry Nodes to distribute the grass across our Landscape object. We will also be making use of weight painting to paint in the density of the grass. Let's do this now.

Creating the individual grass blades

Execute the following steps to create individual grass blades:

1. Create a new plane object by pressing *Shift + A* and select **Mesh | Plane**. This will be one of our grass blades.

2. With this plane object selected, press *G* and then press *X* and move it off to the side away from our landscape and mushroom.

3. Let's rotate this plane object 90 degrees around the *x* axis. To do this, press *R* and then press *X* and type 90. Click in the 3D Viewport to confirm the rotation.

4. Next, let's scale this plane object on the *x* axis by pressing *S* and then press *X* so that we have a thin rectangle object, as shown in the following screenshot:

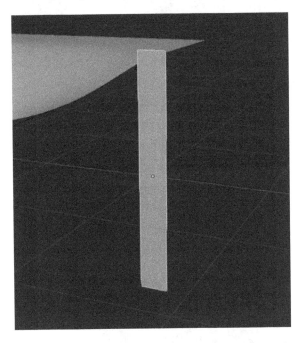

Figure 4.5 – Rotate and scale the plane object until you have something like this

5. Move the grass blade up by pressing *G* and then pressing *Z* so that it's on top of the floor grid. You can hold down the *Ctrl* key while moving to enable **snapping**.

6. With the grass blade selected, press *Tab* to enter **Edit Mode**.

7. Press *2* to enable **Edge Select** mode.

8. Now, let's move the pivot point of our grass blade to the bottom of the mesh. To do this, click the bottom edge of the grass blade to select it.

9. With this edge selected, press *Shift + S* and click **Cursor to Selected**. This will snap the 3D Cursor to this bottom edge.

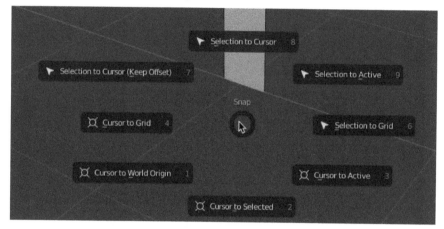

Figure 4.6 – Snapping the 3D Cursor to the bottom edge of the grass blade

10. Press *Tab* to exit **Edit Mode**.

11. Right-click the grass blade object and select **Set Origin | Origin to 3D Cursor**. This will position the pivot point of this object to its bottom edge.

12. Let's apply the object's scale now – with the grass blade selected, press *Ctrl + A* and select **Scale** from the drop-down menu to apply its scale.

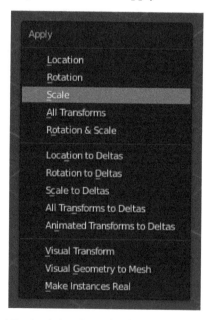

Figure 4.7 – Applying the scale of our grass blade object

13. With the grass blade selected, press *Tab* to enter **Edit Mode** again.

14. Let's add some loop cuts to our mesh – press *Ctrl + R* and hover your mouse pointer over the mesh until you get a horizontal loop cut. Use your mouse wheel to increase the number of loop cuts to 3. You can also use the **Loop Cut and Slide** dialog box in the corner of the 3D Viewport to adjust the number of loop cuts. Click in the 3D Viewport to apply these loop cuts.

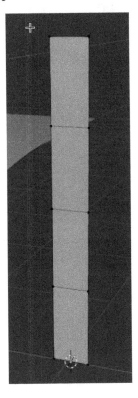

Figure 4.8 – Adding some loop cuts to our grass blade object

15. Press *1* to enable **Vertex Select** mode.

16. Drag the mouse to select the two top vertices, and then press *S* to scale them so we have a sharper point at the top of the grass blade. You should still have **Proportional Editing** active, which will help with this process as it will scale the middle vertices as well – adjust the Proportional Editing circle using *PageUp* and *PageDown* until you have something that looks like the following screenshot:

Figure 4.9 – Shaping our grass blade object

17. Next, let's add a slight curve to our grass blade by selecting two vertices across from each other and moving them in the *y* axis by pressing *G* and then pressing *Y*. Do this until you have a grass blade that looks like this:

Figure 4.10 – Adding a slight curve to our grass blade object

18. Next, we're going to create a few variations of the grass blade by duplicating our grass blade model. Press *Tab* to exit **Edit Mode** and with the grass blade selected, press *Shift + D* and then press *X* to duplicate and move along the *x* axis.

19. With the duplicate copy still selected, press *S* and scale it down slightly.

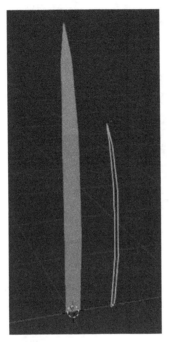

Figure 4.11 – Duplicating the grass blade to create more variations

20. Now rotate this copy on the *z* axis by pressing *R* and then pressing *Z* and moving the mouse. We're adding rotation variations to add randomness to our grass.

21. Create two more duplicate copies and add some variations to their scale and Z rotation by using the shortcut *S* to scale, and pressing *R* and then *Z* to rotate on the *z* axis. Do this until you have four grass blades.

Figure 4.12 – Creating four grass blades for variation

22. Next, we need to apply the scale and rotation of our grass blades. To do this, select all four grass blades, and then press *Ctrl + A* and click **Rotation & Scale** from the drop-down menu.

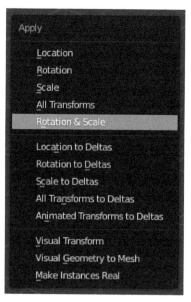

Figure 4.13 – Applying the Rotation & Scale of the grass blades

23. We need to add our grass blades to their own Collection so we can instantiate them using Geometry Nodes later in this chapter. With all four grass blades selected, press *M* and click **New Collection** from the dialog box.

24. Type Grass to give this new collection a name and click **OK** to confirm.

Figure 4.14 – Naming the Collection as Grass

Looking at the **Outliner,** you will see your new Collection called **Grass**, containing each grass blade object. Uncheck the box next to this collection in the **Outliner** to hide it from our scene as we will reference this collection using Geometry Nodes and don't need to see the collection in the scene.

Figure 4.15 – Unchecking the box next to the collection to hide it from our scene

Scattering the grass blades using Geometry Nodes

Let's distribute our grass blade objects across the landscape we've created. For this, we're going to make use of Geometry Nodes. Please go ahead and save your project now:

1. Click the Landscape plane (Ground) to select it and click the **Geometry Nodes** tab at the top of the interface to enter the **Geometry Nodes** workspace.

2. With the plane still selected, click **New** to add a Geometry Nodes modifier to our landscape.

3. The first node we will be creating is the **Point Distribute** node, which will create random points across our landscape. Create this node now by pressing *Shift + A* and selecting **Point | Point Distribute**; slot it in after the **Group Input** node. You will now see the points distributed across our mesh in the 3D Viewport.

4.   Next, we need a **Point Instance** node to instantiate our grass blade objects. Create this node by pressing *Shift + A* and selecting **Point | Point Instance** and slot this node in right before the **Group Output** node.

5.   We need to configure this node to use our Grass collection. At the top of the **Point Instance** node, click **Collection**, and then untick **Whole Collection**.

6.   Click the empty box next to **Collection** on the **Point Instance** node and select the **Grass** Collection from the drop-down list.

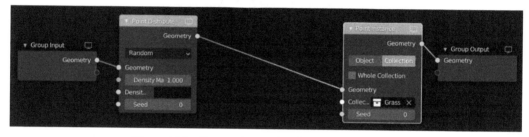

Figure 4.16 – Your node tree should now look like this

7.   You will now see the grass blades in the 3D Viewport but without the landscape mesh. We need to join this mesh before we can see it in the 3D Viewport. Let's create a **Join Geometry** node by pressing *Shift + A* and selecting **Geometry | Join Geometry**. Position this node above the **Point Instance** node but do not connect it to our node tree yet.

8.   Now connect both the **Point Instance** and **Group Input** node to the **Join Geometry** node. The **Group Input** node should also be connected to the **Point Distribute** node. This way, we are joining our Grass instance objects with our original landscape geometry. You should now see the grass objects as well as the landscape in the 3D Viewport.

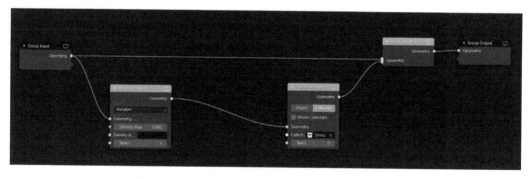

Figure 4.17 – Your node tree should now look like this

9. We can add some variation to the scale of our grass instance objects. To do this, we need an **Attribute Randomize** node. Let's add one by pressing *Shift + A* and selecting **Attribute | Attribute Randomize**. Slot this node in between the **Point Distribute** and **Point Instance** nodes.

10. Click the empty box next to **Attribute** on the **Attribute Randomize** node and select **scale** from the drop-down menu. You can also type the attribute name `scale` in lowercase if you don't see it in the dropdown.

11. On this **Attribute Randomize** node, set the **Min** value to `0.010` and the **Max** value to `0.780`. These settings worked for me but feel free to experiment.

12. Let's increase the amount of grass we see on the landscape. To do this, we can increase the **Density** amount on the **Point Distribute** node. Set this value to `50` but feel free to experiment with different values until you are happy with the number of grass blades you see in the scene.

13. We can also make use of **Weight Paint** to paint the density of our grass! First, let's disable the **Geometry Nodes** modifier for the viewport – click the **Landscape (Ground)** object in the 3D Viewport to select it, and then click the **Modifiers** icon in the side properties panel. Click the **Display modifier in viewport** icon to disable the modifier from the viewport.

Figure 4.18 – Disabling the Geometry Nodes modifier temporarily from the 3D Viewport

14. With the Landscape object still selected, click the **Object Data Properties** panel and click + under **Vertex Groups** to create a new Vertex Group.

15. Rename this new Vertex Group to `GrassDensity`.

16. In the 3D Viewport, click the **Object Mode** dropdown, and then select **Weight Paint** from the list.

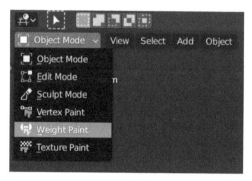

Figure 4.19 – Entering Weight Paint mode

17. Let's set our Brush settings at the top of the 3D Viewport now. Set **Weight** to 1.000, **Radius** to 106 px, and **Strength** to 0.667. Again, feel free to experiment with different settings here.

18. Now, paint on the Landscape object where you want to have more grass. Red areas will have a density of 1 and blue will have a density of 0. Be creative and feel free to experiment here – we can always come back to the weight painting later to change it if needed.

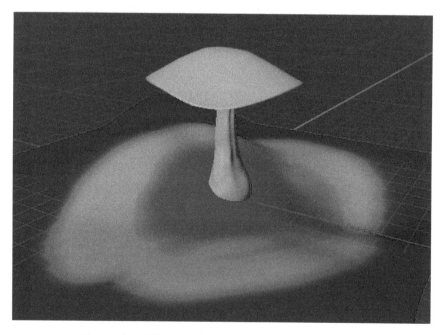

Figure 4.20 – Using weight painting to distribute the grass

19. Click the **Weight Paint** dropdown in the top corner of the 3D Viewport and select **Object Mode** to change back to **Object Mode**.

20. Let's enable our Geometry Nodes modifier again in the Viewport. Click the **Modifier Properties** icon and click the **Display modifier in viewport** checkbox to enable the modifier.

21. We need to configure the **Point Distribute** node so that it's making use of **Weight Paint**. In the Geometry Node tree, on the **Point Distribute** node, click the empty box next to **Density** and select the **GrassDensity** Vertex Group that we created from the drop-down list. You can also type the name of the Vertex Group but note that this field is case-sensitive.

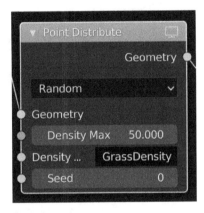

Figure 4.21 – Using the GrassDensity Vertex Group we created to distribute the grass instances

22. Let's add some more random rotation to our grass. For this, we're going to create another **Attribute Randomize** node by pressing *Shift + A* and selecting **Attributes | Attribute Randomize** node. Slot this node in between the first **Attribute Randomize** node and the **Point Instance** node.

23. Click the empty box next to **Attribute** and select **rotation** from the list. You can also type rotation in the box. Note that this is case-sensitive.

24. The **Min** rotation values should be 0.000 / 0.000 / 0.000.

25. For the **Max** rotation values, I used 0.250 / 0.250 / 10.000. This means that our grass blades will be randomly rotated by using these values. They will be rotated a maximum of 0.250 on both the *x* and *y* axes and a maximum of 10 on the *z* axis.

Feel free to experiment with these values until you are happy with the randomness of your grass. Remember that you can always go into **Edit Mode** and adjust the scale of the grass blade meshes. Always adjust the scale of your instance objects within **Edit Mode** and not in **Object Mode**.

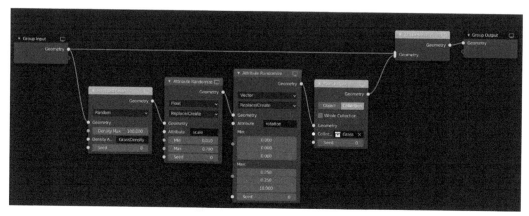

Figure 4.22 – Your final node tree should look like this

The grass should now look more natural and have some nice randomness to it. Feel free to change the values of some of the nodes and see how they affect your scene. Feel free to go back to **Weight Paint** and make adjustments if needed.

Figure 4.23 – Your scene should now look something like this

Congratulations! You have now created an organic-looking landscape as well as grass distributed using Geometry Nodes. Please save your project now.

Summary

You should now have a good understanding of how to create organic-looking landscapes using Proportional Editing. You should now also understand the process of creating individual grass or plant elements and how to distribute them across an object using Geometry Nodes and making use of weight painting to control the density.

In the next chapter, we will focus on shading and how to create realistic materials for our mushroom, landscape, and grass objects.

5
PBR Materials: Texturing our Mushroom Scene

In this chapter, we will be adding materials to our mushroom scene. We will create procedural materials using shading nodes to create realistic-looking materials for the mushroom as well as the grass. For the landscape, we will make use of a texture image. We will also be using the normal map that we baked in *Chapter 3, Organic Modeling P1: Creating a Mushroom,* to add finer details to our mushroom. Let's get started.

The following is a render preview of the materials that we will be creating in this chapter:

Figure 5.1 – A render preview of the materials that we will create in this chapter

The main topics we'll cover in this chapter are as follows:

- Creating procedural materials for both the mushroom and grass using the Shader Editor
- Assigning multiple materials to the same model
- Using a normal map to add details to our mushroom
- Using PBR textures to create realistic-looking materials for our landscape
- Using **High Dynamic Range Imaging** (**HDRI**) and Sky Texture to add realistic-looking lighting

Adding materials to the mushroom

In this section, we will focus on creating materials for our mushroom model. We will be making use of two material slots, one for the stem of the mushroom and one for the top part of the mushroom.

The mushroom stem

Let's begin creating the material for the stem part of the mushroom. We will be creating a gradient color material, as well as adding tiny bumps on the surface of the stem.

Creating a new material

Execute the following steps for creating a new material for the mushroom stem:

1. Let's hide all the objects in our scene except the mushroom model so that we can focus on the mushroom. In the **Outliner**, click the eye icon next to each object to hide them in the 3D Viewport. Do this with all objects, except the **Mushroom_LP** model.

2. Click the **Mushroom** model in the 3D Viewport to select it, then click the **Shading** tab at the top of the interface to open the Shader Editor.

3. In the Shader Editor, with the Mushroom model still selected, click **New** to create a new material. You will see that by default, two nodes are created: the **Principled BSDF** shader node and a **Material Output** node. Note that shading nodes flow from left to right, the same as Geometry Nodes.

4. Rename this new material by clicking on the name **Material** at the top of the Shader Editor window, and renaming it to MushroomStem.

Creating the material nodes

Let's create our first node, a ColorRamp node. To create a new node, press *Shift + A* to bring up the **Add** menu. Here you can either browse for a node or you can use the **Search** option at the top of the **Add** menu:

1. Click **Search** at the top of the **Add** menu and type color, then click **ColorRamp** from the list to add this new node to the node editor.

2. Position the **ColorRamp** node to the left of the **Principled BSDF** shader node.

3. Connect the **Color** output of the **ColorRamp** node to the **Base Color** input on the **Principled BSDF** shader node by clicking the **Color** output dot on the **ColorRamp** node and dragging the mouse to the **Base Color** dot on the **Principled BSDF** shader node.

4. By default, the **ColorRamp** node has two color values: black (on the left) and white (on the right). Let's modify these two colors by clicking the small triangle of the black color value to the left and then clicking the bigger black rectangle at the bottom of the **ColorRamp** node.

5. This will bring up the color wheel – use the sliders and/or color wheel to change this color to light brown.

6. Next, let's change the white color on the right to a darker brown. Click the small triangle of the white color value to the right and then click the bigger white rectangle at the bottom of the **ColorRamp** node.

7. This will again bring up a color wheel – change this color to a darker brown by using the sliders and/or color wheel.

Figure 5.2 – Your ColorRamp node should now look like this

8. Next, let's change the interpolation between the two colors from **Linear** to **B-Spline**. To do this click **Linear** on this node, and select **B-Spline** from the dropdown. This will create a smoother gradient between the two color values.

9. Next, drag both color values closer to each other to change how the gradient will be displayed on our model. To move the color values, click and drag the small triangle above each color value. Experiment with this and see how it affects your material in the 3D Viewport. See the following screenshot:

Figure 5.3 – Drag the color values close to each other to change the gradient

10. Next, let's create a Gradient Texture node, by pressing *Shift* + *A* and using the search function to search for `Gradient`. Click **Gradient Texture** from the drop-down menu to add the node to the node editor.

11. Position the **Gradient Texture** node to the left of the **ColorRamp** node.

12. Connect the **Color** output of the **Gradient Texture** node to the **Fac** input of the **ColorRamp** node.

13. Next, create a **Separate XYZ** node by pressing *Shift* + *A* and using the **Search** function. Position the **Separate XYZ** node to the left of the **Gradient Texture** node.

14. Now, connect the **Z** output from the **Separate XYZ** node to the **Vector** input of the **Gradient Texture** node. The reason we're doing this is to use the *Z axis* of our model for the gradient, thus having a lighter color at the base of the stem and a darker color at the top.

15. Next, let's create a **Mapping** node. This node is used to adjust how our material will be mapped onto our model. Press *Shift + A* and use the search function to search for the **Mapping** node. Position this node to the left of the **Separate XYZ** node.

16. Connect the **Vector** output from the **Mapping** node to the **Vector** input of the **Separate XYZ** node.

17. Lastly, we need to create a Texture Coordinate node. This node is also used for how our material will be mapped to our model – making use of different coordinates, such as **UV Maps** or **Generated**. Press *Shift + A* and use the search function to search for **Texture Coordinate** and position this node to the left of the **Mapping** node.

18. Connect **Generated Output** from the **Texture Coordinate** node to the **Vector** input on the **Mapping** node. We're making use of the Generated coordinates and not the UV Map coordinates, which will give us a vertical gradient across our model.

19. Your mushroom should now have a gradient texture from top to bottom – see the following screenshot to ensure that your node tree has been set up correctly:

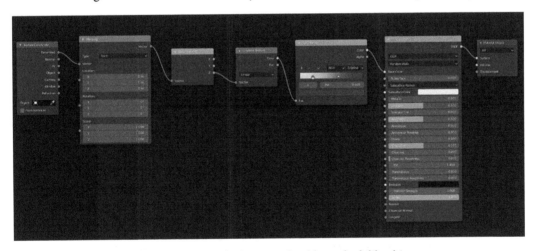

Figure 5.4 – Your shading tree should now look like this

20. Next, let's add tiny bumps to this material by making use of a noise texture and a bump node. This will add some realism to our material. Create a new **Noise Texture** node by pressing *Shift + A* and using the search function to search for **Noise Texture**. Position this node to the left of **Principled BSDF**, but below the **ColorRamp** node.

21. Configure the **Noise Texture** node as follows: change the **Scale** value to 50. The bigger the scale value, the smaller the noise/bumps will be. Set the **Detail** value to 2, **Roughness** to 0.5, and **Distortion** to 0.

Figure 5.5 – Configure the Noise Texture node

22. Next, let's create a **Bump** node by pressing *Shift + A* and using the search function to search for the **Bump** node. Position the **Bump** node in between the **Noise Texture** node and the **Principled BSDF** shader node.

23. Now, let's connect the **Color** output of the **Noise Texture** node to the **Height** input of the **Bump** node.

24. Then connect the **Normal** output of the **Bump** node to the **Normal** input of the **Principled BSDF** node.

25. You should now see the bumps appear on the mushroom model in the 3D Viewport, but the bump texture is way too big. Let's adjust the bump strength by changing the **Strength** parameter on the **Bump** node to 0.100.

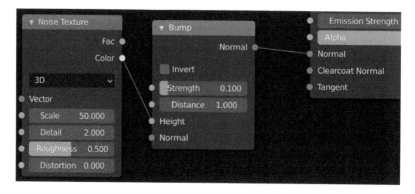

Figure 5.6 – Adding tiny bumps to our material by using a Noise Texture and a Bump node

The bumps should now be much smaller as seen in the following screenshot:

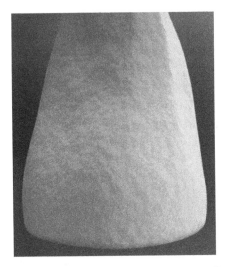

Figure 5.7 – Adding tiny bumps to create realism

We have now created the first material for our mushroom model. In the next section, we will focus on the top part of the mushroom, adding some variation as well as using the normal map that we baked in *Chapter 3, Organic Modeling P1: Creating a Mushroom.* Please save your project now.

Your mushroom material should now look similar to the following screenshot:

Figure 5.8 – The final mushroom material for the stem part

The top part of the mushroom

Let's now focus on the material for the top part of our mushroom. First, we will need to create a new material and assign it to the top part of the mushroom model. We will also learn how to apply the normal map that we have baked to the underside of the top of the mushroom. This will add finer details without increasing the amount of geometry.

Let's get started!

1. In the **Shading** workspace, click the mushroom model in the **3D Viewport** to select it.

2. With the mushroom selected, click the **UV Editing** tab at the top of the interface to bring up the UV Editing workspace.

3. You will now see your UV Map on the left and the mushroom model on the right. With your mouse over the UV Map, ensure that you are in **Face select mode** by pressing the *3* shortcut key.

4. Next, we need to select only the top part of the mushroom model in order to assign a new material to it. We can make use of our UV Map to do this. Hover your mouse pointer over the two large, round UV islands (see the following figure for reference) and press *L* to select all the linked faces of the UV islands. You need to press *L* while hovering over the first round UV island, then hover your mouse over the second round UV island and press *L* again. You should now have both these UV islands selected.

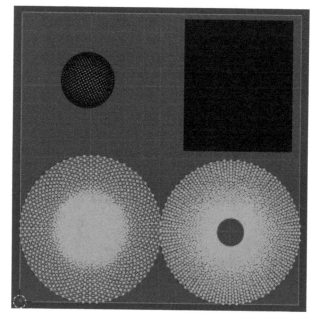

Figure 5.9 – Select both large, round UV islands

5. With these two UV islands selected, you should now see that the top part of the mushroom model has been selected in the 3D Viewport on the right.

Figure 5.10 – The 3D Viewport showing the selected top part of the mushroom

6. Now let's go back to the **Shading** workspace by clicking the **Shading** tab at the top of the interface.

Creating a new material

Execute the following steps for creating a new material:

1. Back in the **Shading** workspace, we need to enter **Edit Mode**. Hover your mouse over the 3D Viewport and press *Tab* to enter **Edit Mode**.

   You will see that the top part of the mushroom is still selected.

Figure 5.11 – The top part of the mushroom is still selected as we enter Edit Mode

2. Click the **Slot 1** drop-down menu at the top of the Shader Editor.

3. Now click + to add a new material slot.

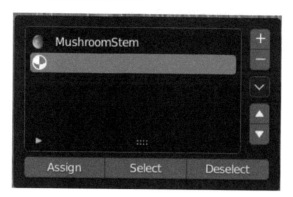

Figure 5.12 – Clicking the + button will create a new material slot

4. Click the **New** button to the right of the **Slot 2** drop-down menu to create a new material.

5. Rename this new material to MushroomTop by clicking on the word **Material** at the top of the Shader Editor.

6. Next, we need to assign this new material to the top part of the mushroom. To do this, click the **Slot 2** drop-down menu, and with the new material, **MushroomTop**, highlighted, click the **Assign** button to assign this new material to the selected faces of the mushroom. The top part of the mushroom should now turn white in the 3D Viewport because we have assigned a blank new material to it.

Figure 5.13 – The top part of the mushroom now has its own material

Creating the material nodes

Execute the following steps for creating material nodes:

1. Let's create our first node – a **ColorRamp** node. Press *Shift + A* and use the search function to search for this node and position it to the left of the **Principled BSDF** shader node.

2. On the **ColorRamp** node, change the colors to a darker brown on the left and a light brown on the right.

3. Change the interpolation from **Linear** to **Ease**. This will create a smoother gradient. Experiment with the different types of interpolation to see how they affect the gradient.

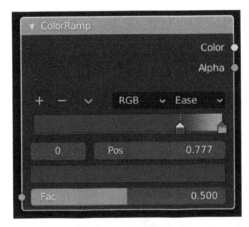

Figure 5.14 – Configure the ColorRamp node like this

4. Now connect the **Color** output of the **ColorRamp** node to the **Base Color** input of the **Principled BSDF** shader node. See how your mushroom model updates in the 3D Viewport once you connect the **ColorRamp** node.

5. Next, add a **Gradient Texture** node and place it to the left of the **ColorRamp** node. Press *Shift + A* and use the search function to add the **Gradient Texture** node. This will allow us to create a gradient across our model.

6. Connect the **Color** output on the **Gradient Texture** node to the **Fac** input of the **ColorRamp** node.

7. Next, add a **Separate XYZ** node and place it to the left of the **Gradient Texture** node. Press *Shift + A* and use the search function to add the **Separate XYZ** node.

8. Connect the **Z** output of the **Separate XYZ** node to the **Vector** input on the **Gradient Texture** node. This will create a gradient using the *z* axis – from the top of the mushroom to the base of the top part of the mushroom.

9. Next, create a **Mapping** node by pressing *Shift + A* and using the search function. Place this node to the left of the **Separate XYZ** node. The **Mapping** node allows us to modify the position, rotation, and scale of a texture.

10. Connect the **Vector** output of the **Mapping node** to the **Vector** input of the **Separate XYZ** node.

11. Lastly, we need a **Texture Coordinate** node to be able to specify which coordinates to use. Press *Shift + A* and use the search function to add this node. Position it to the left of the **Mapping** node.

12. Connect the **Generated** output of the **Texture Coordinate** node to the **Vector** input of the **Mapping** node. The reason we're using the generated coordinates and not the UV Map coordinates is that we want to use the automatically generated texture coordinates of the mushroom mesh.

Have a look at the following screenshot to ensure that your node tree is set up correctly:

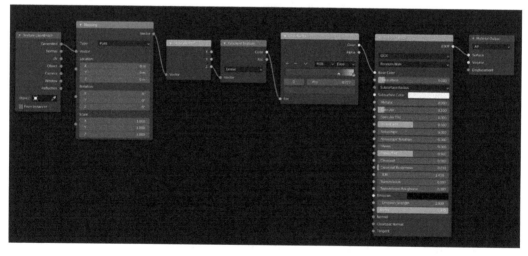

Figure 5.15 – Your node tree should now look like this

13. Next, we're going to adjust the roughness of the top of the mushroom by reusing the gradient texture we currently have as the Base Color. To do this, let's create another **ColorRamp** node by pressing *Shift + A* and using the search function. Position the new **ColorRamp** node under the existing **ColorRamp** node.

14. Configure this **ColorRamp** node as follows: *white on the left* and *light gray on the right*. Drag the right color marker closer toward the white marker on the left as shown in *Figure 5.16*. Note that 100% white represents a value of 1 and 100% black represents a value of 0. A roughness value of 0 is 100% reflective and a roughness value of 1 is 0% reflective.

Figure 5.16 – Configure the ColorRamp to control the roughness

15. Connect the **Color** output from the original **ColorRamp** node to the **Fac** input of this new **ColorRamp** node. This will convert the original gradient to white and gray.

16. Now connect the **Color** output of this new **ColorRamp** node to the **Roughness** input of the **Principled BSDF** shader node.

17. See how this affects the material in the 3D Viewport. The top of the mushroom should now be slightly more reflective than the outer edges and underside of the top part of the mushroom.

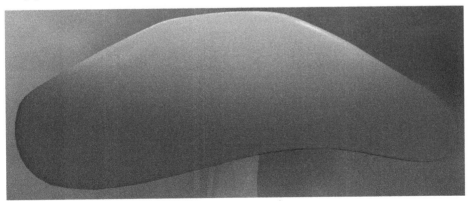

Figure 5.17 – The top of the mushroom is now slightly more reflective

18. Next, we're going to apply the normal map that we created in *Chapter 3, Organic Modeling P1: Creating a Mushroom*. To do this, we'll need a **Normal Map** node. Create one now by pressing *Shift + A* and using the search function. Position this node to the left of the **Principled BSDF** shader node.

19. On the **Normal Map** node, click the empty box below **Tangent Space** and select **UVMap** from the drop-down menu. This is not really necessary but good practice, because if you have more than one UV Map, you will have to specify which one you're going to use. For this example, we only have one UV Map configured.

20. Next, let's create an **Image Texture** node so that we can load the normal map that we created. Press *Shift + A* and use the search function, then position this **Image Texture** node to the left of the **Normal Map** node.

21. On the **Image Texture** node, click **Open** and browse to the location where you have saved the normal map that we have baked. Select the `NormalMap.png` normal map and click **Open Image** to load it into the **Image Texture** node.

22. Still on the **Image Texture** node, change **Color Space** from **sRGB** to **Non-Color**. The reason we're changing **Color Space** is that we won't be using the sRGB colors from the PNG image and are only using the image as a normal map.

23. Next, we need a **Mapping** node – create one by pressing *Shift + A* and using the search function. Position this node to the left of the **Image Texture** node.

24. We also need a **Texture Coordinate** node – create one by pressing *Shift + A* and using the search function. Place this node to the left of the **Mapping** node.

25. Now let's connect the nodes: connect the **UV** output of the **Texture Coordinate** node to the **Vector** input of the **Mapping** node. We're using the UV output because we want to use our UV Map to ensure the normal map will be placed correctly on the model.

26. Connect the **Vector** output on the **Mapping** node to the **Vector** input of the **Image Texture** node.

27. Connect the **Color** output of the **Image Texture** node to the **Color** input of **Normal Map**.

28. And lastly, connect the **Normal** output of the **Normal Map** node to the **Normal** input on the **Principled BSDF** shader node.

29. You can adjust the strength of the normal map by adjusting the **Strength** parameter on the **Normal Map** node – let's change this value to 2.000.

30. Have a look at the mushroom model in the 3D Viewport. See how the normal map is affecting the underside of the top part of the mushroom. We can now see the details that we have sculpted.

Figure 5.18 – See how the normal map is affecting the underside of the top of the mushroom

31. The top of the mushroom is still very smooth – let's add some tiny bumps to it. For this, we will need a few more nodes. First, let's create a **Noise Texture** node and position it below the **Image Texture** node.

32. Configure the **Noise Texture** node as follows: **Scale:** 5.000, **Detail:** 16.000, **Roughness:** 0.500, **Distortion:** 0.000. This should give the bumps a good overall size and detail level.

33. Next, we need a **Bump** node to convert the **Noise Texture** to a normal map. Add a **Bump** node by pressing *Shift + A* and using the search function. Position the **Bump** node to the right of the **Noise Texture** node.

34. Connect the **Color** output on the **Noise Texture** node to the **Height** input on the **Bump** node.

35. Set the **Strength** parameter on the **Bump** node to 0.400. This parameter controls the strength of the bump texture.

36. Next, we need a **MixRGB** node so that we can combine the sculpted normal map details with the overall noise texture bumps. Add a **MixRGB** node by pressing *Shift + A* and using the search function. Position the **MixRGB** node to the right of the **Bump** node.

37. Now connect the **Normal** output of the **Normal Map** node to the **Color1** input on the **MixRGB** node.

38. Connect the **Normal** output of the **Bump** node to the **Color2** input on the **MixRGB** node.

39. Finally, connect the **Color** output of the **MixRGB** node to the **Normal** input on the **Principled BSDF** shader node.

40. You can adjust the **Fac** value on the **MixRGB** node to change the influence or mix of the **Normal Map** and **Bump** data. Let's leave this at 0.500 to have a mix of 50%/50%. Experiment with this value and see how it affects your material.

Figure 5.19 – You should now see bumps on the top of the mushroom

41. Let's make some final adjustments to the **Principled BSDF** shader node. Change the **Subsurface** value to 0.100 and the **Specular** value to 0.100. The **Subsurface** value will allow some of the light to penetrate the surface of the model to create a subtly translucent effect. The lower **Specular** value will limit the number of specular reflections. Feel free to experiment with these values to see how they affect your material.

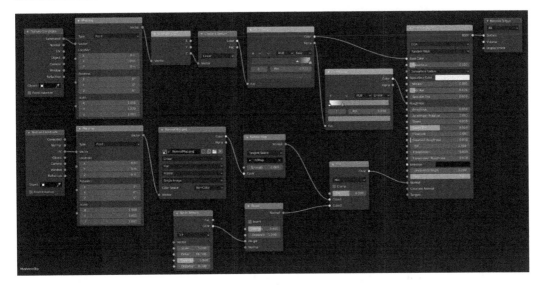

Figure 5.20 – Your final node tree should look like this

Congratulations, you have now successfully created materials for the stem and top part of the mushroom model. You should now have a good understanding of creating materials using the Shader Editor as well as assigning different materials to different parts of a 3D model.

You have also learned how to set up a normal map in the Shader Editor as well as how to use different nodes such as the **ColorRamp, Gradient Texture**, and **Mix** nodes to create procedural materials.

In the next section, we will take a look at how we can use pre-made PBR materials that you can download from various websites. We will be adding materials to the landscape around our mushroom model.

Adding materials to the landscape

Let's add some materials to the landscape. For this, we will be using a PBR texture image consisting of the following passes:

- **Albedo**: Used for the Base Color
- **Ambient Occlusion**: For adding shadows to the Base Color
- **Specular**: Controls specular reflections
- **Roughness**: Controls the overall roughness
- **Bump**: For adding tiny bumps using a normal map

You can either use your own PBR materials or you can download the one we will be using here: `https://github.com/PacktPublishing/Taking-Blender-to-the-Next-Level/blob/main/Chapter05/Patchy_Wild_Grass.zip`

1. Before we start applying materials to our landscape, make sure you unhide the **Ground** object by using the show/hide eye icons in the **Outliner**. You can hide the mushroom model if you prefer, but it's not required.

2. Disable the **Geometry Nodes** modifier on the **Ground** object so that we don't see the grass while we're adding materials. Click the **Ground** object in the 3D Viewport to select it, then click the **Modifier Properties** icon to the right of the 3D Viewport, and then click the **Display modifier in viewport** icon at the top of the **Geometry Nodes** modifier to disable the grass in the 3D Viewport.

3. With the **Ground** object selected, click the **Shading** tab at the top of the interface to enter the shading workspace.

4. With the **Ground** object still selected, click the **New** button above Shader Editor to create a new material.

5. Click the material's default **Material** name at the top of the Shader Editor and rename it to Ground.

6. Next, we're going to drag and drop our material passes into the Shader Editor. If you are using a Mac, open **Finder** and browse to the folder containing the material passes. On Windows, you can do the same using **File Explorer**.

7. Now, we're going to drag the following passes one by one into the Shader Editor. Let's begin with the **Albedo** pass, which we will use for the Base Color of our ground: vb2mdatlw_4K_Albedo.jpg.

8. You will see that Blender automatically creates an **Image Texture** node with the image file when dragging images into the Shader Editor.

    Now do the same with the following material passes:
    - vb2mdatlw_4K_AO.jpg (**Ambient Occlusion**)
    - vb2mdatlw_4K_Bump.jpg (**Bump map**)
    - vb2mdatlw_4K_Roughness.jpg (**Roughness map**)
    - vb2mdatlw_4K_Specular.jpg (**Specular map**)

9. Let's arrange these nodes in the Shader Editor as follows:
    - Place the Albedo map at the top to the left of the Principled BSDF shader node.
    - Position the AO map under the Albedo map.

- Position the Specular map under the AO map.

- Position the Roughness map under the Specular map.

- And lastly, position the Bump map under the Roughness map.

10. Next, we also need a **Mapping** node as well as a **Texture Coordinate** node. Create both of these now by pressing *Shift + A* and using the search function. Place the **Mapping** node to the left of all the material passes, and place the **Texture Coordinate** node to the left of the **Mapping** node. We will be sharing these two nodes with all the material pass nodes.

11. Connect the **UV** output of the **Texture Coordinate** node to the **Vector** input of the **Mapping** node.

12. Next, connect the **Vector** output of the **Mapping** node to each of the five material pass nodes as shown in the following screenshot:

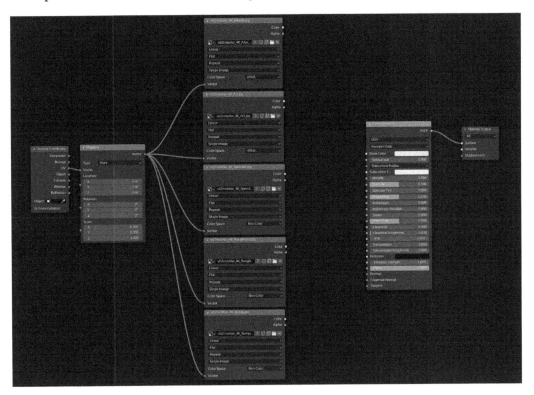

Figure 5.21 – Position the nodes like this

13. Let's start connecting these material passes to the **Principled BSDF** shader node. First, connect the **Color** output of the **Albedo map** node to the **Base Color** input on the **Principled BSDF** shader node.

14. Next, let's connect the **Specular map**. Connect the **Color** output on the **Specular map** node to the **Specular** input on the **Principled BSDF** shader node.

15. On the **Specular map** node, change **Color Space** from **sRGB** to **Non-Color** as we don't need any color information, only black and white data.

16. Next, we can connect the **Roughness** map. Connect the **Color** output on the **Roughness map** node to the **Roughness** input on the **Principled BSDF** shader node.

17. Change **Color Space** on the **Roughness** map node to **Non-Color** as we just need the black and white data from this image.

18. Next, we're going to connect the **Bump map**. For this, we also need a **Bump** node to convert our image texture to a normal map. Create a **Bump** node now by pressing *Shift + A* and using the search function. Position this **Bump** node between the **Bump map Image Texture** node and the **Principled BSDF** shader node.

19. On the **Bump map Image Texture** node, change **Color Space** to **Non-Color** as we also don't need any color values, only black and white color data.

20. Next, connect the **Color** output on the **Bump Image Texture** node to the **Height** input on the **Bump** node.

21. Then connect the **Normal** output on the **Bump** node to the **Normal** input on the **Principled BSDF** shader node.

22. On the **Bump** node, set **Strength** to 0.2. Experiment with this value to adjust the influence of this bump map and see how it affects your material in the 3D Viewport.

23. We can easily make some adjustments to how these different passes affect our material by adding a **ColorRamp** node to change the contrast of these black and white passes. Let's do this now by adding a new **ColorRamp** node by pressing *Shift + A* and using the search function.

24. Drag this **ColorRamp** node onto the line between the **Roughness map** node and the **Principled BSDF** shader node. Dragging a node onto a line will automatically connect it to the node tree.

25. Now let's adjust the white and black sliders on this **ColorRamp** node to change the contrast of the **Roughness** map, thus changing the way it affects the roughness of our material. Feel free to experiment with the **ColorRamp** values to see how it changes the roughness of the material.

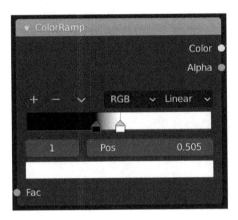

Figure 5.22 – Use ColorRamp to make quick adjustments to the material passes

26. Next, we're going to mix the **Albedo map** with the **AO map** to add darker shadows to our landscape by multiplying the AO map with the Albedo map. Let's begin by creating a **MixRGB** node by pressing *Shift + A* and using the search function.

27. Drag this **Mix** node over the line between the **Albedo map** node and the **Principled BSDF** shader node. This will automatically connect the node to the node tree. The **Albedo map** should now be connected to the **Color1** input on the **Mix** node and the **Color** output on the **Mix** node should be connected to the **Base Color** input on the **Principled BSDF** shader node.

28. Now connect the **Color** output on the **Ambient Occlusion map** node to the **Color2** input on the **Mix** node.

29. Let's change the **Blending Mode** setting of the **Mix** node from **Mix** to **Multiply** by clicking the drop-down menu at the top of the **Mix** node. **Multiply Blending Mode** will multiply the color values allowing us to increase or decrease the number of shadow details.

30. By default, the **Fac** value on the **Mix** node is set to 0.500 giving us a 50/50 mix between the two inputs. Leave this **Fac** value at 0.500 but feel free to experiment with this value to see how it affects the overall look of the landscape material.

31. Let's neaten up our node tree by collapsing all the Image Texture nodes by clicking the small triangle icon at the top left of each of these nodes. This will save some layout space and it looks a bit nicer as well.

Figure 5.23 – You can collapse a node by clicking the small triangle in the top-left corner

Congratulations, you have created your first PBR material!

Figure 5.24 – Your landscape should now look similar to this

Look at the following screenshot to ensure you have all the nodes that we have covered in this section:

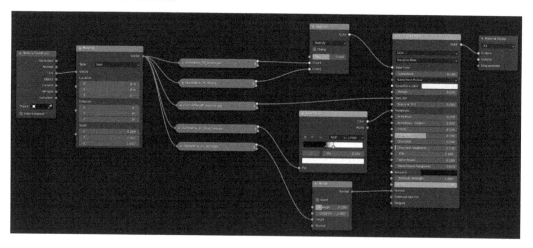

Figure 5.25 – Your final node tree for the landscape should look like this

In the next section, we will create a procedural material for the grass. Please save your project now.

Creating a procedural grass material

In this section, we will be creating a procedural material for our grass blades. We will be making use of a **ColorRamp** node as well as a **Wave Texture** node to create the grass materials.

Let's get started!

1. First, let's ensure you are in the **Layout** workspace by clicking the **Layout** tab at the top of the interface.

2. Click the **Ground** object in the 3D Viewport to select it, then click the **Modifier Properties** icon to the right of the 3D Viewport and click the **Display Modifier in Viewport** icon to activate it.

3. Unhide the Mushroom model by clicking the eye icon next to it in the **Outliner**.

4. Next, let's enable **Grass Collection** by checking the box next to the **Grass** collection name in the **Outliner**. You will now see the individual grass blades in the 3D Viewport that we created in *Chapter 4, Organic Modeling P2: Creating the Landscape around the Mushroom*.

5. Let's focus on the first grass blade object by selecting it in the 3D Viewport and pressing . (period) on the numpad. If you don't have a keyboard with a numpad, you can also use the tilde ' (above the *Tab* button) shortcut and then select **View Selected** from the **Radial** menu. This will focus the 3D Viewport on the selected object.

6. With the first grass blade still selected, click the **Shading** tab at the top of the interface to enter the Shading workspace.

7. In the Shading workspace, click the **New** button to create a new material.

8. Rename this material to GrassBlade by clicking the default material name at the top of the **Shader Editor**.

9. You should see the default **Principled BSDF** shader node. Let's create our first node, a **ColorRamp** node, by pressing *Shift + A* and using the search function.

10. Position this node to the left of the **Principled BSDF** shading node.

11. On this **ColorRamp** node, change the interpolation from **Linear** to **B-Spline**. This will give us a smooth gradient.

12. Next, let's configure the colors of this **ColorRamp** node. We're creating grass, so let's create a gradient from light green to a slightly darker green. Try and match it with the following screenshot but feel free to experiment:

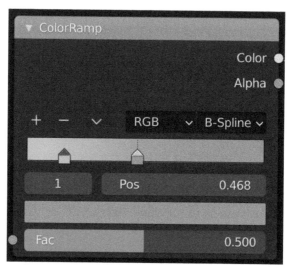

Figure 5.26 – Creating a gradient using a ColorRamp node

13. Connect the **Color** output on the **ColorRamp** node to the **Base Color** input on the **Principled BSDF** shading node.

14. Next, we need to create a **Wave Texture** node. This will allow us to create bands or lines across our grass blade model. Create one now by pressing *Shift + A* and using the search function.

15. Position the **Wave Texture** node to the left of the **ColorRamp** node.

16. Now connect the **Color** output on the **Wave Texture** node to the **Fac** input on the **ColorRamp** node.

17. Let's configure the **Wave Texture** node as follows: **Scale:** 1.000, **Distortion:** 2.000, **Detail:** 4.000, **Detail Scale:** 7.000, **Detail Roughness:** 0.500, **Phase Offset:** 0.000. These settings will give your material thin vertical lines, but again, feel free to experiment with these values to see how they affect the material.

Figure 5.27 – Configure the Wave Texture node

18. Next, we need a **Mapping** node – create one now by pressing *Shift + A* and using the search function.

19. Position the **Mapping** node to the left of the **Wave Texture** node.

20. Connect the **Vector** output on the **Mapping** node to the **Vector** input on the **Wave Texture** node.

21. We also need a **Texture Coordinate** node – create one now by pressing *Shift + A* and using the search function.

22. Position the **Texture Coordinate** node to the left of the **Mapping** node.

23. Connect the **Generated** output on the **Texture Coordinate** node to the **Vector** input on the **Mapping** node. The reason we're using the **Generated** output is we did not create a proper UV Map for the grass blade objects, so we're making use of the **Generated** coordinates from the original plane object we used to create the grass blade object. You may use the UV output as well but it might give you slightly different results. Feel free to experiment and see how it affects your material.

24. Next, let's create some slight unevenness on the grass blade by creating a bump map using a **Noise Texture** node. Press *Shift + A* and using the search function, create a **Noise Texture** node.

25. Position this **Noise Texture** node underneath the **Wave Texture** node.

26. Let's configure the **Noise Texture** node as follows: **Scale**: 4.000, **Detail**: 2.000, **Roughness**: 0.500, **Distortion**: 0.000.

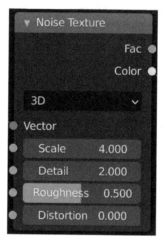

Figure 5.28 – Configure the Noise Texture node to add tiny bumps to the grass blade model

27. Connect the **Vector** output from the **Mapping** node to the **Vector** input on the **Noise Texture** node. Note that we can share the same **Vector** output from one node with multiple nodes.

28. Next, we need a **Bump** node to convert the color data from the **Noise Texture** into a normal map. Create a **Bump** node by pressing *Shift + A* and using the search function.

29. Position this **Bump** node between the **Noise Texture** node and the **Principled BSDF** shader node.

30. Now connect the **Color** output on the **Noise Texture** node to the **Height** input on the **Bump** node.

31. Set the **Strength** property of the **Bump** node to 0.100 – this will affect the amount of bump we have on the grass blade. Experiment to see how it affects the grass material.

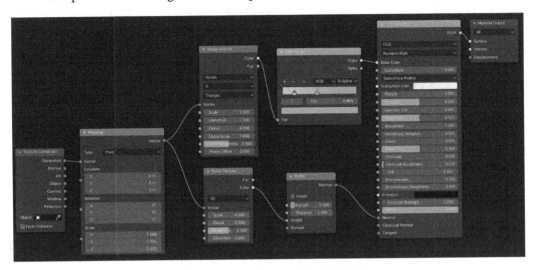

Figure 5.29 – The final grass material shading tree

32. Now let's apply this material to the other three grass blade objects in the **Grass Collection**. Click the second grass blade object in the 3D Viewport to select it, then click the drop-down menu next to the **New** button, at the top of the **Shader Editor**, and choose **GrassBlade** from the drop-down menu to assign this material to the selected grass blade.

Now do the same for the last two grass blade objects. Notice that the grass objects on the landscape are now using this material.

Figure 5.30 – The final look of our grass material in the 3D Viewport

Congratulations, you have now created a procedural grass material. Feel free to experiment with the colors and other parameters of the different nodes. The best way to learn is to play around with the node parameters to see what they do. Don't worry, you can't break them, but always remember to save your project before trying something. Please go ahead and save your project now.

Using an HDRI, Sky Texture, and Sun to light our scene

In this section, we will be setting up our scene lighting using an HDRI map, a Sky Texture, as well as a Sun. Let's do this now:

1. Ensure you are in the Shading workspace by clicking the **Shading** tab at the top of the interface.

2. In the top-left corner of the **Shader Editor**, you will see a drop-down menu with the name **Object**. This is the **Shader Type** menu. Here you can switch between the three different shader types: **Object**, **World**, and **Line Style**. Click this drop-down menu and select **World** from the list.

3. By default, you should see two nodes, a **Background** node and a **World Output** node.

4. We're going to use an HDRI map from Poly Haven that you can download for free from here: `https://polyhaven.com/a/forest_slope`.

    You don't have to use this HDRI – feel free to use any HDRI map you want.

5. Now drag and drop your **HDRI map** from Finder or File Explorer into the Shader Editor. You will see that an **Image Texture** node will be created.

6. Position this **Image Texture** node to the left of the **Background** node.

7. Connect the **Color** output on the **Image Texture** node to the **Color** input on the **Background** node.

8. We're going to mix our HDRI map with a Sky Texture map, so we need a **MixRGB** node to mix them together. Create a new **MixRGB** node by pressing *Shift + A* and using the search function.

9. Drag the **Mix** node onto the line connecting the **Image Texture** node and the **Background** node. This will connect the **Mix** node between these two nodes.

10. Next, we need a **Sky Texture** node to get a nice dynamic sky texture we can use to light our scene. Create a **Sky Texture** node by pressing *Shift + A* and using the search function.

11. Position the **Sky Texture** node below the **Image Texture** node.

12. Configure the **Sky Texture** node as follows: **Sky Type**: **Hosek / Wilkie**, **Turbidity**: `8.000`, **Ground Albedo**: `0.300`. Again, please feel free to experiment with these parameters to see how they affect your scene's lighting.

Figure 5.31 – Configure the Sky Texture node like this

13. Connect the **Color** output on the **Sky Texture** node to the **Color2** input on the **Mix** node.

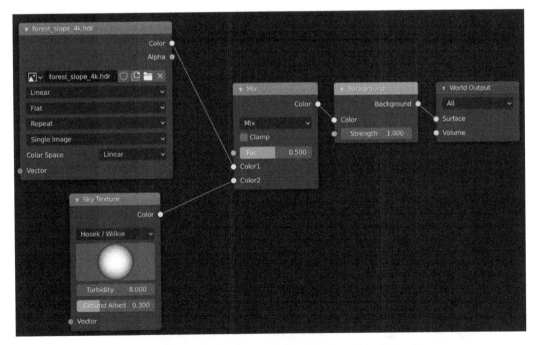

Figure 5.32 – Your final World shading tree should look like this

14. You can now use the **Fac** slider value on the **Mix** node to adjust the mix between **HDRI Image Texture** and **Sky Texture**. Let's leave the **Fac** value as 0.500 to get a 50/50 mix between them. Feel free to experiment to see how this affects your scene.

15. Next, let's create sunlight. For this, let's change over to the **Layout** workspace by clicking the **Layout** tab at the top of the interface.

16. To create a sun, press *Shift + A*, click **Light**, and then click **Sun**. This will create a new sun in your scene.

17. Let's move the sun up by pressing *G* and then pressing *Z* and moving the mouse until the sun is above your scene.

18. Now click and drag the yellow dot under the sun to adjust the angle of the light rays. Move it slightly off to the side so that we're getting light from an angle and not from above. This will give us some nice dramatic-looking shadows.

19. Let's hide **Grass Collection** by unchecking the box next to **Grass Collection** in the **Outliner**. This will hide the four individual grass blades next to our scene.

20. Next, let's change the render engine to **Cycles** by clicking the **Render Properties** icon to the right of the 3D Viewport, and selecting **Cycles** from the drop-down menu next to **Render Engine**.

21. Finally, let's change the 3D Viewport to a Rendered preview mode by hovering your mouse cursor over the 3D Viewport, pressing *Z*, and selecting **Rendered** from the radial menu.

Congratulations! You have now successfully created and applied materials to your mushroom scene, as well as natural-looking scene lighting. Feel free to move the sun around until you are happy with the results. Please save your project now.

Figure 5.33 – Rendered view of our scene

Summary

You should now have a good understanding of how to create your own procedural materials using different shading nodes such as the **ColorRamp** node, as well as adding texture to your materials by using a bump node. You have also learned how to use PBR materials, which you can download from various websites, and how to connect them to the **Principled BSDF** shader. We've also looked at how you can control these PBR maps using **ColorRamp** to adjust how they affect the different parameters on the **Principled BSDF** shader. And lastly, you have also learned how to apply an HDRI to light your scene, as well as mixing an HDRI texture with a Sky Texture to add an extra level of detail.

Congratulations on completing this chapter and please remember to practice your shading skills – it's the only way to get better. Experiment with different nodes and try creating materials you see around you in the real world. I believe that's the best way to become better at creating amazing materials.

In the next chapter, we will be looking at 3D scanning and photogrammetry. You will learn how you can create 3D models of real objects by taking multiple photos and making use of photogrammetry software.

6
3D Scanning and Photogrammetry: Creating Your Own 3D Scans

In this chapter, we will be looking at 3D scanning and photogrammetry! **Photogrammetry** is the process of taking many photos of an object from multiple angles and then using software, such as **Meshroom**, to convert those photos into a 3D model. We will then clean up the scanned model in Blender and optimize the topology using a free program called **Instant Meshes**.

Once we have an optimized model, we will bake the textures from the original high-poly scanned model onto the low-poly optimized model. Let's get started!

The main topics we'll cover in this chapter are as follows:

- Taking photos for 3D scanning/photogrammetry
- Using Meshroom to convert photos into a 3D model
- Cleaning up a model using Blender
- Optimizing the topology of a model using Instant Meshes
- UV unwrapping and baking textures from an original high-poly model to an optimized low-poly model

Taking photos for 3D scanning/ photogrammetry

In this section, we will focus on taking photos of our object that we would like to 3D scan. We will look at which camera settings to use and also best practices to get the best possible 3D scans.

Camera settings and best practices

When it comes to 3D scanning or photogrammetry, you can make use of any good-quality camera. You can even use your mobile phone's camera if you don't have a dedicated DSLR or some other digital camera. If you do make use of your mobile phone, I would suggest looking at camera apps that let you change the camera settings manually, such as the **shutter speed**, **ISO**, and **aperture**. There is a great free option in iOS called **Mavis** that would work really well as it gives you manual control of the iPhone camera.

Here are some settings and best practices when taking photos for photogrammetry:

- **Avoid direct sunlight**: When capturing photos outside, you always want to avoid harsh sunlight on the object you are scanning. Harsh shadows and light will be captured in the texture and cause problems when you're trying to light your object in your 3D environment. Overcast days are usually the best when doing 3D scanning outside, as you will get soft and even lighting across the object. You can also make use of a diffuser to stop any direct sunlight from hitting the object. If possible, shoot your photos indoors, using lights. This way, you can control the lighting and also be sure that you will get perfect lighting during this process.

- **High shutter speed**: Try to use a high shutter speed when taking your photos. A high shutter speed will produce sharp images without much motion blur. I usually try to use a shutter speed above 100.

- **Avoid a shallow depth of field**: When taking the photos, you want the whole object to be in focus, so try to avoid a shallow depth of field. I usually set my aperture to anything above 5 or 6. This setting depends on the lens you are using, but take a few test photos to ensure that the object is completely in focus.

- **Use a low ISO**: Try to use a low ISO setting as this will give you cleaner images. A high ISO setting will cause noise in your images and result in noisy-looking textures. When shooting indoors, make use of lights in order to use a low ISO setting. I would recommend an ISO setting of 100, but this will depend on the camera. Some cameras can take clean images with high ISO values such as 1,200, but do a few tests to see how your camera performs with different ISO settings.

- **Use a tripod if possible**: This is not necessary but will give you better results. Making use of a tripod will ensure that your photos are sharp and that they don't have any motion blur. A tripod will also help a lot if you can't set your shutter speed to a high value. If you can't make use of a tripod, you need to set your shutter speed above 100 to prevent any shaking or motion blur.

- **Consider the number of photos**: This depends a lot on the size of the object you are 3D scanning, but I usually aim for around 50 to 100 photos. You want to make sure that you capture every little detail of the object from all angles. Any part of the object you don't capture will result in missing geometry or holes in the object.

- **Taking the photos**: Start taking photos of the object at a low angle and slowly move around the object as you take photos. Once you have completed a circular movement around the object, increase the height of the angle and move around the object again, taking more photos. Then, increase the angle once again, ensuring you cover the top of the object as well. Once you have taken photos from every angle of the object, you can move in closer and start taking more close-up photos to get the best possible details. The main focus here is to take as many good photos as possible of the object, slowing moving around the object. You want to make sure that you capture every little detail of the object.

- **Avoid reflective objects**: Try to avoid any reflective objects because the software will struggle when it comes to reflections on the object. The software will try to calculate reflections rather than geometry and you might get strange-looking 3D scans. This also goes for the surface the object is placed on. Do not place the object on a reflective surface as this will cause problems.

Once you have captured all the photos, you are ready to move to the next step. We're going to use a free program called **Meshroom** to convert the photos into a 3D model. In the next section, we will look at how to use Meshroom to create a 3D model from your photos.

Using Meshroom to convert photos into a 3D model

In this section, we will be using a free program called Meshroom to convert still images into a 3D model.

Note that Meshroom is currently only compatible with Windows and Linux. Unfortunately, there is no Mac version right now. There are a few other options to use if you are on a Mac but most of them are not free.

Let's get started:

1. Download and install Meshroom from the following URL:
    `https://alicevision.org`.

2. Next, you need to copy the photos to your computer. Create a new folder (this
    folder can be created anywhere on your computer) and copy all your photos from
    your camera into this folder.

3. Launch **Meshroom**.

4. First, you need to import all the photos you have taken into Meshroom. On
    the left side of the interface, you will see a window with the text **Drop Images
    Files / Folders**. Now, open **Windows Explorer** and locate the folder containing
    all your photos.

5. Select all the photos in the folder and drag them into Meshroom over the **Drop
    Images Files / Folders** window.

    The following is a screenshot of the Meshroom user interface. On the left side,
    you will see all the photos you have imported, and on the right side, you will
    see a full-size preview of the selected image.

Figure 6.1 – Imported photos appearing in the Meshroom interface

6. Next, you need to save your Meshroom project so that the program can create the required folders where it will export the OBJ and texture files to. Do this now by clicking **File | Save As**. Browse to a location on your computer where you would like to save the Meshroom project, give it a name, and click **Save**.

    Usually, you can leave all the settings as default in Meshroom and you will get good results, but there is one setting I would like you to activate.

7. At the bottom of the Meshroom interface, you will see the **Graph Editor** window displaying **Nodes**. Click the last node in the node tree, called **Texturing**.

    Clicking this node will display the node properties in the bottom right of the interface.

8. In this window, scroll down until you see **Correct Exposure**. Tick the box next to **Correct Exposure** to enable this setting. With this setting active, Meshroom will try and smooth out any lighting issues on your model.

    You don't have to enable this setting but do experiment with it and see what gives you the best results.

9. Before we start the process, let's save the Meshroom project once more by clicking **File | Save**.

    Now we are ready to run the photogrammetry process.

10. At the top of the Meshroom interface, click the green **Start** button to start the process.

    You will see a progress bar at the top of the interface. This process can take some time depending on your computer as well as your GPU. It also depends on the number of photos and the complexity of the model. Be patient as this process can take a couple of hours to complete.

11. During this process, you will see the 3D mesh being built in the **3D Viewer** window on the right side of the interface. You will also see multiple cameras representing all the angles you took the photos from.

Figure 6.2 – The 3D Viewer window showing the mesh being constructed

12. Allow this process to complete. As I mentioned, this can take a couple of hours. The progress bar at the top of the Meshroom interface will turn completely green – when that happens, you know the process has completed. Meshroom will automatically save the model and texture files once the process is complete, so you don't have to do anything but wait.

In the next section, we will jump back into Blender, import the 3D model created by Meshroom, and start the clean-up process.

Cleaning up a model using Blender

In this section, we will focus on the clean-up process. We will import the 3D model created by Meshroom into Blender. Then, we will orient the model so it's aligned to our floor grid. Lastly, we will delete any unwanted geometry and fix any visible holes in the model.

Importing the model created by Meshroom

Let's begin by importing the model created by Meshroom:

1. Launch a new Blender project.

2. Delete all the current objects by pressing *A* and then pressing *X* and clicking **Delete** to confirm.

3. Now, let's import the model created by Meshroom. In Blender, click **File | Import** and select **Wavefront (.obj)** from the list.

4. Browse to the folder where you saved the Meshroom project. You will see a folder called `MeshroomCache`. Inside this folder, you will see multiple subfolders. Browse to the `Texturing` folder. Inside this folder, you will see a randomly generated folder that looks something like this: `df0c69b046db42c2d5bae036267b79fbffce2af0`.

5. Inside this folder, you will see both the OBJ file as well as the material file. Click the `.obj` file and click **Import OBJ** at the bottom of the window to import the model into your Blender project.

6. The orientation of the imported model will probably not align with the floor grid. Let's rotate it so that it sits flat on the floor grid. You will get the following:

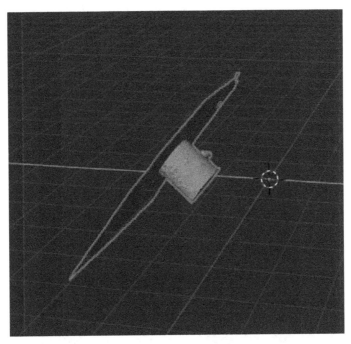

Figure 6.3 – The imported model not aligned to the grid

I find it easier to align the model by using the front, side, and top views. You can toggle between these views by either using the *1*, *3*, and *7* shortcut keys on your numpad to switch between front, side, and top view, or by clicking the different axes in the top-right corner of 3D Viewport as shown in the following screenshot:

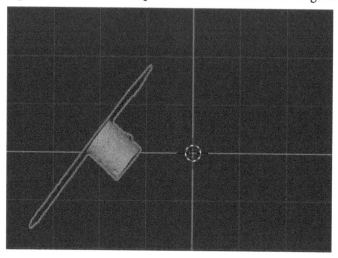

Figure 6.4 – Using the front, side, and top views to easily align the object with the grid

7. Using the front view, click on the model to select it, then press *R* and rotate the object so it aligns with the grid. Press *G* to move the object to the center of the grid.

8. Now, using the side view, do the same by pressing *R* to rotate the model so it aligns with the grid. Use *G* to move it to the center of the grid.

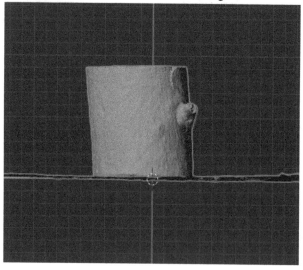

Figure 6.5 – Using the front and side views to align the model with the grid

9. You can also make use of the top view to rotate the object so it aligns with the grid. This does not have to be 100% perfect: we're only trying to align it as best as we can.

10. Once the object is aligned, we need to remove any unwanted geometry as photogrammetry will sometimes detect background objects in your scene or the floor under and around the object. I find it easier to use the top view to remove unwanted geometry. Press the shortcut *7* on the numpad to go into the top view, or you can click on the *z* axis in the top-right corner of 3D Viewport.

11. Click the model to select it and press *Tab* to enter **Edit Mode**.

12. Let's use the **Select Lasso** tool by clicking and holding the **Select Box** icon on the left of 3D Viewport and selecting **Select Lasso**. You can also use the shortcut key *W* to toggle between the four different select modes.

13. Press *1* to ensure you are in vertex select mode.

14. Enable **X-Ray** mode by clicking the icon to the left of the **Wireframe Viewport Shading** icon at the top of 3D Viewport. You can also use the shortcut *Option / Alt + Z*. **X-Ray** mode will ensure that you are selecting all the vertices and not just the visible ones.

15. Now, in the top view, using the **Select Lasso** tool, click and drag to draw a lasso selection around your object as in the following figure:

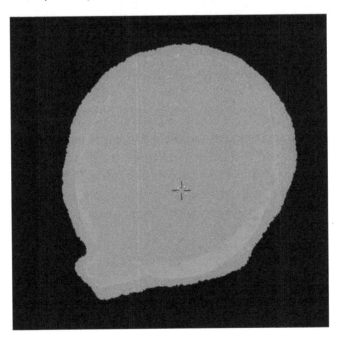

Figure 6.6 – Using the lasso tool to draw around your object

16. Next, let's invert the selection by clicking the **Select** menu at the top of 3D Viewport and selecting **Invert** from the drop-down menu. You can also use the shortcut *Cmd / Ctrl + I*. This will select all the vertices we don't want to keep.

Figure 6.7 – Inverting the selection to select all the vertices we want to discard

17. Now, let's delete these vertices by pressing *X* and selecting **Vertices** from the drop-down menu.

Sometimes you might see holes in your 3D-scanned model. It's very easy to fix these holes but it can take some time to find them. Orbit around your object and zoom in close to find any holes. To fill these holes, press the shortcut *2* to enable **Edge Selection** mode, then click two edges across from each other. Click the first edge, then hold *Shift* and click the second edge. Press *F* to create a new face between these two edges. Repeat this process to fix any holes in the mesh:

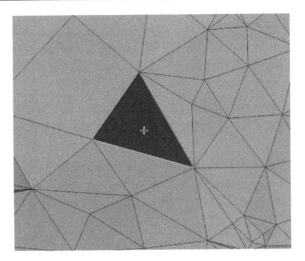

Figure 6.8 – Easily fixing holes by selecting two edges to create a new face

Let's flatten the bottom of the scanned object – this step depends on the kind of model you have scanned. With my wooden log example, I want the base of the log to be perfectly flat with the grid.

18. Let's go into the front view by pressing *1* on the numpad or clicking the axis in the top-right corner of 3D Viewport.

19. Change **Select Tool** back to the default **Select Box** by clicking and holding the **Select Tool** icon to the left of 3D Viewport and clicking **Select Box** from the list, or you can use the shortcut key *W* to toggle between the different select tools.

20. In the front view, press *1* to enable **Vertex Select** mode, then drag a box at the base of your model to select the bottom vertices.

Figure 6.9 – Using the Box tool to select all the bottom vertices of your model

21. Delete these vertices by pressing *X* and clicking **Vertices** from the drop-down menu.

22. Press *Tab* to exit **Edit Mode**.

23. Deactivate **X-Ray** mode by clicking the icon to the left of the **Wireframe Viewport Shading** icon at the top of 3D Viewport. You can also use the shortcut *Option / Alt + Z*.

24. Let's center the pivot of our model. Click the model in 3D Viewport to select it, then right-click on the model, click **Set Origin**, and select **Origin to Geometry** from the drop-down menu.

25. You should now have a clean high-poly model without any unwanted geometry. You can now also preview the material of your model by clicking **Material Preview** at the top of 3D Viewport or using the shortcut *Z* and selecting **Material Preview** from the radial menu.

In the following figure, you can see the material preview of the scanned model.

Figure 6.10 – Viewing the material of the model by enabling Material Preview

26. Next, we need to export our clean, high-poly model for the retopology or topology optimization process. To do this, click the model in 3D Viewport to select it, then click **File | Export | Wavefront (.obj)**.

27. Browse to a folder where you want to save the model.

28. Now let's give it a name – let's call it Model_HP.obj by typing that at the bottom of the dialog box. The **HP** stands for **high-poly**.

29. Tick the box next to **Selection Only** to ensure you are not exporting any other objects.

30. Click **Export OBJ** at the bottom of the window to export the model.

You should now have a good understanding of importing your scanned model into Blender and orienting the model in 3D space to ensure that it's flat on the world grid. We've also looked at how to clean up your model by deleting any unwanted geometry. You have also learned how to fix any holes in your model.

In the next section, we will be looking at optimizing the topology of the model. Please save your project now.

Optimizing the topology of a model using Instant Meshes

In this section, we will focus on optimizing the topology of our scanned model. For this process, we're going to use a free program called **Instant Meshes**! Instant Meshes is compatible with Windows, Mac, and Linux.

Instant Meshes is an amazing program that can lower the vertex count of a model, as well as optimizing the topology from triangles to quads. **Quads** are faces with 4 edges and are usually much easier to work with.

Please download and install Instant Meshes from `https://github.com/wjakob/instant-meshes`:

1. Launch Instant Meshes once you have downloaded and installed it.
2. In the top-left corner of the user interface, click the **Open Mesh** button, then click the **PLY / OBJ** button.

Figure 6.11 – Importing the model

3. Browse to the folder where you have exported the clean OBJ model from Blender.
4. Select the exported OBJ (**Model_HP.obj**) and click **Open** to load it into Instant Meshes.

    You will now see the cleaned-up, high-poly model in the viewport. You can click and drag to orbit around the model or right-click and drag to pan. You can also use the mouse wheel to zoom in and out.

The original model from Meshroom has a very high-poly count, and we need to lower this in order to use our model for animation or even as a game asset. It's very easy to lower the poly count in Instant Meshes.

5. Let's do this now by using the **Target Vertex Count** slider in the side menu to the left of the interface. The target number depends on the size and complexity of the model, but for this example let's aim for a number close to 30,000. Drag the slider under **Target vertex count** and lower it to around 3 0K.

6. Once you have set the desired **Target vertex count** value, click the **Solve** button to apply.

Figure 6.12 – Lowering Target vertex count by using the slider

7. Once this step is done, you can click the **Solve** button under **Position Field** to apply.

Note how the model changed in the viewport. You should be able to see the quad faces on its surface.

Figure 6.13 – Updated model with quad faces

8. We can now export this new, low-poly model with a much better topology as an OBJ. To do this click the **Export Mesh** button at the bottom of the side menu.

9. Next, click **Extract Mesh** in the pop-out menu to create the new mesh we will export.

10. Click **Save** – then, browse to the same folder where you exported the high-poly mesh and name this new export `Model_LP.obj`. The **LP** stands for **low-poly**. Click **Save** again to export the model and close Instant Meshes.

Great, you have now created a low-poly model with a much better quad topology. In the next section, we will import this low-poly model into our Blender project and begin the texture-baking process.

UV unwrapping and texture baking

In this section, we will focus on UV unwrapping our low-poly model as well as texture baking. We will be baking textures from the high-poly scanned model into our low-poly model. Let's get started!

UV unwrapping

Let's begin by importing the low-poly model that we have exported from Instant Meshes into Blender:

1. Open the Blender project you saved earlier in this chapter. Then, click **File | Import | Wavefront (.obj)** and browse to the folder where you have exported it.

2. Select **Model_LP.obj** and click **Import OBJ** at the bottom of the dialog box.

The low-poly model will appear exactly at the same location as the high-poly model that's currently in this project. You will notice the slight overlap in 3D Viewport:

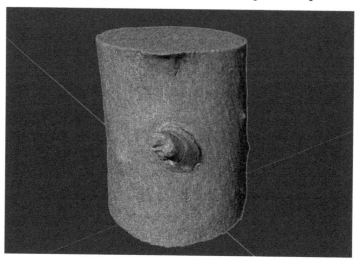

Figure 6.14 – The low-poly and high-poly models overlap slightly in 3D Viewport

3. Let's make sure our models are named properly in **Outliner**. The low-poly object should be named `Model_LP`. Double-click the high-poly model in **Outliner** and rename it `Model_HP`. You can give it any name as long as you remember to put `_LP` or `_HP` after the name to know which one is which.

4. Click the low-poly object in the **Outliner** or in 3D Viewport to select it, then click the **UV Editing** tab at the top of the interface.

> **Note**
>
> It will probably be easier to select it via **Outliner** and not in 3D Viewport because of the overlap. You can try clicking it in 3D Viewport but keep an eye on **Outliner** to ensure that the correct model is selected. If the high-poly model is selected, just click the model in 3D Viewport again to select the low-poly model.

5. In **Outliner**, click the eye icon next to the high-poly model to hide it from 3D Viewport.

6. In the UV editor workspace, we will be switched to **Edit Mode** automatically. You will notice green edges across the low-poly model. These are sharp edges marked by Instant Meshes. We can clear these. Press the shortcut key *2* to switch to **Edge Select** mode.

7. Hover your mouse cursor over the model in 3D Viewport and press *A* to select all the edges on the model.

8. Right-click on the model and click **Clear Sharp** to remove the sharp edges as we don't need them to be marked as sharp edges.

    Next, we need to specify which edges are seams in order for Blender to know how to unwrap the UVs. In my example of a log, which is cylindrical in shape, I would mark the top edge as a seam, as well as a seam down the side of the log. Think of how you would cut this model with scissors if it was made out of paper and you wanted to lay it flat on a surface. In my example, I would mark the top edge around the log.

9. Still in **Edge Select** mode, click on an edge and hold *Ctrl* and click another edge to select all the edges in between. Do this until you have selected all the edges around the top of the model.

10. Right-click the model in 3D Viewport and select **Mark Seam** from the drop-down menu to mark these edges as seams.

11. Now click away from the model to de-select everything, and let's select our next seam. Again, for my example of the wooden log, I will create another seam down the side of the log. Click any edge at the top of the log pointing down, then press *Ctrl* and click an edge at the bottom to select all the edges in between.

12. Right-click the model and select **Mark Seam** to mark these as seams as well, as shown in the following figure:

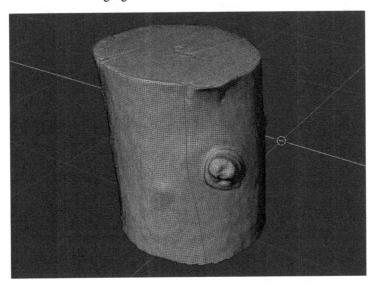

Figure 6.15 – Marking seams to UV unwrap your model

Now we are ready to unwrap the model.

13. Switch to **Face Select** mode by pressing the shortcut key *3*.

14. Hover your mouse over the model in **3D Viewport** and press *A* to select all the faces.

15. Now, right-click on the model in 3D Viewport and select **UV Unwrap Faces**, then click **Unwrap**. This will make use of the marked seams to unwrap the model.

    Note that if you are not too familiar with marking seams, you can also try **Smart UV Project** without marking any seams. This works quite well for complex models that are usually difficult to unwrap. Again, feel free to experiment with the different types of unwrapping projections. UV unwrapping can be a difficult topic and is an artform on its own, so please experiment and practice. It's the only way to get better at UV unwrapping.

    In the following figure, you will see the unwrapped UV Map. The circular shape represents the top part of the log, while the rectangular shape represents the sides of the log.

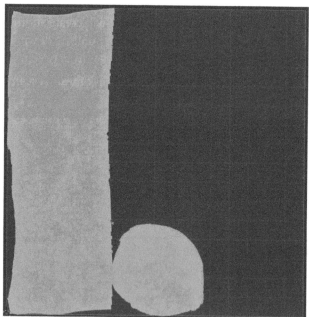

Figure 6.16 – The UV Map for my wooden log model

16. Click the **Layout** tab at the top of the interface to return to the default workspace.

17. In **Outliner**, click the eye icon next to the high-poly model to unhide it from 3D Viewport.

Congratulations, you have now successfully UV unwrapped your model. In the next section, we will look at baking the high-poly texture details, including a normal map, into this low-poly model. Please save your project now.

Texture baking

Now that we have successfully UV unwrapped our model, it's time to bake some textures. We're going to bake two textures, a **diffuse map** and a **normal map**. The diffuse map will hold the color information while the normal map will contain the bump or normal data, giving our low-poly object more detail.

Let's get started!

1. In 3D Viewport, click the model until you have the low-poly model selected. Keep an eye on **Outliner** to ensure you select the correct model. As mentioned earlier, just click the model again if the wrong one gets selected.

2. With the low-poly model selected, click the **Shading** tab at the top of the interface to enter the shading workspace.

3. In the shading workspace, click **New** above **Shader Editor** to create a new material for the low-poly model.

4. Give the material a name by clicking the default material name at the top of **Shader Editor**. Call it anything you like.

   By default, you should see two nodes in **Shader Editor**: a **Principled BSDF** node and a **Material Output** node. We need to create two **Image Texture** nodes, one for the diffuse map and one for the normal map.

5. Create the first **Image Texture** node by pressing *Shift + A* and using the search function. Position this node above and to the left of the **Principled BSDF** node. This will be our diffuse map or base color.

6. On this **Image Texture** node, click **New** to create a new texture.

7. Change the **Width** and **Height** values of the texture to 2048. This will create a blank 2K resolution image. Feel free to increase this to 4K if you feel that's needed, but I don't need anything higher than 2K for my log example.

8. Give it a name by clicking the word **Untitled** at the top of the node. Call it anything you like. This will be the main texture map of your model, holding color data.

9. Click **OK** to confirm these parameters.

   Let's create another **Image Texture** node. This one will be for the normal map.

10. Press *Shift + A* and use the search function to create another **Image Texture** node. Place this node below the top **Image Texture** node.

11. On this second **Image Texture** node, click **New** to create a new texture.

12. Set both **Width** and **Height** to 2048. Feel free to increase this to 4K if you need a bigger texture.

13. Give it a name – you can call it anything, but remember this is the normal map, so maybe add _normal to the end of the name so it's easier to know which texture is which.

14. Untick the box next to **Alpha** as we don't need an alpha channel for the normal map.

15. Lastly, tick the box next to **32-bit Float**. This will give us a 32-bit texture, holding more color data, which is great for something like a normal map.

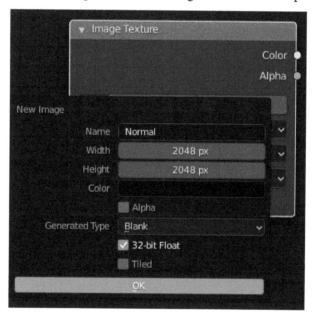

Figure 6.17 – Configuring the texture for the normal map

16. Click **OK** to confirm these settings.

Now we are almost ready to bake our textures.

17. First, let's change the render engine to the **Cycles** render engine by clicking **Render Properties** (the camera icon) to the right of the interface. Click the drop-down menu next to **Render Engine** and select **Cycles**.

18. Under **Sampling**, set **Render samples** to 256.

19. Scroll down and expand **Bake**.

20. Click the drop-down menu next to **Bake Type** and select **Diffuse** from the list. You can specify here which map you want to bake. For now, we're baking a diffuse map.

21. Expand **Influence** below **Bake Type** and untick the boxes next to both **Direct** and **Indirect**. This allows us to bypass any lighting in the scene, direct or indirect lighting. We don't want to bake any lighting into our texture.

22. Next, expand **Selected to Active** below **Influence** and also tick the box next to **Selected to Active**. This means we are baking textures from the selected model into the active model.

23. Under **Selected to Active**, set **Extrusion** to 0.1 and **Max Ray Distance** to 0.1.

    These values depend on the amount of overlap between the high-poly and low-poly models. The size of the models will also affect these values, but I usually get good results with both set to 0.1. Feel free to experiment with both of these values if you get any unwanted results.

24. Now, a very important step: select the **Image Texture** node in **Shader Editor** to specify which texture we're baking into. Let's bake the diffuse map first. In **Shader Editor**, click the top **Image Texture** node to select it. It should be highlighted with a white outline.

    Next, we need to select the high-poly model, then hold *Shift* and select the low-poly model. Remember, the first model you select will be the **Selected** model and the last model you select will be the **Active** model. The **Active** model will always have a brighter orange outline. The **Selected** model will have a dark orange/red outline.

25. To do this, click the model in 3D Viewport and keep an eye on **Outliner**. We want to select the high-poly model first. If the low-poly model is selected, just click the model in 3D Viewport again, and the high-poly model will be selected.

26. Now hold *Shift* and click the model again in 3D Viewport to select the low-poly model last.

27. Finally, we are ready to bake our diffuse map! In the **Render Properties** panel, click the **Bake** button under the **Bake** section.

28. Notice the **Texture Bake** progress bar at the bottom of the interface. Wait for this to finish before moving on to the next step.

29. To preview the baked texture, click the **UV Editing** tab at the top of the interface. You should see your baked diffuse map on the left. If you see any issues, you can try to re-bake the texture using different **Extrusion** and **Max Ray Distance** settings.

The following figure shows the diffuse map that we have baked from the high-poly model into the low-poly model.

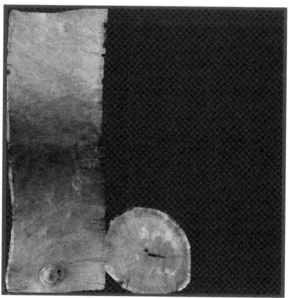

Figure 6.18 – You can preview the baked diffuse map in the UV editing workspace

30. Next, let's bake the normal map. Click the **Shading** tab at the top of the interface to go back to the shading workspace.

31. Click the second **Image Texture** (the blank normal map) in **Shader Editor** to select it. You always need to select the texture node you are baking into.

32. You should still have both the high-poly and low-poly models selected. If not, select the high-poly model first to set it as the **Selected** model, then hold *Shift* and click the low-poly model to set it as the **Active** model.

33. In the **Render Properties** panel, click the **Bake Type** drop-down menu and select **Normal** from the list.

34. Click **Bake** to bake the normal map.

35. Wait for the progress bar at the bottom of the interface to complete before moving on to the next step.

36. Click the **UV Editing** tab to preview the baked normal map. You should see something similar to the following figure:

Figure 6.19 – The baked normal map

37. Let's connect our baked textures to our shader node so we can see our material on our model. Click the **Shading** tab at the top of the interface to enter the shading workspace.

    Make sure you have only the low-poly model selected.

38. You should see the two **Image Texture** nodes in **Shader Editor**. First, connect **Color output** from the top **Image Texture** (the diffuse map) to **Base Color input** on the **Principled BSDF shader** node.

39. Next, we need one more node before we can connect the normal map **Image Texture** node. Create a **Normal Map** node by pressing *Shift + A* and using the search function. Position this node between the bottom **Image Texture** node and the **Principled BSDF** node.

40. Connect **Color output** on the **Image Texture** node (the normal map we baked) to **Color input** on the **Normal Map** node.

41. Then, connect **Normal output** on the **Normal Map** node to **Normal input** on the **Principled BSDF** node.

42. You can adjust the **Strength** value on the **Normal Map** node to adjust the influence of the normal map on your model.

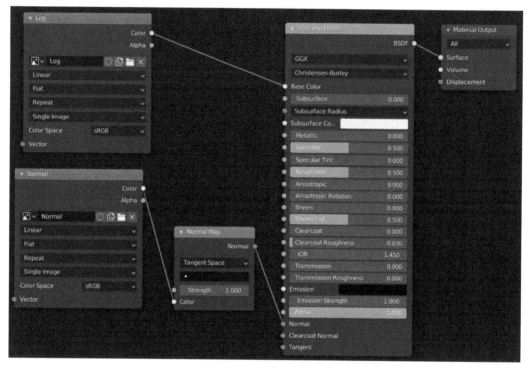

Figure 6.20 – Your node tree should look similar to this

You should now be able to see the material on the low-poly model in 3D Viewport.

43. Click the eye icon in **Outliner**, next to the high-poly model, to hide it from 3D Viewport so we can admire our low-poly material.

Congratulations! You have successfully baked a diffuse map and a normal map from the high-poly 3D-scanned model into the optimized low-poly model. Please save your project now.

The following figure shows the log model with both the diffuse map and the normal map applied to it.

Figure 6.21 – Your low-poly model should now have a diffuse map and a normal map applied

You should now have a good understanding of how to take photos for photogrammetry as well as how to use Meshroom to convert your still photos into a 3D model. You have also learned how to clean up your model and fix any holes that might be present. You should also know how to optimize the topology using Instant Meshes.

Lastly, we looked at how to bake textures from a high-poly model into a low-poly model. With this information, you will be able to scan almost any object in the real world and convert it into a usable model for use in your own animations or even game assets.

Summary

Congratulations! You now have the power to create a 3D model of almost anything in the real world by taking photos and converting those photos into a 3D model using Meshroom. You should also have a good understanding of cleaning your model in Blender and optimizing the topology using Instant Meshes. We also looked at how to bake textures from an original high-poly model into an optimized low-poly model. Now, go out there and scan anything and everything that you can find. Save them in your library and use them in your next animation, short film, or video game!

In the next chapter, we will be focusing on character modeling. We will be creating an alien character using reference images.

7
Modeling an Alien Cartoon Character

In this chapter, we will 3D-model an alien cartoon character from scratch! First, we will create our own reference images of our character, which will make the modeling process a lot easier. Then, we will import these reference images into Blender and start modeling our character, using the front and side views of our character. You can also download reference images from the internet if don't feel like drawing your own.

It all depends on whether you want to create your own original character or if you are modeling a known character from a video game or movie. Let's get started!

The main topics we'll cover in this chapter are as follows:

- Creating front and side reference images of your character
- Setting up your Blender project using the reference images you created
- Modeling the character in Blender

Creating reference images of your character

In this section, we will look at how to create reference images of your character using any drawing application you are comfortable with. I am using Adobe Photoshop to create my reference images, but there are many free alternatives that you can use. One of the best open source drawing applications available is **GIMP**, which you can download for free from the following URL: `https://www.gimp.org`.

You can also make use of Procreate if you have an iPad.

The following is the reference image that I created, which we will use during this chapter. Feel free to either create your own reference image or download my reference image from the following URL: `https://github.com/PacktPublishing/Taking-Blender-to-the-Next-Level/blob/main/Chapter07/Chapter%2007%20-%20MyAlienRef.png`.

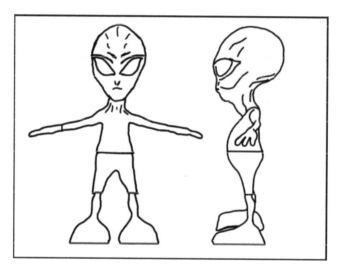

Figure 7.1 – My character reference image

As you can see, I am not the best artist when it comes to drawing anything! But remember – we're not creating a masterpiece; this is only a reference, and you can always add more details to your character in Blender. The main purpose of your reference image is to provide you with the shape or outline of your character.

In the preceding reference image, I'm making use of rulers in Photoshop to ensure that the parts of my character line up in the front and side view. I used the ruler to align the following parts of my character: the top of the head and the eyes, and below the eyes, the chin, the arms, the waist, the pants, and the feet. This will ensure that these areas of your character line up correctly in the front and side views. It's very important to make sure that your front and side views line up correctly.

I would suggest you start drawing the front view of your character first. Then, line up the rulers and draw the side view, using the rulers as reference lines.

The following is the process we will follow to create the reference images:

1. Create a blank project in the drawing application of your choice. You don't have to create a super high-resolution image, as this is only a reference. I used quite a low-resolution image of only 800 x 600 pixels, but feel free to use a higher resolution if you want. My reference image is not very detailed, as I am going for a very basic cartoon-style character – and I also can't draw very well.

2. The next step in the process is to focus on the front view of your character. Try to draw the outline of the character without any details, such as the eyes, nose, and mouth. We can add those details later. Position the front view of your character to the left of the canvas, leaving enough space at the right side of the canvas for the side view of your character.

3. Let's start drawing the head, neck, body, arms, legs, and feet. Keep it simple, as you can always make adjustments as you add more details:

Figure 7.2 – Creating a front-view outline of your character

4. Next, let's draw the eyes! Keep it basic for now; we just need the outline for the eyes. Here is a very handy tip if you really can't draw – try to find reference images of eyes or any other body parts you need and then trace them. Try not to copy other people's work exactly; make slight adjustments to make it your own!

Figure 7.3 – Drawing the eyes

5. Let's add the mouth and nose – as you will see in the following figure, I'm keeping it very simple. Again, feel free to download a reference image of a mouth and trace over it! Make small adjustments when tracing to make it your own:

Figure 7.4 – Adding the mouth and nose

6. Next, let's add some smaller details, such as the eyebrows. Feel free to add any small details you would like to see on your final 3D model. Remember – you can always add more details in Blender, so try to keep it simple for now:

Figure 7.5 – Adding smaller details, such as the eyebrows

7. Once you are happy with the front view, we can start adding the ruler lines. This will help us when drawing the side view. Add as many ruler lines as you need – one for each feature of your character. This will ensure that the front and side views line up correctly:

Figure 7.6 – Adding ruler lines to each feature of your character

8. Now, we can begin drawing the side view of our character. Making use of the ruler lines, create a new layer and start drawing the side view of the head. Only focus on the outline for now:

Figure 7.7 – Drawing the outline of the side view of the head

9. Draw the rest of the body in the side view. Focus on the ruler lines to align the neck, the waist, the bottom of the pants, and the bottom of the feet:

Figure 7.8 – Drawing the outline of the side view – focus on the ruler lines to align the different parts of the body

10. Lastly, let's add some details to the side view, such as the eyes, the nose, and the mouth. Make sure to use the ruler lines to align these details to the front view:

Figure 7.9 – Adding details to the side view

11. Once you are happy with both the front and side views of your character, we are ready to export the reference image as a PNG image. This process depends on the software you are using, but you will usually find it under *export*. In Adobe Photoshop, you click **File** | **Export** | **Quick Export as PNG**. Browse to a location on your hard drive where you would like to save your reference image and give it a name, and then click **Save** to export your reference as a PNG image.

12. Also, remember to save your Photoshop or other application project file. This will allow you to go back to the reference image and make adjustments to the layers if needed.

Congratulations! You have now successfully created the front and side reference images of your cartoon character! This is a vital step in creating a 3D model of more complex objects such as a character and will make the process much easier.

In the next section, we will create our Blender project and learn how to set up the reference images we have created.

Setting up the reference images in Blender

In this section, we will set up our Blender project using the 2D reference images we created in the previous section. This will allow you to easily start the modeling process using the front and side reference images. Let's get started!

1. Create a new Blender project and delete all the default objects in the scene by pressing *A*, then pressing *X*, and clicking **Delete** to confirm.

2. Next, drag and drop your character reference image from the Windows Explorer or Finder if you are using a Macintosh into your Blender scene. This will import the reference image as an empty object.

3. With the empty object selected, press *N* to display the side menu in the 3D Viewport. Click the **Item** tab on the side menu to show the **Location, Rotation,** and **Scale** parameters.

4. Set the **Location** parameters to **X – 0, Y – 0**, and **Z – 0** to position the reference image to the center of the grid.

5. Set the **Rotation** parameters to **X – 90, Y – 0**, and **Z – 0** to rotate the reference image 90 degrees on the *x* axis:

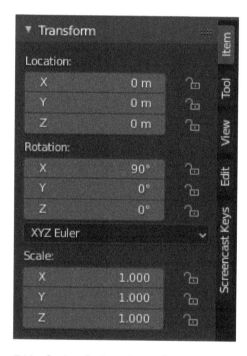

Figure 7.10 – Setting the Location and Rotation parameters

6. Press *N* again to hide the side menu for now.

7. With the empty object still selected, click the **Object Data Properties** icon at the right of the 3D Viewport.

8. Under **Object Data Properties**, click the tick box next to **Opacity** and set the amount to **0.1**. This will set the opacity of the reference image to 10%, which will make it easier to see through the reference image, making modeling a lot easier.

9. To align the front reference image to the grid, let's go into the front view by pressing *1* on the numpad. If you use a keyboard without a numpad, you can also click on the **X** (side) and **-Y** (front) axis icons at the top right of the 3D Viewport to switch between the front and side views.

10. With the empty object selected, press *G* to move the reference image, and position the front view of your character to the center of the grid. Ensure the bottoms of the feet are on the red *x* axis line. The blue *z* axis line should split the front view of your character in half, as shown in the following figure:

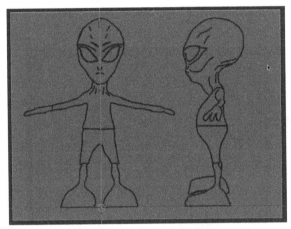

Figure 7.11 – Aligning the front view of your character to the center of the grid lines

11. Double-click the empty object in **Outliner** and rename it `Front`. This will make it easier to know which empty object is which.

12. Next, let's duplicate this empty object to create a second reference for the side view. With the empty object selected, press *Shift + D* to duplicate the empty object, then press *R*, then *Z*, and finally, type `90` to rotate the empty object 90 degrees on the *z* axis.

13. You should now have two empty objects in your scene:

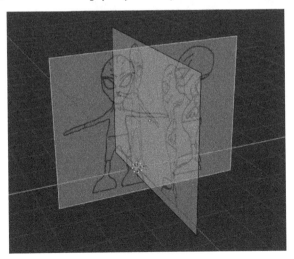

Figure 7.12 – The two empty objects

14. Press *3* on the numpad to go into the side view or click the **-Y** axis icon at the top-right corner of the 3D Viewport.

15. With the empty object still selected, press *G* to move the reference image and align it to the **Y** and **Z** axis lines. Try and position the side reference of the character at the center of the blue **Z** axis line. Also, ensure the undersides of the feet are on the green **Y** axis line:

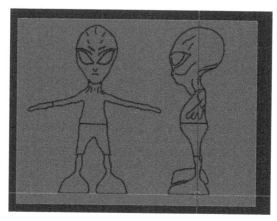

Figure 7.13 – Aligning the side reference image to the Y and Z axis lines

16. Double-click on the empty object in **Outliner** and rename this empty object `Side`.

17. Now, let's move both these reference images back so that they don't overlap each other. This will make it a bit easier when modeling. Orbit your view so that you can see both reference images in the scene:

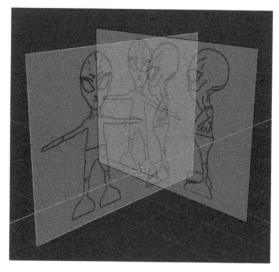

Figure 7.14 – Orbiting the 3D Viewport so that you can see both image references

18. Click the **Side** reference image in the 3D Viewport to select it. Press *G* and then press *X* to move it back on the *x* axis.

19. Click the **Front** reference image in the 3D Viewport to select it. Press *G* and then press *Y* to move it back on the *y* axis:

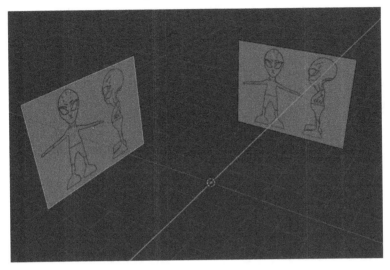

Figure 7.15 – Moving both reference images back so they don't overlap

20. Let's set both these reference empty objects to **non-selectable**, meaning you can't accidentally click on them in the 3D Viewport. To do this, click the **Filter** drop-down menu at the top of **Outliner**, and then click the **Selectable** icon (the pointer second from the left) to enable it:

Figure 7.16 – Enabling the Selectable icon using the Filter dropdown above Outliner

21. Now, click the two **Selectable** icons next to **Front** and **Side** in **Outliner** to disable this for both the **Front** and **Side** empty objects. Now, you won't be able to select these objects in the 3D Viewport, which makes the modeling process less obstructed. You can enable **Selectable** for both objects again if you need to select them:

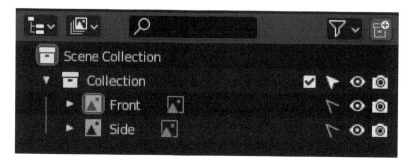

Figure 7.17 – Disabling Selectable for both the Front and Side empty objects in Outliner

Our reference images are now set up correctly. In the next section, we will start modeling our alien cartoon character. Please save your Blender project now.

Modeling an alien cartoon character

In this section, we will make use of the reference images we've set up in Blender to create a 3D model of an alien cartoon character. During the modeling process, we will constantly toggle between the **front** and **side** views. An easy way to do this is to use the *1* and *3* shortcut keys on the numpad. If you don't use a keyboard with a numpad, you can also click the **X (side)** and **-Y (front)** axis icons at the top-right corner of the 3D Viewport to switch between the front and side views. Let's get started!

Modeling the body

Let's begin to model the body of our character:

1. Ensure you are in the Front view by pressing *1* on the numpad or clicking the **-Y** axis icon in the 3D Viewport.

2. Create a new cylinder mesh by pressing *Shift + A* and then selecting **Mesh | Cylinder**.

3. Expand the **Add Cylinder** dialog box at the bottom left of the 3D Viewport.

4. Set the number of **vertices** to **8**, as we only need eight sides for the cylinder object.

5. Next, enable **Toggle X-Ray** mode. This will allow you to see through the mesh to see the reference images behind the object:

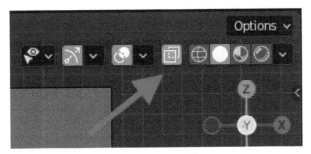

Figure 7.18 – Enabling Toggle X-Ray

6. Click the **Cylinder** object in the 3D Viewport to select it, press *G*, and move it up to the character's neck area.

7. Scale the cylinder down by pressing *S* and dragging with the mouse:

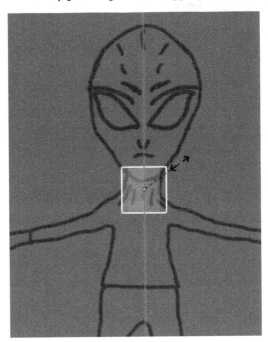

Figure 7.19 – Scaling the cylinder down to approximately the size of the character's neck

8. With the **Cylinder** object still selected, let's apply the scale by pressing *Ctrl + A* and selecting **Scale** from the drop-down menu.

Next, we're going to apply a **Mirror modifier** to our Cylinder object. The **Mirror** modifier will allow us to only edit one side of our character while the other side will be mirrored automatically. I prefer to use the **Auto Mirror** add-on, which makes this process a bit easier. Let's enable this add-on now.

9. Click **Edit** at the top of the interface and click **Preferences** from the drop-down menu.

10. Click the **Add-ons** tab at the left side of the **Preferences** dialog box.

11. Type the word `mirror` in the search box at the top of this window to search for the **Auto Mirror** add-on.

12. Tick the box next to **Mesh: Auto Mirror** to enable this add-on:

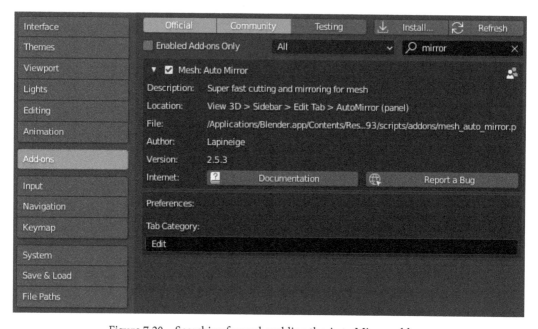

Figure 7.20 – Searching for and enabling the Auto Mirror add-on

13. Close the **Preferences** window.

14. With the **Cylinder** object selected, press *N* to open the side menu, and then click the **Edit** tab on the side of this menu:

Figure 7.21 – Auto Mirror is available at the top of the side menu under the Edit tab

15. You should now see the **Auto Mirror** add-on at the top of this menu. Click the small triangle next to **Auto Mirror** to expand its properties.

16. Here, you can choose across which axis you want to mirror your mesh. We want to use the *x* axis to mirror any modifications on the right side of the model to the left. Click the **X** button below **Auto Mirror** to choose the *x* axis.

17. Now, click the **Auto Mirror** button at the top of this menu to enable mirroring for the **Cylinder** object.

18. Press *N* again to close the side menu.

19. With the **Cylinder** object still selected, press *Tab* to enter **Edit Mode**.

20. Press *1* at the top of the keyboard to activate **Vertex Select mode**.

21. Click and drag a box around the top vertices to select them. Press *G* and then press *Z* to move them down. Align these vertices to the top of the neck, just above the chin. Note how the vertices on the left side of the model move automatically because of the **Mirror** modifier:

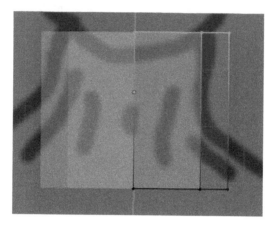

Figure 7.22 – Aligning the top vertices to the neck, just behind the chin

22. Next, drag a box around the four vertices on the right side of the cylinder to select them. Press *G*, then *X*, and move them inward to align with the side of the neck:

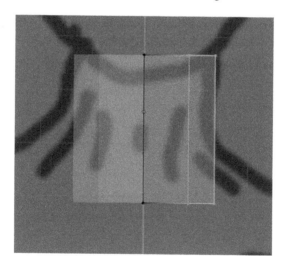

Figure 7.23 – Aligning the side vertices to the side of the neck

23. Select the bottom vertices and press *E* to extrude them downward to just above the waist of the character:

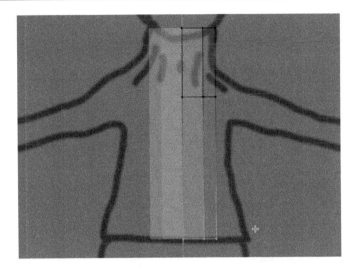

Figure 7.24 – Extruding the bottom vertices down to the waist

24. With these vertices still selected, press *S* and then *X* to scale them along the *x* axis and align them to the character's body:

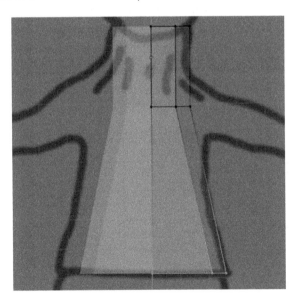

Figure 7.25 – Scaling the bottom vertices to align them to the body of the character

25. Create a **loop cut** in the middle of the body by hovering your mouse over the body and pressing *Ctrl + R*. Left-click to confirm the loop cut's position. Now, move your mouse to adjust the position of the loop cut and left-click again to confirm its location.

26. Select the two outer vertices of this loop cut and press *G* to move and align them with the side of the character's body. See the following figure:

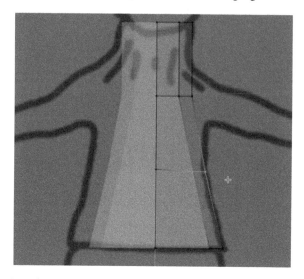

Figure 7.26 – Creating a loop cut and aligning the outer two vertices to the body of the character

27. Create another loop cut above the one you have just created by hovering your mouse over the area and pressing *Ctrl + R*. Left-click to slide the loop cut into position and left-click again to confirm.

28. Select the outer two vertices of this new loop cut and align them to the side of the body, just under the arm, by pressing *G*:

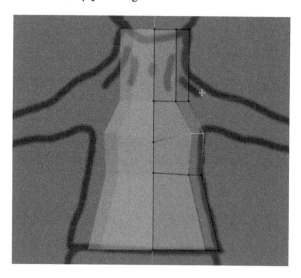

Figure 7.27 – Adding another loop cut and aligning the two outer vertices to the body under the arm

29. Select the two outer vertices above this loop cut and move them to the top of the arm by pressing *G*. Note that you can also rotate them by pressing *R*. Move and rotate these vertices until they're aligned with the top of the arm:

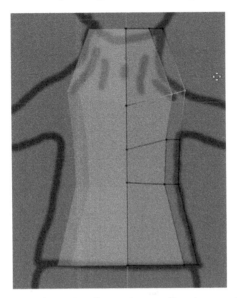

Figure 7.28 – Moving and rotating the vertices to align them to the top of the arm

30. Create another loop cut (*Ctrl + R*) between the top of the neck and the top of the arm. Move and rotate the outer two vertices to align with the neck and shoulder by pressing *G* to move and *R* to rotate:

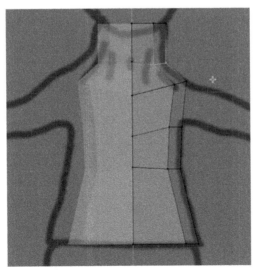

Figure 7.29 – Creating another loop cut to shape the neck and shoulder area

31. Now is a good time to orbit around your object to see it in 3D space. Note how it's slowly starting to take the shape of our character.

32. Let's switch to the side view now by pressing *3* on the numpad or clicking the **X axis** icon in the 3D Viewport. Note how the mesh is not aligned to the front and back of our reference image:

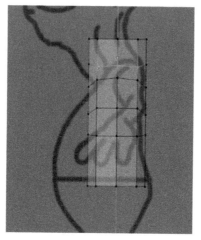

Figure 7.30 – Viewing our mesh from the side

33. Select the three bottom-left vertices and align them to the front of the body by pressing *G*.

34. Select the two bottom-right vertices and align them to the back of the body by pressing *G*:

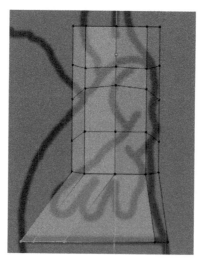

Figure 7.31 – Aligning the bottom vertices to the front and back of the reference image

35. Next, we're going to align these vertices, one by one, to match the shape of our reference image. This can take some time, but once you get used to the process, it can be very satisfying. Select the vertices and move them into place by using the *G* shortcut. Feel free to select multiple vertices at once if you need to. Try to match my reference:

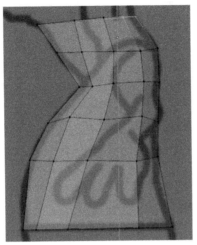

Figure 7.32 – Moving vertices around to match our reference image

Before we continue, let's quickly talk about **edge flow** and **good topology** in 3D modeling. Edge flow is the way that the edges *flow* around your mesh. You want to try and keep the edges flowing in a natural way, eliminating any jagged edges if possible. This will keep the shape of your mesh smooth and without any hard edges. Good topology is not always easy to achieve, but keeping an eye on your edge flow is the easiest way to produce good topology. This will make more sense as we continue to add more geometry to our mesh, which will make visualizing the edge flow easier.

36. Now, add another loop cut just above the bottom edge of your mesh by pressing *Ctrl + R*. Move these vertices into place by selecting them and pressing *G*. This loop cut will help shape the belly of our character better. Move the vertices around to create a natural edge flow:

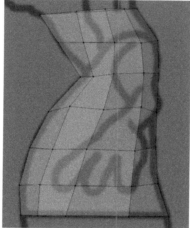

Figure 7.33 – Adding another loop cut to shape the belly of our character

37. Let's go back to the front view by pressing *1* on the numpad or clicking the -**Y** axis icon in the 3D Viewport.

38. Move the vertices to re-align them to the reference image. It's always good practice to switch between the side and front views to ensure the mesh is still aligned with the reference image:

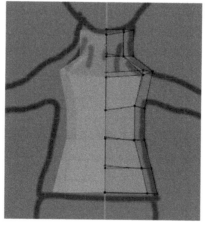

Figure 7.34 – Using the front view to re-align the vertices to the reference image

This concludes the basic shape of the character's upper body. In the next section, we will focus on modeling the head of our character. Please save your project now.

Modeling the head

In this section, we will focus on the shape of the head for our character:

1. Let's extrude the head of our character. To do this, select all the vertices at the top of the neck and press *E* to extrude them upward. Move the mouse until these vertices reach the top of the head.

2. Next, add three loop cuts across the head by using the *Ctrl + R* shortcut and move the outer vertices to the edge of the reference image by using the *G* shortcut. Try to match the following reference image:

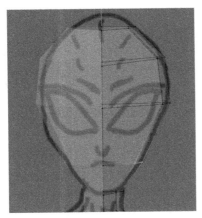

Figure 7.35 – Extruding the head and adding three loop cuts to create the shape of the character's head

3. Go into the side view by pressing *3* on the numpad or clicking the **X axis** icon in the 3D Viewport. Then, by using the *G* shortcut, move the vertices to align with the side view of the head. Note the natural edge flow as you move the vertices. Try to match the following reference image:

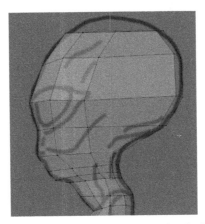

Figure 7.36 – Using the side view to shape the head of the character

4. Next, let's fix the top of the head. To do this, orbit out of the side view and select the middle edge at the top of the head. Right-click and select **Subdivide** from the drop-down menu to split the edge into two edges, creating a new vertex in the middle:

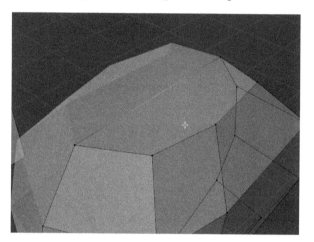

Figure 7.37 – Subdividing the top edge to create a new vertex

5. Now, we can connect the three outer vertices to this new middle vertex. Click one of the outer vertices and hold *Shift*, and click the middle vertex to select them both. Now, press *J* to connect them with a new edge. Do the same with the other two outer vertices. See the following reference image:

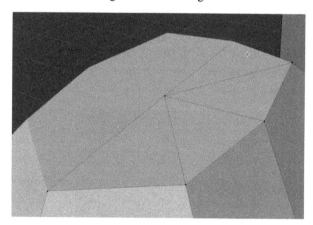

Figure 7.38 – Connecting the outer vertices to the middle vertex at the top of the head

6. Click the top middle vertex to select it, and then press *1* on the numpad to enter the front view or click the **-Y axis** icon in the 3D Viewport. Press *G*, then *Z*, and move the middle vertex up and align it to the top of the head of our character reference image:

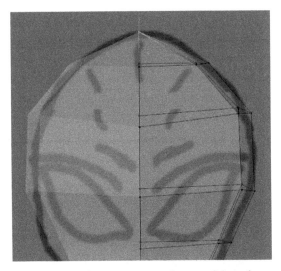

Figure 7.39 – Aligning the top vertex to the top of the reference image

7. Next, we need to add a loop cut at the top of the head, but to do this, we will need to use the **knife tool**. Orbit the view to the top of the head and press *K* to activate the knife tool. Click on the edge connecting the front of the head to the middle vertex to create the first vertex. Now, click on each edge as you move around to the back of the head. Once you have clicked on the last edge, press *Enter* to confirm the cut you made with the knife tool:

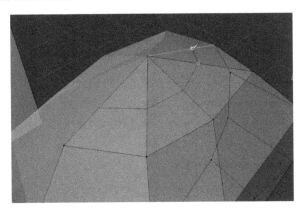

Figure 7.40 – Creating a loop cut at the top of the head using the knife tool

8. Go into the front view again by pressing *1* on the numpad and align these new vertices to the reference image.

9. Go into the side view by pressing *3* on the numpad and align these vertices to the reference image as well. Look at the rest of the vertices and move them around if needed.

As you will notice, modeling a character, or any complex shape, requires a lot of tweaking – constantly toggling between the front and side views, aligning vertices to the reference image, adding loop cuts, and moving the new vertices around to shape our character. In the next few steps, I will move a bit quicker, not always mentioning the shortcuts for switching between the front and side views or common shortcuts such as **Move**, **Scale**, and **Rotate**, as you should know these by now. Let's go!

10. Go into the side view and add two more loop cuts around the head. Move the vertices into place. Focus on the edge flow when moving vertices around:

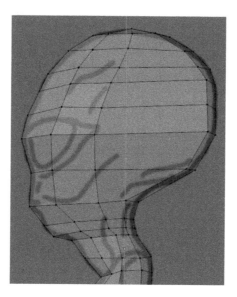

Figure 7.41 – Adding two more loop cuts around the head

This concludes the modeling of the head. In the next section, we will focus on modeling the legs and feet of our character. Please save your project now.

Modeling the legs and feet

In this section, we will focus on the legs and feet of our character:

1. Go into the front view, and let's move down to the legs. Select the bottom row of vertices just above the waist and press *E* to extrude them downward to just above the groin:

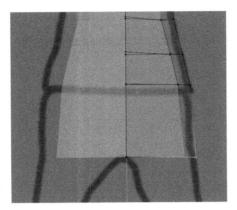

Figure 7.42 – Extruding the waist area downward

2. Orbit to the underside of the body and select the bottom face. Press *I* (capital *i*) to create an inset face:

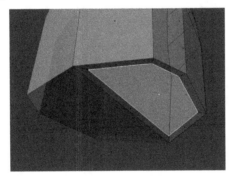

Figure 7.43 – Creating an inset face under the body of the character

3. Select this new inset face and press *E* to extrude downward to create the upper thigh. Go into the front view and align the vertices to the reference image:

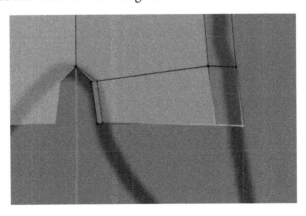

Figure 7.44 – Extruding the inset face to create the upper thigh

4. The thigh has five vertices and five edges around the bottom, but we need to increase this to eight so that we have enough geometry the create the legs and feet of our character. To achieve this, we can subdivide three of the five edges. Press *2* to enter **Edge Select mode**. Select the inner edge, the front-facing edge, and the back-facing edge by holding *Shift*. Then, right-click on one of these three edges and select **Subdivide** from the drop-down menu. Now, we have eight vertices and eight edges around the thigh, which will be enough for the legs and feet. Press *1* again to enter vertex select mode.

5. Go into the front view and select the bottom vertices of the leg. Press *E* to extrude them downward to the middle of the thigh. Do this once more by pressing *E* again and extruding further down to the edge of the pants:

Figure 7.45 – Extruding these vertices downward to form the upper leg

6. Go into the side view and align the vertices to the reference image of the character. Feel free to orbit the view around the model and make small adjustments as needed. Move vertices around to try and match the shape of the character, but also look at the model in 3D and adjust where you feel it is needed. Remember – it's all about constant tweaking, slowing shaping the character:

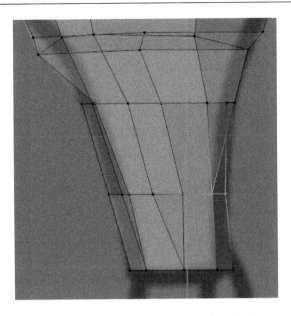

Figure 7.46 – Aligning the vertices in the side view

7. Go back into the front view and select the bottom loop of vertices. Press *E* to extrude them down toward the middle of the leg. Press *E* again and extrude down to the top of the foot. Move the vertices around and align them to the reference image.

8. Go into the side view and align the vertices to the reference image. Go back into the front view and make adjustments if needed:

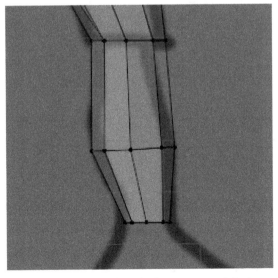

Figure 7.47 – Modeling the bottom part of the leg

9. Go into the side view again, select the bottom loop of vertices, and make four extrusions downward. The first one is for the ankle, then the middle of the foot, then another one a bit further down, and finally, at the bottom of the foot. Move the vertices to align with the character reference. See the following figure:

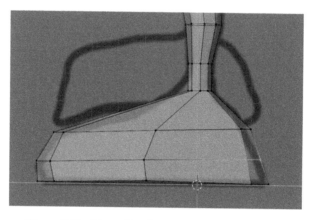

Figure 7.48 – Extruding downward to create the foot

10. Go into the front view and align the vertices to the reference image. Remember to keep a natural edge flow when moving the vertices around:

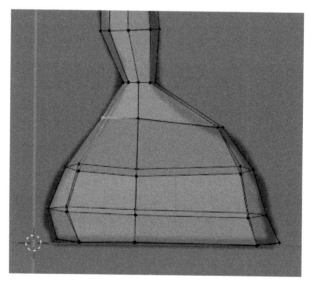

Figure 7.49 – Shaping the foot using the front view

11. Create one more loop cut above the middle edge loop on the foot. Align the vertices to the reference again. Go into the side view and align the vertices again. See the following figure:

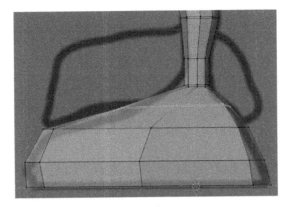

Figure 7.50 – Creating another loop cut to shape the foot

This concludes the character's legs and feet. In the next section, we will model the arms and hands of our character. Please save your project now.

Modeling the arms and hands

In this section, we will focus on modeling the arms and hands of our character:

1. Next, we're going to model the arms of our character. In the side view, orient the 3D Viewport so that you have the shoulder area in frame. First, we need to move some vertices around to maximize the size of the face that can be extruded for the arm. Move the vertices and try to match the following reference image. Note the edge flow above the shoulder:

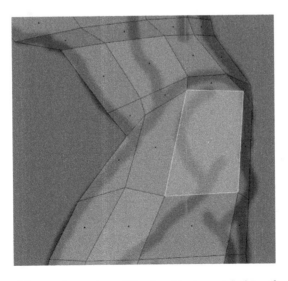

Figure 7.51 – Moving the vertices of the shoulder to match this reference image

2. Press *3* to enter **Face Select mode**, and click the face highlighted in the preceding reference image to select it. Press *I* to create an inset face. This is the face we will extrude for the arm:

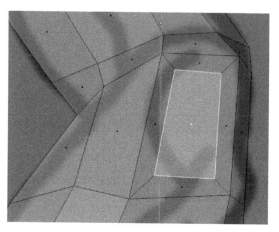

Figure 7.52 – Creating an inset face that we will later extrude for the arm

3. Next, we need to subdivide the two side edges of the selected face to create more geometry for the arm. Currently, this face has four edges, and we need six for the arm. Press *2* to enter edge select mode, select the left edge of the face, and then right-click and select **Subdivide** from the drop-down menu. Do the same for the edge on the right of the selected face. You should now have a face with six sides.

4. Move the vertices of this face so that the face is more circular:

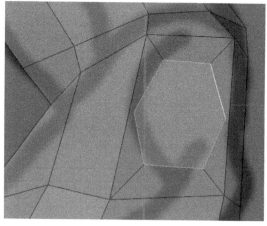

Figure 7.53 – Moving the vertices of the face to create a more circular face

5. Now, we're ready to extrude the arm. Press *3* to enter face select mode and select the six-sided face. Go into the front view and press *E* to extrude the arm to just above the elbow. Press *1* to enter vertex select mode and move the vertices around to match the following reference image. Feel free to make adjustments to the neck and shoulder area if needed:

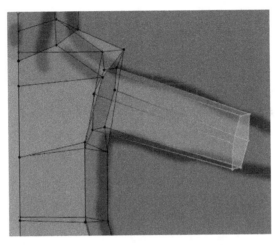

Figure 7.54 – Extruding the arm of the character

6. Switch to the side view and align the face we have extruded to the character reference image:

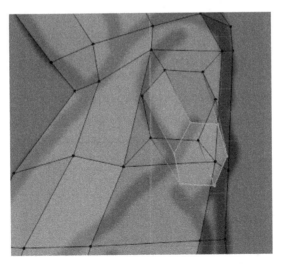

Figure 7.55 – Aligning the extruded arm in the side view to match the reference image

7. Switch to the front view and select the arm vertices we have extruded. Press *E* to extrude the lower part of the arm. Align these vertices to the wrist of the character:

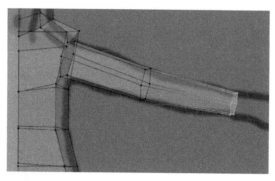

Figure 7.56 – Extruding the lower part of the arm and aligning the vertices to the wrist of the character

8. Go into the side view and align these vertices to the character wrist using the reference image:

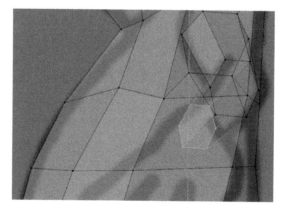

Figure 7.57 – Aligning the vertices in the side view to the wrist of the character

9. Next, let's extrude the hand. Go into the front view, and with the preceding vertices still selected, press *E* and extrude these vertices to the middle of the hand:

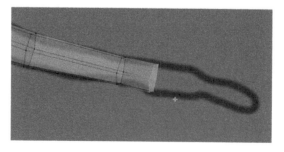

Figure 7.58 – Extruding the vertices to the middle of the hand

10. Go into the side view and align these extruded vertices to the hand.

11. Orbit out of the side view and position the hand in view. Move the vertices so that this face is more rectangular in shape. This will allow us to extrude the fingers easily in the next few steps. Look at the following reference image and try to match the shape of the hand:

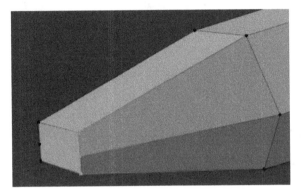

Figure 7.59 – Shaping the face at the end of the hand to be more rectangular

12. Next, we need to split this face into three faces so that we can create the three fingers. Press *2* to enter edge select mode. Select the top edge of this rectangular face, and then right-click and select **Subdivide** from the drop-down menu. Expand the **Subdivide** dialog box in the bottom-left corner of the 3D Viewport and set **Number of Cuts** to **2**:

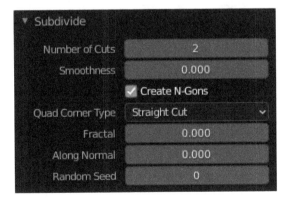

Figure 7.60 – Subdividing the top edge into two cuts to create geometry for the three fingers

13. Now, do the same for the bottom edge on this rectangular face. Select the bottom edge, right-click, and select **Subdivide** from the drop-down menu. Expand the **Subdivide** dialog box in the bottom-left corner of the 3D Viewport and set **Number of Cuts** to **2**:

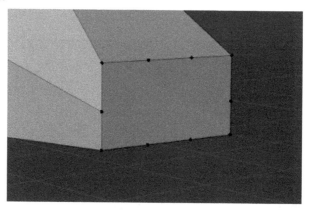

Figure 7.61 – Creating two extra vertices on the top and bottom edge

14. Next, let's connect the two new vertices on the top edge to the two new vertices on the bottom edge. Press *1* to switch to vertex select mode, and select one of the top vertices and also the vertex below it. Then, press *J* to connect the two vertices with an edge. Do this to the second pair of vertices as well:

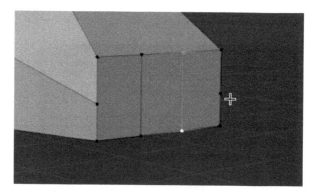

Figure 7.62 – Connecting the top and bottom vertices to create three new faces

15. Let's extrude the three fingers now. Press *3* to switch to face select mode and select the three faces we have created. Press *Alt + E* or *Option + E* and select **Extrude Individual Faces** from the drop-down menu. This option will extrude each face individually:

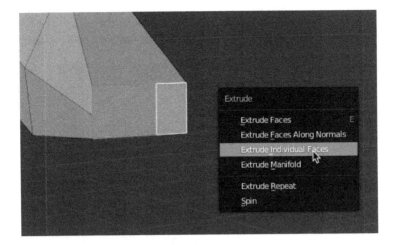

Figure 7.63 – Extruding the three faces individually to create the fingers

16. Now, select each of the three faces one by one and move them slightly away from each other to separate the fingers from each other:

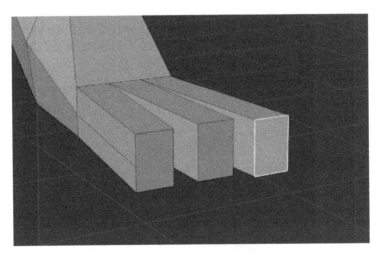

Figure 7.64 – Separating the fingers by moving the faces away from each other

Modeling hands and fingers can be really tricky, but always remember to constantly toggle between the front and side views and make small adjustments. Orbit around the hand and fingers in 3D space to visualize them better while tweaking their shape.

17. Go into the side view again and move the three faces at the tips of the fingers downward to match the character reference image:

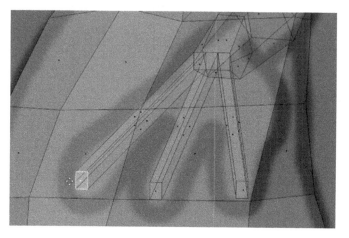

Figure 7.65 – Moving the faces at the tips of the fingers downward to match the reference image

18. Go back into the front view and then scale, rotate, and move the vertices of the fingers and hands until they match the reference image. Try to position the fingers to match the middle of the reference image, as we're going to add more loop cuts to create the fingertips:

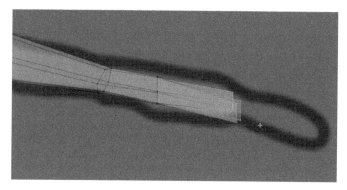

Figure 7.66 – Positioning and scaling the fingers to match the reference image

19. Orbit out of the front view, and create a new loop cut on each finger by using the *Ctrl + R* shortcut. Scale these three loop cuts by selecting their edges and using the *S* shortcut to make the fingers a bit bigger in the middle:

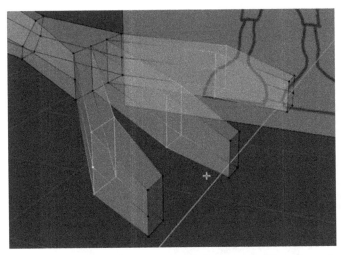

Figure 7.67 – Creating a loop cut on each finger and scaling these edges
to make them a bit bigger in the middle

20. Let's create the fingertips now. Select the three faces at the tips of the fingers and press *E* to extrude them by a small amount. With the new extruded faces still selected, press *S* to scale them down so that they are a bit smaller, creating smoother fingertips:

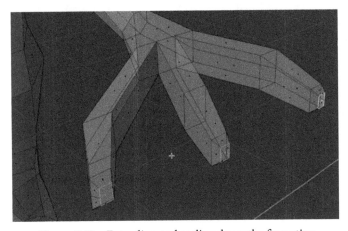

Figure 7.68 – Extruding and scaling down the fingertips

21. Go into the top view by using the *7* shortcut on the numpad or by clicking the **Z axis** icon in the 3D Viewport. Move, scale, and rotate the vertices to shape the hands and fingers:

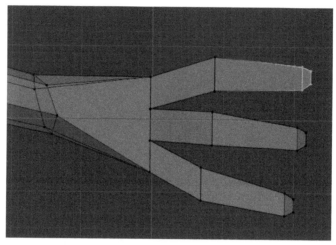

Figure 7.69 – Using the top view to shape the hands and fingers

22. Try and shape the fingers until you get a shape that is close to the following reference image:

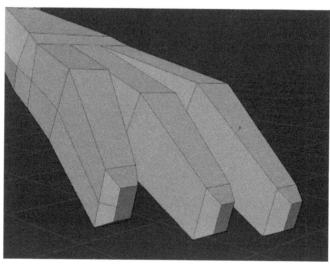

Figure 7.70 – Shaping and rotating the fingers until you have something similar to this reference image

This concludes the modeling of the arms and hands of our character. In the next section, we will focus on modeling the eyes. Please save your project now.

Modeling the eyes

In this section, we will focus on modeling the eyes of our character:

1. Go into the front view and position the view so that the face of our character is visible. Now, move the vertices so that they don't overlap the eye area. Position the vertices right above and below the eye area:

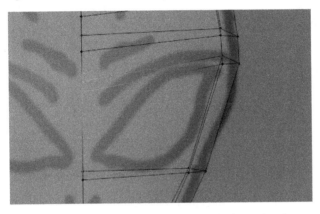

Figure 7.71 – Moving the vertices so that they don't overlap the eye area

2. Now, go into the side view and move the vertices around the eye area. The goal here is the have two faces overlapping the eye. Feel free to add more loop cuts if needed. Toggle between the front and side views to make sure the eye is covered by two faces. Try and keep a natural edge flow when moving vertices around:

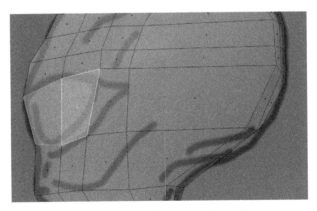

Figure 7.72 – Moving the vertices around the eye until you have two faces covering it

3. Let's create an inset where the eye will be. Select both faces covering the eye as per the previous figure and press *I* to create an inset. If both faces are inset individually, press *I* again to create one combined inset. Move the mouse to adjust the size of the inset until you have something similar to the following reference image:

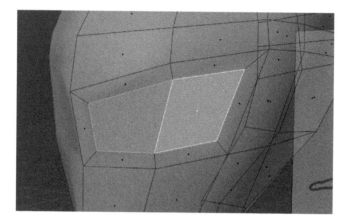

Figure 7.73 – Inset the two faces covering the eye

4. We can now delete these two inner faces where the eyeballs will be positioned. With these two faces selected, press *X* and select **Faces** from the drop-down menu to delete them both:

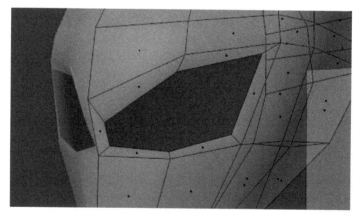

Figure 7.74 – Deleting the two inner faces to create space for the eyeballs

5. Go into the front view again and move the vertices around the eye and inner eye areas to match the shape of the reference image better:

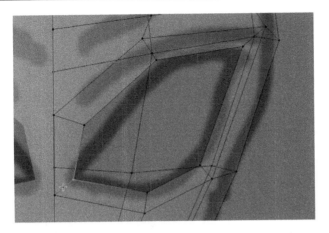

Figure 7.75 – Using the front view again to shape the inner eye

6. Next, we're going to extrude the edge around the inner eye inward. To do this, select the edge loop around the inside of the eye. You can either hold *Shift* while clicking the edges one by one or hold *Alt* (for Windows) or *Option* (for Macintosh) and click on one of the edges to select the edge loop. With this selected, press *E* and move the mouse slowly to extrude them inward toward the back of the head. Press *S* to scale the extruded edges so that they are slightly smaller than the inner eye area:

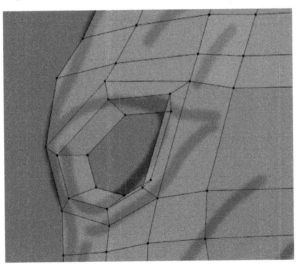

Figure 7.76 – Extruding the inner eye inward and scaling the edge loop down

7. Now, let's create the eyeballs! Exit **Edit** mode by pressing *Tab*.

8. Create an icosphere by pressing *Shift + A*, selecting **Mesh | Ico Sphere**, and positioning it where the eye should be.

9. Rotate, scale, and move the eyeball as best you can so that it fits nicely into the eye socket:

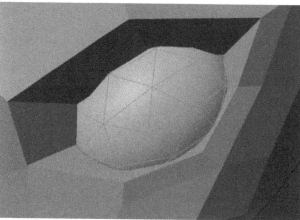

Figure 7.77 – Creating an icosphere for the eye and positioning it in the eye socket

10. Once you are happy with the shape, size, and position of the eyeball, we can join it to our character mesh. To do this, click the eyeball to select it, then hold *Shift*, and click the character to select it as the active object. Now, right-click in the 3D Viewport and select **Join** from the drop-down menu to join the eyeball to our character mesh. Note how the eyeball is mirrored automatically to the other side because it's now part of the character mesh:

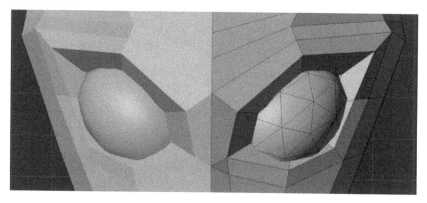

Figure 7.78 – The eyeball will be mirrored automatically when joined to the character mesh

This concludes the modeling of the eyes of our character. In the next section, we will focus on creating the mouth. Please save your project now.

Modeling the mouth

In this section, we will focus on modeling the mouth of our character:

1. Now, let's create the mouth of our character. To do this, we need another loop cut just above the mouth area, looping around to the back of the head. Press *Ctrl + R* and position the loop cut just above the mouth area:

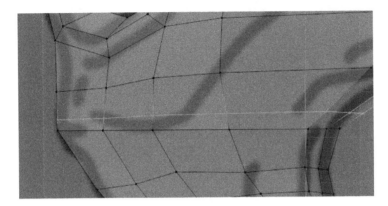

Figure 7.79 – Creating another loop cut right above the mouth

2. Select the face where the mouth is and press *I* to inset this face to create the cavity for the mouth. We need this inset to be connected where the mesh is being mirrored. To do this, press *B* before clicking to confirm the inset:

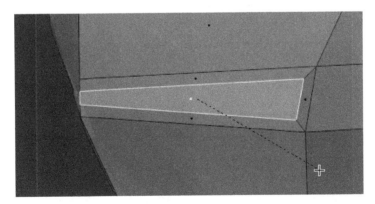

Figure 7.80 – Creating an inset where the mouth will be

3. With this mouth face still selected, press *S* to scale it down until you are happy with the size of the mouth.

4. With the mouth face selected, press *G* and then *Y* to move the face inward to create the mouth cavity. Move and scale the mouth until you are happy with its shape and size:

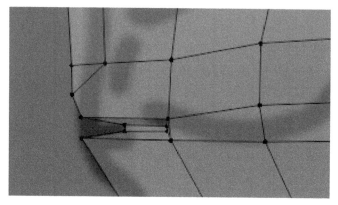

Figure 7.81 – Shaping the mouth until you are happy with its size

This concludes the modeling of the mouth. In the next section, we will focus on creating smaller details for our character. Please save your project now.

Adding smaller details to our character

Let's finish our character by adding a few smaller details to refine its body:

1. Add a loop cut right under the character's pants and scale it inward to create a sharper edge that will define the leg shape better:

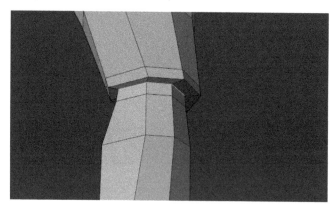

Figure 7.82 – Adding a loop cut under the pants

2. Create a few loop cuts around the ankle and scale them down to define the leg going into the character's boots:

Figure 7.83 – Adding loop cuts around the ankle

3. Create a few loop cuts around the wrist to create a sharp edge where the hand connects with the arm:

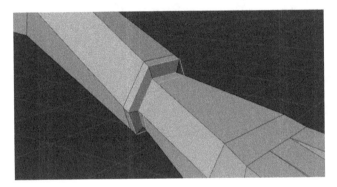

Figure 7.84 – Adding a few loop cuts around the wrist to create a sharper edge

4. Create a couple of loop cuts where the arm connects to the shoulder to create a sharper edge:

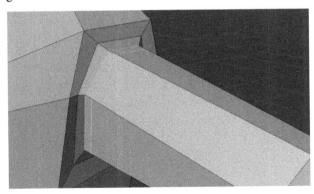

Figure 7.85 – Creating a few loop cuts where the arm connects to the shoulder

5. Feel free to add other details to your character by adding more loop cuts. Try to create a belt around your character's waist. Create another loop cut around the waist area, select the faces where you would like to create the belt, use the *Alt + E* (for Windows) or *Option + E* (for Macintosh) shortcuts, and select **Extrude Faces Along Normals** from the drop-down menu to extrude the belt outward:

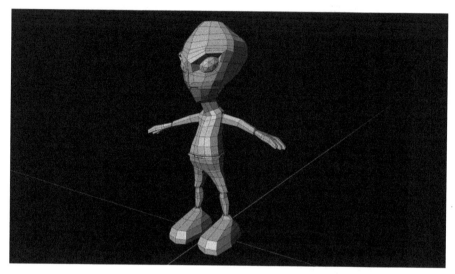

Figure 7.86 – A wireframe view of the character

6. Finally, let's add a **Subdivision Surface** modifier to our character to smooth out the geometry. Press *Tab* to exit out of edit mode. With the character model selected, click the **Modifier Properties** icon at the right of the 3D Viewport, click **Add Modifier** at the top, and select **Subdivision Surface** from the drop-down menu. Set the levels for **Viewport** and **Render** to **2**.

7. Right-click on your model in the 3D Viewport and select **Shade Smooth** to render the faces smooth.

This concludes the modeling process of our alien cartoon character. By following the steps in this chapter, you should feel more confident to try and model different types of characters. Try experimenting by drawing a reference image of an animal or creature, and see whether you can create a 3D model from it. Remember – practice makes perfect, so spend some time creating a few different-looking characters, as it is the only way to get better at character modeling.

Summary

Congratulations! You have now successfully modeled your own 3D character! Using the techniques covered in this chapter, you will be able to create a 3D model of almost anything that you can imagine. It's a constant process of tweaking and toggling between the front, side, and 3D views of your model, shaping it to your reference images. Remember to keep an eye on the edge flow, trying to maintain a natural flow around your mesh. The most important part of 3D modeling is practice; that is the only way to get better at it! Start by creating simple, basic characters and slowly try to create more complex characters and other objects.

In the next chapter, we will rig our character using bones, which will allow us to bring our character to life using animation!

8

Rigging and Animating Your 3D Cartoon Character

In this chapter, we will bring our cartoon character to life by applying an animation rig to it and animating a walk cycle using keyframes. Rigging consists of adding bones to our character and converting the bones to an animation rig. This will allow us to animate the individual bones of our character to create animations such as a walk cycle. For the rigging process, we will make use of a free add-on that comes with Blender called **Rigify**.

Rigify will automatically setup **Inverse Kinematics (IK)** and **Forward Kinematics (FK)**, which will make the animation process a lot easier – but more on that later in this chapter. Let's get started!

The main topics we'll cover in this chapter are as follows:

- Installing the Rigify add-on
- Importing our character and getting it ready for the rigging process
- Rigging our character using Rigify
- IK versus FK and rig layers
- Animating a walk cycle using key poses

Installing the Rigify add-on

In this section, we will activate the Rigify add-on that comes pre-installed with Blender. The Rigify add-on will allow you to easily convert bones (armatures) into functional rig controls. Rigify will also apply **Inverse Kinematics (IK)** to certain parts of our character for easy animation, but more on that later.

Let's first install the add-on:

1. Launch Blender if it's not open already. You can start with a new project.
2. Click **Edit | Preferences** to open the Blender **Preferences** window.
3. Click the **Add-ons** tab at the left side of the **Preferences** dialog box.
4. In the search box at the top right, type the word `rigify` to search for the add-on.
5. Tick the box next to **Rigging: Rigify**, which will appear below the search box:

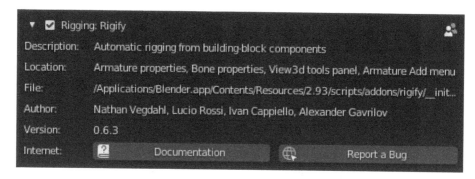

Figure 8.1 – Activating the Rigify add-on

6. Click the three horizontal lines icon at the bottom-left corner of the **Preferences** dialog box and click **Save Preferences**:

Figure 8.2 – Saving the preferences

7. You can now close the Blender **Preferences** dialog box.

The Rigify add-on has now been installed! In the next section, we will get our character model ready for the rigging process and start adding bones to our character. Feel free to bookmark the Rigify documentation URL if you want to reference it later: `https://docs.blender.org/manual/en/2.81/addons/rigging/rigify.html`.

Importing our character and getting it ready for the rigging process

In this section, we will import our character model and get it ready for the rigging process. First, we will import our cartoon character from the project file that we have saved in *Chapter 7, Modeling an Alien Cartoon Character*. We will then apply any active modifiers that we have added to our character to ensure that it's ready for rigging. We will also apply the scale of our character model to ensure there are no scaling issues during the rigging process.

Let's get started!

Importing our character model

Let's begin by importing our character model from the project file we saved in *Chapter 7, Modeling an Alien Cartoon Character*. You can also download my character model if you want from the following URL: `https://github.com/PacktPublishing/Taking-Blender-to-the-Next-Level/blob/main/Chapter08/Chapter%2008%20-%20AlienModel.obj`. First press *A* to select everything in the scene, then press *X*, and click **Delete** to confirm. We now have a blank scene:

1. Click **File | Append**.
2. Browse to the Blender project that you created in *Chapter 7, Modeling an Alien Cartoon Character*, and double-click the `.Blend` file to show its contents.
3. Double-click the **Object** folder to open it.
4. In the folder, you should see your cartoon character model. It will have the same name that you gave it in the Outliner of that Blender project.
5. Select the model from the list and click **Append** to import it into this new Blender project.
6. Save your Blender project now.

Applying any active modifiers

First, we need to ensure that we don't have any active modifiers on our character model. We might still have the **Mirror** modifier as well as a **Subdivision Surface** modifier that we need to apply before we can start the rigging process. Let's do this now:

1. Click your character model in the 3D Viewport to select it.

2. Click the **Modifier Properties** icon to the right of the 3D Viewport.

3. Here, you should see any active modifiers. At the top of the list, you should see the **Mirror** modifier that we used during the modeling process. Let's apply this **Mirror** modifier now by clicking the drop-down menu next to its heading and then clicking **Apply**.

4. You should also see a **Subdivision Surface** modifier in the list, which we added at the end of *Chapter 7, Modeling an Alien Cartoon Character*.

5. Ensure **Levels** are set to **2** for both **Viewport** and **Render**, and then click the drop-down menu next to the Subdivision Surface heading and click **Apply**. Using a **Subdivision Surface** modifier with a level of **2** should give us enough geometry for animating our character.

6. With your character selected, press *Tab* to enter **Edit Mode**. Look at the geometry – note that we now have a lot more faces because of the **Subdivision Surface** modifier that we have applied. This will allow the character to be animated and deformed better when applying a rig.

7. My character has about 18,000 faces. Try to keep this number around 15,000 to 30,000, as we don't want a model with too much geometry, which will slow down the process. Enable **Statistics** by clicking the **Overlays** dropdown at the top of the 3D Viewport and ticking the box next to **Statistics**. This will enable the Statistics overlay in the 3D Viewport, showing you the number of faces, edges, and vertices:

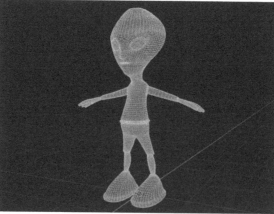

Figure 8.3 – Applying the Subdivision Surface modifier

8. Press *Tab* again to exit **Edit Mode**.

9. With your character still selected in the 3D Viewport, press *Ctrl + A* and select **Scale** from the drop-down menu. This will set the scale of our character to **1**, which is always good practice before starting the rigging process.

Congratulations! Your character is now ready for the rigging process. In the next section, we will start adding bones to our character and converting the bones into a control rig, ready for animation. Please save your project now.

Rigging the character using Rigify

In this section, we will focus on the rigging process. We will start by adding bones or armature to our character, aligning the bones to our character's mesh. We will then convert the bones into a control rig using the Rigify add-on. At the end of this section, we will test the Rigify control rig, and we will also look at the difference between Inverse Kinematics and Forward Kinematics.

Rigging the upper part of the character

Let's get started:

1. Ensure your character is in the middle of the world space and on top of the floor grid. Go into the front view by pressing *1* on the numpad or clicking the **-Y axis** icon in the 3D Viewport. Move the character using *G* and ensure that it's in the center, as shown in the following screenshot:

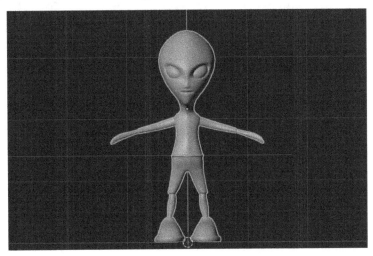

Figure 8.4 – Positioning your character model at the center of the grid

2. Let's center the 3D Cursor by pressing *Shift + S* and selecting **Cursor to World Origin** from the snapping menu. This will snap the 3D Cursor to the center of the grid and will ensure that our armature is created in the correct position.

3. Now let's create our armature by pressing *Shift + A* and selecting **Armature**. Select **Human (Meta-Rig)** from the drop-down menu, which will create a new human-type armature.

4. Click **Armature** in the 3D Viewport to select it, and then click the **Object Properties** icon at the right of the 3D Viewport.

5. Scroll down and expand **Viewport Display**, and tick the box next to **In Front**. This will ensure that the armature is always visible and will not be displayed inside or behind your character model, making it easier to adjust the bone positions.

6. With **Armature** still selected in the 3D Viewport, press S and scale it so that the shoulders align with your character model, as shown in the following screenshot:

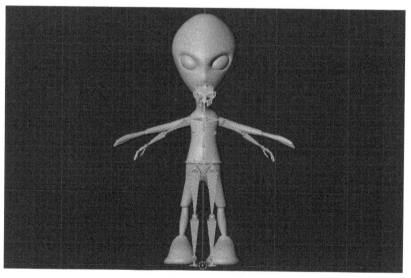

Figure 8.5 – Scaling the armature to align it with the character's shoulders

7. With the armature still selected, press *Tab* to enter **Edit Mode**. In **Edit Mode**, we will be able to move the individual bones as well as delete any bones that we don't need.

    Next, we're going to delete all the face bones, as we will only focus on the character's body animation.

8. Go into the side view by pressing the shortcut on the numpad or clicking the **X Axis** icon in the 3D Viewport. Zoom in to have a better view of the face bones. Select them by dragging a box around them, then press *X*, and select **Bones** to delete them, as shown in the following screenshot:

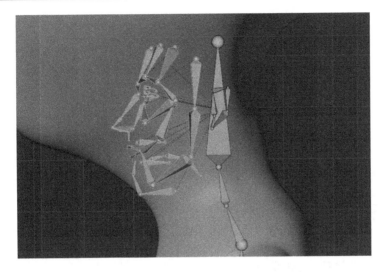

Figure 8.6 – Selecting and deleting the face bones

9. Go into the front view by pressing *1* on the numpad or clicking the -**Y Axis** icon in the 3D Viewport.

10. Select the ear bones on both sides and delete them as well by pressing *X* and selecting **Bones** from the drop-down menu.

    Next, we need to delete the face bone. This bone is located inside the large, top spine bone.

11. Let's enable **Wireframe** mode by pressing *Z* and clicking **Wireframe** from the radial menu to see this bone. Now select it, press *X*, and click **Bones** to delete it, as shown in the following screenshot:

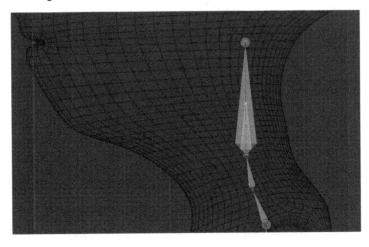

Figure 8.7 – Locating and deleting the face bone

12. Change back to Solid view by pressing *Z* and selecting **Solid** from the radial menu. You can also use **Wireframe** mode if you prefer.

    Now, we can start aligning the bones to our character. Let's start with the head bone.

13. Select the top connector of the head bone. Press *G* and then press *Z* to move it up toward the top of the character's head:

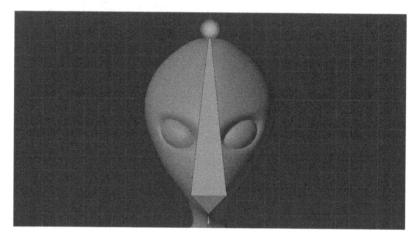

Figure 8.8 – Positioning the top of the head bone to the top of the character's head

14. Go into the side view by pressing the shortcut on the numpad or by clicking the **X Axis** icon in the 3D Viewport. Position the head bone so that it follows the shape of the head. The easiest way to move a bone is to select the round connector at the top of the bone and press *G* to move it. Always try to move the round connector and not the bone itself, as this will keep linked bones together and thus avoid any rigging errors:

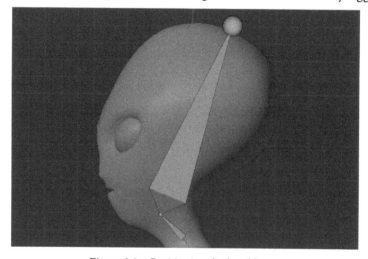

Figure 8.9 – Positioning the head bone

15. Next, let's enable **bone mirror** mode by clicking the **X** icon at the top right of the 3D Viewport, above the axis icons. This will mirror any changes you make on one side of the bones to the opposite side, which makes alignment much easier:

Figure 8.10 – Enabling bone mirroring by clicking the X button at the top of the 3D Viewport

Rigging the lower part of the character's body

Now that we have rigged the upper part of the character, we will rig the lower part of the character's body in this section:

1. Next, let's align the spine bones to our character's body shape. I find it easier to select the bone connectors in the perspective view and then change to the side view to align them. This process is similar to the modeling process where you constantly switch between the side, front, and perspective views to align the bones as best as you can. It's good practice to rotate the bones in either the side, front, or top view, rather than in the perspective view. This way, the bones will rotate around the viewing axis:

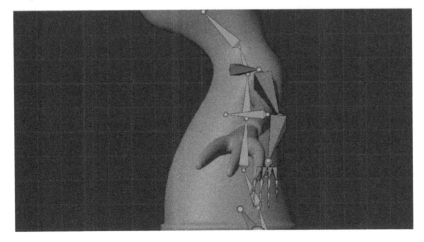

Figure 8.11 – Aligning the spine bones to the character's body shape

2. Next, let's align the pelvis and thigh bones. Go into the front view and move the bones into place. Match the bottom of the thigh bone to the character's knee, as shown in the following screenshot:

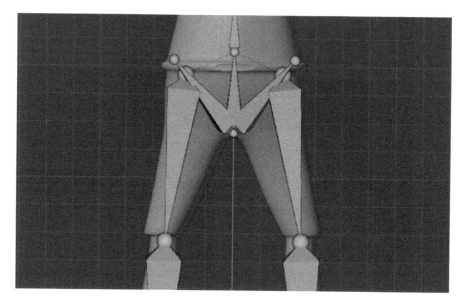

Figure 8.12 – Aligning the pelvis and thigh bones using the front view

3. Still in the front view, align the shin bones to match the character's legs.

4. Still in the front view, scale the heel bone (the bone at the bottom of the foot) so that it matches the width of our character's foot. Click the bone to select it and press *S* to scale it accordingly:

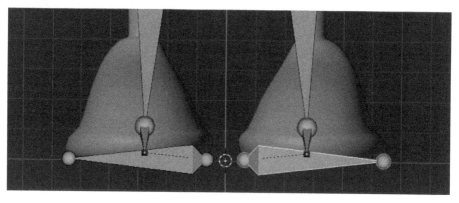

Figure 8.13 – Aligning the shin and heel bones of our character

5. Switch over to the side view and align the heel bone to the rear of our character's foot, and also position the toe and foot bone so that it matches the following screenshot:

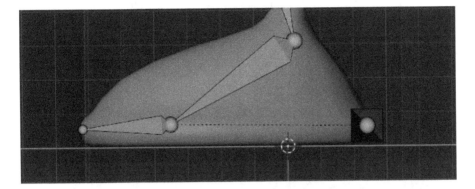

Figure 8.14 – Aligning the heel and foot bones

6. Still in the side view, position the thigh bone as shown in the following screenshot. Note how the bone bends with the character's knee. This will allow the knee to bend in the correct way:

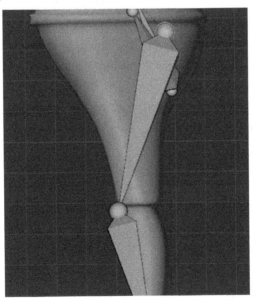

Figure 8.15 – Adding a slight bend to follow the character's knee bend position

Rigging the torso, arms and hands of our character

We will continue further to rig the torso, arms and hands of our character

1. Go into the front view and position the breastbone so that it's slightly to the side, and close to the armpit of our character:

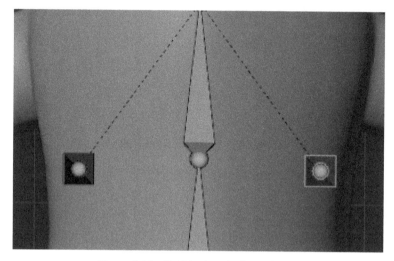

Figure 8.16 – Positioning the breastbone

2. Still in the front view, move the shoulder, upper arm, and forearm bones into place. With the hand bones selected, press *R* to rotate them to match our character's hand rotation:

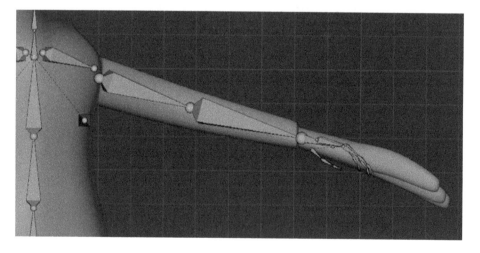

Figure 8.17 – Aligning the shoulder, upper arm, and forearm bones into position

3. Go into the top view by pressing *7* on the numpad or clicking the **Z Axis** icon in the 3D Viewport. Now align the shoulder, upper arm, forearm, and hand bones to match our character. Don't spend too much time on the hand bones yet; we will align them soon. Feel free to switch to wireframe mode, as it might be easier to align the bones. Note the slight elbow bend when aligning the arm bones:

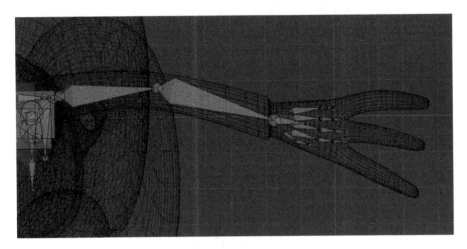

Figure 8.18 – Aligning the arm bones using the top view

4. Next, we're going to align the hand and finger bones. Our character only has three fingers, and the default human armature comes with five fingers. We can go ahead and delete the pinky and thumb finger bones. Select these bones and press *X*, and then select **Bones** from the drop-down menu to delete these fingers.

5. Align the finger bones to the character's fingers:

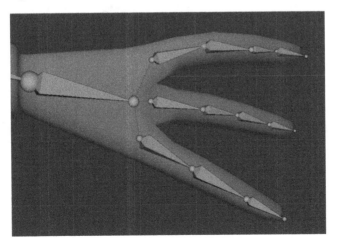

Figure 8.19 – Aligning the three finger bones to our character's hand

6. Now, go into the front view and align the first finger to the character's first finger. The trick is to constantly toggle between the front, top, and perspective views to ensure that the fingers are aligned from all views. This can take some time:

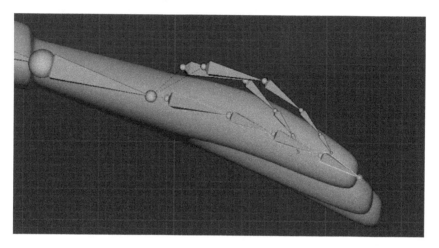

Figure 8.20 – Aligning the first finger bone using the front view

7. Continue to toggle between the front and side views and align the other fingers to the character mesh. Take your time with this step to ensure that the finger bones are in the center of the mesh. Note the slight bend of the finger bones – this will ensure that the fingers bend in the correct direction. An easy way to select all the bones in each finger is to select the last bone at the tip of the finger and then press *CMD + + on the numpad. This will increase the selection by one bone. Keep pressing the *CMD + +* numpad shortcut until you have selected all the bones of the finger:

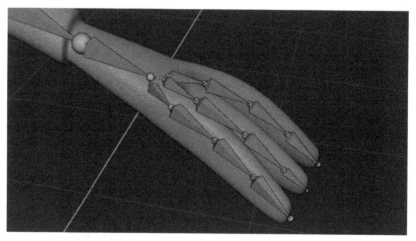

Figure 8.21 – Aligning the other finger bones to the mesh

Final rig alignment

And for the final rig alignment, excute the following steps:

1. Now, let's ensure that all the bones are aligned to our character mesh. Go into the front view and confirm that all the bones are aligned. Use the following reference diagram:

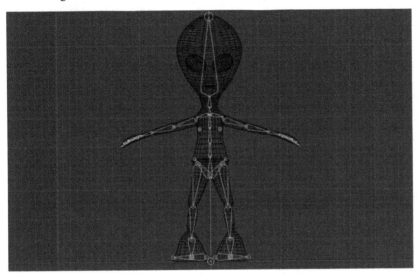

Figure 8.22 – Using the front view to align the bones

2. Go into the top view and ensure that all the bones are aligned:

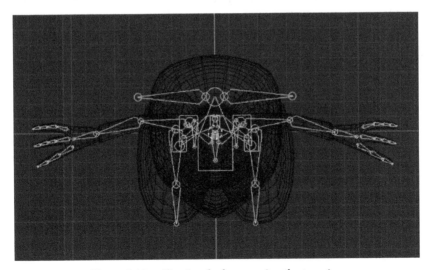

Figure 8.23 – Aligning the bones using the top view

3.   Switch to the side view and ensure that the bones are aligned:

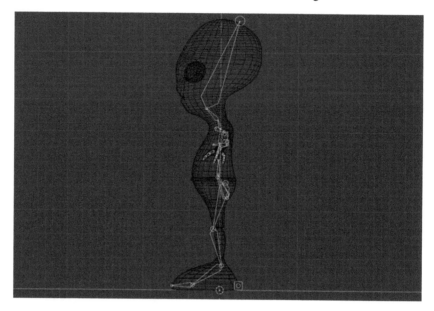

Figure 8.24 – Aligning the bones using the side view

4.   After aligning all the bones of the character, press *Tab* to exit **Edit Mode**.

5.   With **Armature** still selected in the 3D Viewport, let's apply its scale to avoid any scaling issues. Press *Ctrl + A* and select **Scale** from the drop-down menu.

6.   Next, we're going to generate the Rigify control rig. To do this, click **Armature** in the 3D Viewport to select it.

7.   Click the **Object Data Properties** icon at the right of the 3D Viewport.

8.   Scroll down to **Rigify Buttons** and click **Generate Rig**:

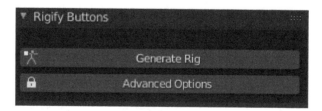

Figure 8.25 – Generating the control rig

The Rigify control rig will now be generated in the 3D Viewport:

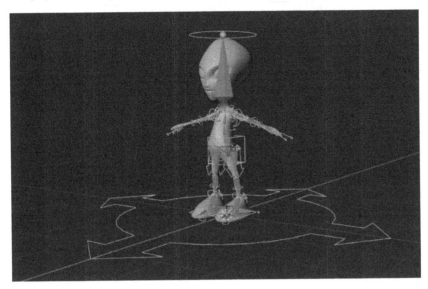

Figure 8.26 – The Rigify control rig appearing in the 3D Viewport

If you receive an error at this stage, select the bones again and press *Tab* to get into **Edit Mode**. Ensure that the bones (especially the spine bones) are connected to each other and that their round connector points are connected and not separated from each other. Try generating the rig again after making adjustments, if needed.

9. Next, let's hide the bones (armature) from the 3D Viewport. Select the **Armature** (not the rig) and press *H* to hide it from the 3D Viewport.

10. Click the rig to select it in the 3D Viewport, and then click the **Object Data Properties** icon at the right of the 3D Viewport. Expand **Viewport Display** and tick **In Front**. This will ensure that the rig is always visible and not obscured by the mesh.

11. We can now parent the rig to our character. To do this, deselect everything in the 3D Viewport by clicking in an empty area.

12. Click the character to select it first, then hold *Shift*, and click on the rig to select it as the active object.

13. Right-click in the 3D Viewport, select **Parent**, and click **With Automatic Weights** from the drop-down menu:

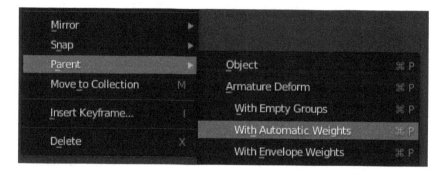

Figure 8.27 – Parenting the rig to our character using Automatic Weights

Congratulations! You have now successfully rigged your character using Rigify! In the next section, we will look at the differences between IK and FK, as well as how to use rig layers. Please save your project now.

IK versus FK and rig layers

In this section, we will look at the difference between IK and FK, as well as how to hide certain rig controls from the 3D Viewport. Let's get started!

IK versus FK

Before we start creating our walk cycle, let's quickly talk about IK and FK and their differences.

When IK is used, you can move a certain limb (for instance, the hand), and the parent bones, the forearm, and the upper arm will move accordingly, adjusting the elbow bend automatically in relation to the position of the hand. When using IK, the child limb will not be affected when the parent bones are moved or rotated. A good example would be the movement of a character's upper torso not affecting the position of its hand. This is useful if you want to animate the character's body without affecting a certain limb, such as the hand.

When FK is used, the child limb will follow the parent bones – for instance, when the upper torso of a character is animated, the arm and hand will move in relation to the upper torso.

By default, Rigify uses IK for both the hands and the feet, but this can be adjusted as needed.

Let's have a look at how this works and how this will affect the way we animate our character:

1. Click the control rig in the 3D Viewport to select it and press *Ctrl + Tab* to enter **Pose Mode**. This is similar to **Edit Mode**, but it is used when animating a character rig or armature and adjusting its pose.

2. Press *N* to bring up the side menu and click the **Item** tab to display the **Rigify** properties.

3. We can now start manipulating the different controls in the 3D Viewport to change the pose of our character. Click the cube-shaped control near the center of our character to select it. This is the **torso control**.

4. With the torso control selected, press *G* and move the mouse. See how your character moves. Note how the character's knees and elbows bend automatically. You will also notice that the feet and hands do not move in relation to the torso control. This is because both the feet and hands are set to use IK. Press *Esc* to cancel the move operation.

5. Let's see how IK works when moving the child limb. Click the foot control to select it. This is the oval-shaped control below the foot, as shown in the following screenshot:

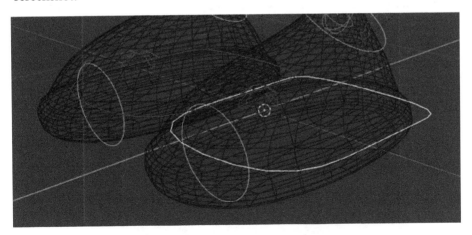

Figure 8.28 – Selecting the foot control

6. With the foot control selected, press *G* and move the mouse. Note how the knee automatically bends as you move the foot control up and down. Press *Esc* to cancel the move operation:

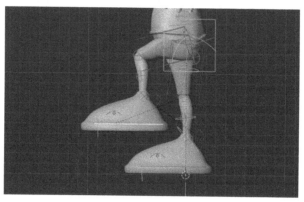

Figure 8.29 – Automatically bending the knee when the foot control is moved because of IK

7. Let's change the foot control from IK to FK. With the foot control still selected, look at the side menu to the right of the 3D Viewport. You will see a slider called **IK-FK (foot.L)**. Currently, its value is 0.000, which means that it's configured for IK. Click and drag this slider all the way to 1.000. This control is now set to use FK.

8. With the foot control still selected in the 3D Viewport, press *G* again and move the mouse. Note that the foot does not move. This is because we changed from IK to FK and, thus, we need to move the parent controls to adjust the foot's position. Let's see how we can do that.

9. We can now use the following four FK control points to adjust the position of the foot. Click to select one of these four control points, and then press *R* to rotate the control. Note how the foot will follow along in the following screenshot:

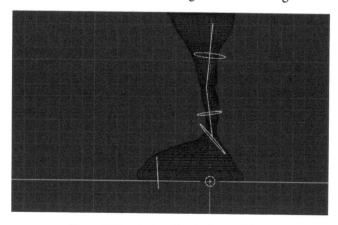

Figure 8.30 – Animating the leg and foot

10. Rotate these four FK controls and see whether you can match the following image:

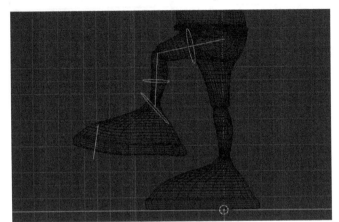

Figure 8.31 – Changing the pose using FK controls

11. Click the torso control in the 3D Viewport to select it again. This is the cube-shaped control near the middle of our character.

12. Press *G* and move the mouse. Note how one foot is moving with the character's torso. This is because we're using FK to control that foot.

13. Before moving on, let's reset all the rig controls back to default. Still in **Pose Mode**, press *A* to select all the controls. Right-click anywhere in the 3D Viewport and select **Clear User Transforms** from the drop-down menu to reset the position, rotation, and scale of all selected controls.

14. Let's set the foot control back to IK, as we will be making use of IK for both the hands and feet when animating the walk cycle. Click the oval-shaped foot control again to select it.

15. In the side menu at the right of the 3D Viewport, change the **IK-FK (foot.L)** slider back to 0.000. This will set the foot control to use IK.

IK and FK can be a bit confusing to understand at first, but all you need to know for now is that with IK, you move the child limb and the parent controls will follow. But with FK, you need to move the parent controls to move the child limb.

As with everything in 3D, experiment with IK and FK to see which works best for the situation at hand. In the next section, we will look at how we can hide certain rig controls from the 3D Viewport. Please save your project now.

Rig layers

Rigging controls can be tricky to work with when animating many different parts of your character. Luckily, there is an easy way to hide and show only the rig controls you need to see in the 3D Viewport.

Staying in **Pose Mode**, look at the side menu at the right of the 3D Viewport. You will see a section called **Rig Layers**. Note that the **Rig Layers** section is available in both **Pose Mode** and **Object Mode**, so you don't have to be in **Pose Mode** to show and hide layers:

Figure 8.32 – Rig Layers as shown in the side menu

Let's see how we can use these layers to easily show and hide different rigging controls from the 3D viewport:

1. Clicking the following layers will hide and unhide a specific rig control.

    Let's hide all the layers except the **Arm.L (IK)** control. This will only keep the IK control for the left arm in the 3D Viewport:

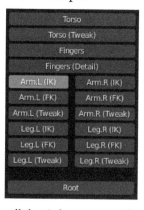

Figure 8.33 – Hiding all the rig layers except the Arm.L (IK) control

2. It's a lot easier now to animate the hand position without all the other controls distracting you. Try to match the following screenshot by moving and rotating the hand control using *G* and *R*:

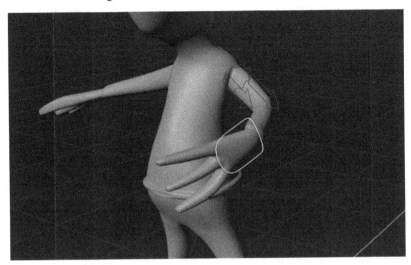

Figure 8.34 – Matching the pose of the hand and arm

3. Unhide all the rig layers by clicking their control names in the side menu.

4. Press *A* to select all the controls in the 3D Viewport, then right-click anywhere, and select **Clear User Transforms** from the drop-down menu to reset the rig controls back to their default position.

You should now be fairly familiar with how this rig works, and we are now ready to start creating the walk cycle animation! Feel free to play with the rig controls. Move, rotate, and scale the different controls and see how they affect your character. Remember – practice makes perfect, and as always, have fun and see what interesting poses you can create! Please save your project now.

In the next section, we will begin animating the walk cycle.

Animating the walk cycle

In this section, we will bring our character to life by animating a walk cycle using keyframes. The amazing part of keyframe animation is that we only need to create a few easy poses and Blender will automatically fill in the gaps by adding the frames between each of our key poses. I will show you how you can create a complete walk cycle by just creating four poses!

In the following reference diagram, you can see the four key poses. These are the only poses we need to create in order to animate a full walk cycle. We will first create these four poses and then invert these poses to create additional poses for the opposite side of the character. We will create these four key poses on frames 1, 10, 20, and 30, and we will position the inverted poses on frames 40, 50, 60, and 70. Let's get started!

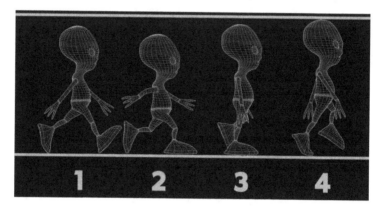

Figure 8.35 – The four key poses needed for a walk cycle

Setting up key pose number one

Let's begin by setting up key pose number one:

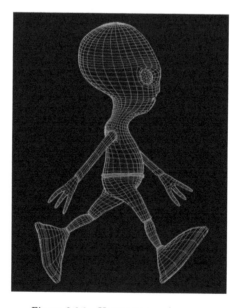

Figure 8.36 – Key pose number one

1. First, ensure that you are in **Pose Mode**. Select the rig in the 3D Viewport and press *Ctrl + Tab* to enter **Pose Mode**.

2. Make sure that you are on frame number **1** on the timeline at the bottom of the Blender interface. This is where the first key pose will be created:

Figure 8.37 – Positioning the play head at frame number 1

3. Go into the side view so that your character is facing right. To do this, you can click the **-X Axis** icon at the top-right corner of the 3D Viewport.

Now, let's try and match pose number one using *Figure 8.36*. Let's focus on the right foot first. Select the foot control and move and rotate it to match the reference diagram. Make sure that the heel of the foot makes contact with the floor grid:

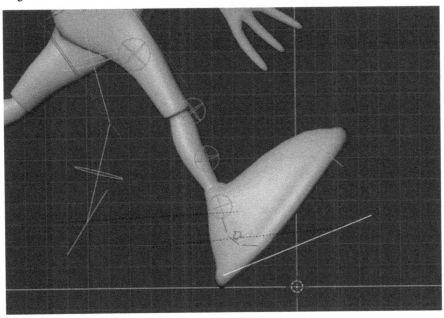

Figure 8.38 – Moving and rotating the right foot control to match key pose number one

Next, let's position the left foot. Move and rotate the left foot control to match the following screenshot. You can also rotate the foot spin control, highlighted in white in the following screenshot. The foot spin control looks like a circle with four arrows. This control allows you to rotate the foot independently from the foot control. Try to match the slight bend in the knee:

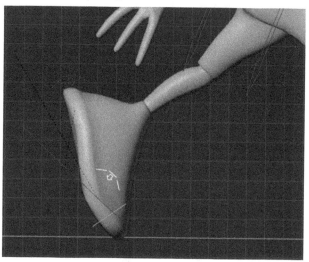

Figure 8.39 – Moving and rotating the left foot control to match key pose number one

Let's move on to the right hand. Using the hand control, move and rotate until it matches the following screenshot:

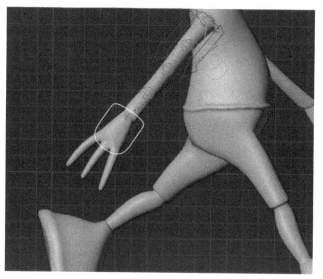

Figure 8.40 – Moving and rotating the right-hand control to match key pose number one

4. Next, let's move the left hand into position to match the following screenshot:

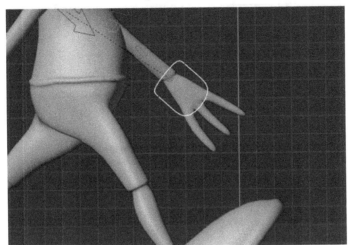

Figure 8.41 – Moving and rotating the left-hand control to match key pose number one

5. Once you are happy with key pose number one, we can set our keyframes to save the control positions onto frame **1**. First, ensure that all the rig controls are visible by enabling them all under **Rig Layers** in the side menu.

6. Press *A* to select all the rig controls in the 3D Viewport and press *I* (capital *i*) to bring up the **Insert Keyframe** menu. Select **Whole Character (Selected Bones Only)** from the drop-down menu to set a keyframe for each of the selected rig controls:

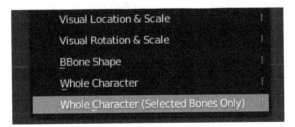

Figure 8.42 – Setting a keyframe for each selected rig control

7. Note that a keyframe has been created on the timeline at the bottom of the interface:

Figure 8.43 – Creating a keyframe on frame number 1

Congratulations! You have successfully created your first key pose for the walk cycle animation! Only three more key poses to create! Let's have a look at key pose number two. Please save your project now.

Setting up key pose number two

Let's have a look at key pose number two. The character's right foot is now flat on the ground, the left foot is pointing downward, both hands are slightly higher up, and the whole body is lower to the ground:

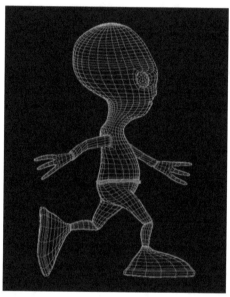

Figure 8.44 – Key pose number two

If you look at *Figure 8.35* at the beginning of this section, you will note that our character is the lowest to the ground in pose number two.

Let's begin creating this pose:

1. We're going to create this key pose on frame number 10. On the timeline at the bottom of the interface, click frame **10** to move the play head to this position.

2. Staying in **Pose Mode**, select the torso control, which has a cube shape and is located in the middle of the character. Press G, then press Z, and move the mouse slightly to lower our character's body closer to the ground.

3. Next, use the right-foot control to rotate and move its right foot until it's flat on the grid. Note the slight bend in its knee.

4. Select the left-foot control, and then move and rotate it until the left foot is pointing downward. Note the slight bend in its left knee.

5. Select both hand controls and move them slightly higher up.

6. Now let's create the keyframes for this pose. Press *A* to select all the controls. Press *I* and select **Whole Character (Selected Bones Only)** to create a keyframe for each control. Note the new keyframe created on the timeline:

Figure 8.45 – The keyframe for key pose number two

Congratulations! You have successfully created key pose number two. Let's have a look at key pose number three.

Setting up key pose number three

The right foot is flat on the ground and right underneath the body. The left foot is also under the body but bent downward and not touching the ground. Both hands are next to the sides, pointing downward. The body is slightly higher up than key pose number one but only slightly:

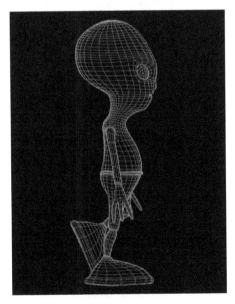

Figure 8.46 – Key pose number three

Let's create the pose:

1. We're going to create this key pose on frame number **20**. On the timeline at the bottom of the interface, click frame **20** to move the play head to this position.

2. Staying in **Pose Mode**, select the torso control. Press *G* and then press *Z* to move its body up slightly. Refer to *Figure 8.35* at the beginning of the main section.

3. Click the right-foot control to select it. Move and rotate if needed until the foot is flat underneath the body. Note there is almost no bend in the knee.

4. Select the left-foot control and move and rotate it until the foot is almost under the body, with the toes pointing downward.

5. Select both hand controls and move them downward, next to the side, and rotate the hands so that the fingers are pointing downward as well.

6. Let's create the keyframes. Press *A* to select all the controls. Press *I* and select **Whole Character (Selected Bones Only)** to create a keyframe for each control. Note the new keyframe created on the timeline.

Congratulations! You have successfully created key pose number three. Let's have a look at key pose number four – the final key pose!

Setting up key pose number four

The right foot and leg of our character are slightly toward the back, and its toe is flat on the ground with the heel lifted slightly. Its left knee is bent, and its left foot is pointing down slightly. Its right hand is slightly forward, with its left hand toward the back. Its body is quite high up, as the character is positioned on its toe:

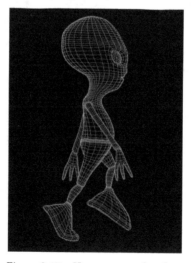

Figure 8.47 – Key pose number four

Let's create the final pose!

1. We're going to create this key pose on frame number **30**. On the timeline at the bottom of the interface, click frame **30** to move the play head to this position.

2. Staying in **Pose Mode**, select the torso control. Press *G* and then press *Z* to move its body up slightly. Refer to *Figure 8.35* at the beginning of the main section.

3. Select the right-foot control and move it toward the back of the character. Rotate the heel and toe controls to get the desired pose for its foot. These controls are highlighted in white in the following screenshot:

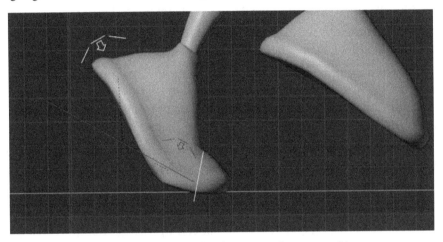

Figure 8.48 – Using the heel and toe controls to create this pose

4. Select the left-foot control and move this foot forward and up. Rotate this foot so that it points downward. Note the bent knee.

5. Select the right-hand control and position this hand to the front of the character.

6. Select the left-hand control and position this hand to the back of the character.

7. Let's create the keyframes. Press *A* to select all the controls. Press *I* and select **Whole Character (Selected Bones Only)** to create a keyframe for each control. Note the new keyframe created on the timeline.

Congratulations! You have successfully created all four key poses for the walk cycle! Next, we need to invert these key poses to create the poses for the opposite side of the animation. This is fairly easy to do in Blender! But first, let's preview our four-keyframe animation to see what we have created.

Click frame **1** in the timeline at the bottom of the interface. Then, press the *spacebar* to play the animation. Enjoy the first half of your walk cycle animation! Let's create the inverted keyframes now after saving your project.

Creating inverted keyframes

We're going to copy key pose number 1, which is on frame **1**, and paste the inverted pose at frame **40**. Then, we will take key pose number 2, which is on frame **10**, and paste the inverted pose at frame **50**. Then, we will take key pose number 3, which is on frame **20**, and paste the inverted pose at frame **60**. Lastly, we'll copy key pose number 4, which is at frame **30**, and paste the inverted pose at frame **70**:

1. Staying in **Pose Mode**, make sure that all the rig controls are visible by activating them all in the **Rig Layers** section in the side menu.

2. In the timeline, go to frame number **1** by clicking on frame **1**.

3. Hover your mouse over the 3D Viewport and press *A* to select all the rig controls. Press *Ctrl + C* to copy them all.

4. Now, go to frame number 40 by clicking on frame **40** in the timeline, hover your mouse over the 3D Viewport again, and press *Shift + Ctrl + V* to invert-paste this pose. This shortcut will paste the opposite version of this pose where every limb's position will be inverted to the other side of the character.

5. We still need to save the keyframe. Press *A* to select all the controls, then press *I*, and select **Whole Character (Selected Bones Only)** to create a keyframe for each control. Note the new keyframe created on the timeline at frame **40**.

6. Next, go to frame **10**.

7. Hover your mouse over the 3D Viewport, press *A* to select all the rig controls, and press *Ctrl + C* to copy them.

8. Now, go to frame **50**, hover your mouse over the 3D Viewport, and press *Shift + Ctrl + V* to invert-paste this pose.

9. Press *A* to select all the controls, then press *I*, and select **Whole Character (Selected Bones Only)** to create a keyframe for each control. Note the new keyframe created on the timeline at frame **50**.

10. Next, go to frame **20**.

11. Hover your mouse over the 3D Viewport, press *A* to select all the rig controls, and press *Ctrl + C* to copy them.

12. Now, go to frame **60**, hover your mouse over the 3D Viewport, and press *Shift + Ctrl + V* to invert-paste this pose.

13. Press *A* to select all the controls, then press *I*, and select **Whole Character (Selected Bones Only)** to create a keyframe for each control. Note the new keyframe created on the timeline at frame **60**.

14. Next, go to frame **30**.

15. Hover your mouse over the 3D Viewport, press *A* to select all the rig controls, and press *Ctrl + C* to copy them.

16. Now, go to frame **70**, hover your mouse over the 3D Viewport, and press *Shift + Ctrl + V* to invert-paste this pose.

17. Press *A* to select all the controls, then press *I*, and select **Whole Character (Selected Bones Only)** to create a keyframe for each control. Note the new keyframe created on the timeline at frame **70**.

Congratulations! You have created all the inverted poses required for the walk cycle! Press the *spacebar* to play your animation. It's great, but let's create a seamless looping animation!

Looping the walk cycle

For the walk cycle to loop, we're going to copy the first key pose and paste it at the end of our walk cycle, but we're only going to loop the frames up until one frame before this final pose. It will make more sense once you see it on the timeline:

1. Staying in **Pose Mode**, go to frame **1** on the timeline.

2. Hover your mouse over the 3D Viewport, press *A* to select all the rig controls, and press *Ctrl + C* to copy them.

3. Now, go to **frame 80**, hover your mouse over the 3D Viewport, and press *Ctrl + V* to paste this pose. Note that we're doing a normal paste command and not an inverted paste command. This is because we want to loop the walk cycle, and we need to return to the first exact pose.

4. Press *A* to select all the controls, then press *I*, and select **Whole Character (Selected Bones Only)** to create a keyframe for each control. Note the new keyframe created on the timeline at frame **80**.

5. Let's set our timeline to loop frames **1** to **79**. The reason why we're only looping **1–79** and not **1–80** is that the pose at frame **80** is exactly the same as the pose at frame **1**. Including frame **80** will cause a double frame of the exact same pose.

6. In the top right of the timeline, you will see the frame **Start** and **End** numbers. Set the **End** frame to **79**, as shown in the following screenshot:

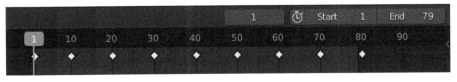

Figure 8.49 – Setting the animation to loop frames 1–79

You have successfully created your first walk cycle! Press the *spacebar* and enjoy your looping walking animation. You can always go back to your key poses and adjust the rig controls as required. Remember to overwrite the keyframes by pressing *I* if you make any changes to the rig controls.

If you want to move the character forward or backward, you can move or rotate the **Root rig control** located at the base of the character. It's in the shape of a large circle and has four arrows pointing in each direction.

Summary

Congratulations! You now have all the tools and knowledge to create any type of animation you can dream of. You should now have a good understanding of adding bones to your character and generating an animation rig from these bones using the Rigify add-on. We've also learned how to add keyframes on these rig controls to create amazing animations for our character.

We've also created a walk cycle using this process by referencing different key pose images. Remember that you can use this technique for non-character animations as well – for example, you can add bones and an animation rig to a construction crane robot or vehicle to allow you to easily animate a crane arm.

As with everything else in the 3D world, experiment and practice. It's the only way to get better at animation. Most importantly, have fun creating amazing animations for your characters, robots, and other models.

In the next chapter, you will learn how to use physics to destroy a statue and break it into pieces.

Part 2:
Let's Do Some
Physics

In this part of the book, we will be focusing on different types of Physics Simulations such as Rigid Body, Cell Fracture, Cloth, as well as Hair Particle Simulations.

We will cover the following chapters in this section:

- *Chapter 9, Rigid Body Simulation: Destroying a Statue Using Physics*
- *Chapter 10, Dynamic Cloth Simulations*
- *Chapter 11, Creating Dynamic Hair Using Particles*

9
Rigid Body Simulation: Destroying a Statue Using Physics

In this chapter, we will be destroying a statue model using **Rigid Body physics**! First, we will break our statue into smaller pieces by using a free Blender add-on called **Cell Fracture**. Then, we will apply physics properties to these fractured pieces and link them together using **Rigid Body constraints**. We will also animate an impact object that will activate the physics simulation and destroy our model. Let's get started!

In this chapter, we will cover the following topics:

- Installing the required add-ons
- Setting up the scene
- Using Cell Fracture to break our model into smaller pieces
- Fracturing the impact point using the Annotation Pencil
- Applying Rigid Body physics to the fractured pieces

- Linking fractured pieces together using Rigid Body constraints
- Animating a Rigid Body impact object
- Baking the final physics simulation

Installing the required add-ons

Let's begin by activating the required Blender add-ons we're going to use in this chapter. There are two add-ons we need to activate. First, we need the **Cell Fracture** add-on, which will break our model into smaller fragments. The second add-on, called **Import-Export STL**, is optional and is only required if you are importing an STL model. We'll look at STL models in more detail in the next section.

Let's begin by installing these two add-ons:

1. Create a blank new Blender project and delete all the default objects by pressing *A* and then *X*. Then, click **Delete** to confirm this.

2. Click **Edit | Preferences** to open the **Blender Preferences** dialog box.

3. Click the **Add-ons** tab on the side of this window to display the active add-ons.

4. In the search box, type `cell`. Then, tick the box next to **Object: Cell Fracture**. This will activate this add-on.

5. Again, in the search box, type `stl`. Then, tick the box next to **Import-Export: STL format**. As we mentioned previously, this add-on is optional and is used for importing STL 3D models.

6. Next, click the three horizontal lines and select **Save Preferences**.

Figure 9.1 – Save Preferences

Great – you now have all the required add-ons installed! In the next section, we will begin setting up our scene. Please save your project now.

Setting up the scene

In this chapter, we will import the statue model that we're going to destroy. You can download my statue model from `https://github.com/PacktPublishing/` `Taking-Blender-to-the-Next-Level/blob/main/Chapter09/` `Chapter%2009%20-%20Statue.obj` or you can use your own 3D model instead. You can also download free models from various websites. **MyMiniFactory** has some great free statue models that you can download for free from their **Scan The World** collection. These models are 3D scans of real statues from around the world.

Please note that these 3D scanned models are high-poly and may need some work to bring their poly count down. I will explain how to do that in this section. These 3D scanned models are mostly in STL format, and that's why we're activating the **Import-Export: STL format** add-on. Let's get started:

1. Click **File | Import | Wavefront (.obj)**.

   Note that if you are importing an **STL** model that you have downloaded from **MyMiniFactory**, you need to click **File | Import | Stl (.stl)**.

2. Browse to the location where you have downloaded my 3D model called `Statue.obj`.

3. Select the `Statue.obj` file and click **Import OBJ** to import the model into your scene.

   Let's apply the transforms of the imported object to ensure the rotation, position, and scale are set correctly.

4. Click the model in the 3D Viewport to select it, then press *Ctrl + A* and select **All Transforms** from the menu.

5. Press *N* to bring up the side menu and click the **Item** tab on the side of this menu to show the item properties.

6. With the statue still selected in the 3D Viewport, press *S* to scale it until you are happy with its size. Keep an eye on the **Dimensions** section in the side menu. I scaled my statue so that it's about 10 meters tall. Remember that **Z** is the height of your statue.

Dimensions:	
X	1.38 m
Y	1.38 m
Z	10 m

Figure 9.2 – Scaling your statue model so that it's around 10 meters tall

7. Now, let's apply the scale of our object. With the statue still selected in the 3D Viewport, press *Ctrl + A* and select **Scale** from the menu. This will ensure that the **Scale** value of our object is **1**. This is very important when you're doing physics simulations because the scale of an object will affect the way it interacts with gravity and other forces.

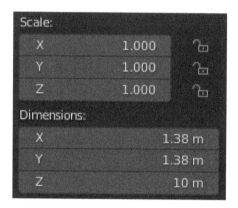

Figure 9.3 – Applying Scale will reset the Scale parameter to 1 but keep its Dimensions properties

8. Double-click on its name in the **Outliner** section to rename it Statue.

Figure 9.4 – Renaming the statue in the Outliner section to Statue

9. Let's create the floor for our scene – press *Shift + A* to select **Mesh | Plane**.

10. With the plane selected, press *S* and scale it to a reasonable size.

11. With the plane object selected in the 3D Viewport, press *Ctrl + A* and select **Scale** to apply its scale.

12. Rename the plane object to Floor by double-clicking it in the **Outliner** section.

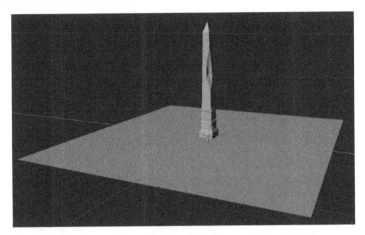

Figure 9.5 – Your scene should look something like this

With that, we have imported our statue model and also created a floor object. Now, we are ready to move on to the next section, where we will be breaking our statue into smaller fragments. Please save your project now.

Using Cell Fracture to break our model into smaller pieces

In this section, we will be using the Cell Fracture add-on to break our statue model into smaller pieces. We will be breaking different parts of our model multiple times to create variation in the fragment sizes, so think about which parts of your model should have smaller fragments and which parts should have larger fragments. This way, the simulation will look more realistic, and the pieces won't be uniform in size.

Let's get started:

1. Click the statue model in the 3D Viewport to select it. Then, click the **Object** menu at the top of the 3D Viewport, select **Quick Effects**, and then click **Cell Fracture**.

2. The **Cell Fracture** dialog box should open. At the top, under the **Point Source** section, click **Own Verts**. This will use the object's vertices to generate the fragments.

3. Increase **Source Limit** to 200. This is the number of fragments that will be generated.

4. Next, increase **Noise** to `1.00`. This will introduce noise to the fragments so that they are all different in shape and size.

5. Toward the bottom of this dialog box, under **Scene**, enter a **Collection** name; that is, `Fracture`. This option will create a new collection in the **Outliner** section and move all the fragments into this new collection. The key with physics simulations is to keep your project organized and the best way to do this is by using collections.

6. Click **OK** to begin generating the first set of fragments. Keep an eye on the 3D Viewport as the fracturing process is quite interesting to watch.

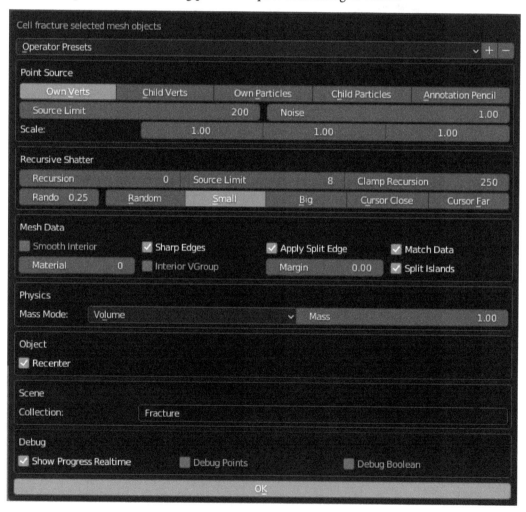

Figure 9.6 – Cell fracture settings

7. Looking at the **Outliner** section, you will see a new collection called **Fracture**. All the fragments we have just created are stored under this collection. You will see that the original statue model is still active and is overlapping the fragments in the 3D Viewport. Hide the original statue model from the **Outliner** section by clicking the **Eye** and **Camera** icons next to it. This will hide it from the 3D Viewport, as well as from any renders.

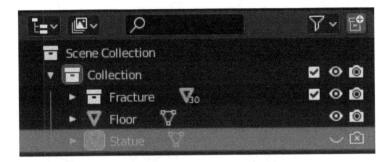

Figure 9.7 – Hiding the original statue model

Next, we're going to break some of the fragments into even smaller pieces. Look at the fractured statue in the viewport and select a single piece that you would like to break up into smaller fragments. I chose the top part of the statue but feel free to select any fragment you want.

8. With this fragment selected, press *M* to bring up the **Move to Collection** dialog box. For the name, enter Temp and click **OK** to confirm. This will create a new collection called **Temp**; the selected fragment will be moved into this new collection. This way, it's easy to delete this fragment once we have fractured it into smaller pieces. This will make more sense in a moment.

9. With this fragment still selected, click the **Object** menu again, select **Quick Effects**, and then click **Cell Fracture** to bring up the **Cell Fracture** dialog box.

10. Change **Source Limit** to 50 as we will be breaking this fragment into 50 smaller pieces.

11. Make sure the collection under the **Scene** section is still set to Fracture as we want to move these smaller fractures into the same **Fracture** collection.

12. Click **OK** to begin the Cell Fracture process.

13. Now, we can delete the fragment that we moved to the **Temp** collection. In the **Outliner** section, expand the **Temp** collection. Click the fragment under this collection to select it and press *X* to delete it since we don't need it anymore.

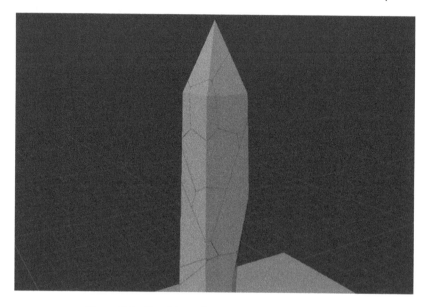

Figure 9.8 – Breaking a fragment into smaller pieces

Now, let's repeat this process.

14. Click on any larger fragment to select it. Again, think of how you want the statue to break. I am selecting a fragment from the middle area of the statue, but feel free to select any fragment.

15. Press *M* to bring up the **Move to Collection** dialog box and select **Temp** from the drop-down menu to move this fragment into the **Temp** collection so we can easily delete it later.

16. With this fragment still selected, click the **Object** menu again, select **Quick Effects**, and then click **Cell Fracture** to open the **Cell Fracture** dialog box.

17. We're going to break this fragment into 50 pieces, so make sure that **Source Limit** is set to 50.

18. Under the **Scene** section, make sure that the collection is still set to Fracture as we want to move these fragments into the **Fracture** collection as well.

19. Click **OK** to begin the Cell Fracture process.

20. Once the Cell Fracture process is done, delete the fragment from the **Temp** Collection in the **Outliner** by selecting it and then pressing *X* to delete.

Let's repeat this process one more time! Select another large fragment in your scene.

21. Press *M* to bring up the **Move to Collection** dialog box and select **Temp** from the drop-down menu.

22. With this fragment still selected, click the **Object** menu and then select **Quick Effects | Cell Fracture**.

23. We're going to break this piece into 50 fragments again, so make sure **Source Limit** is set to 50.

24. Also, make sure that the collection is still set to Fracture.

25. Click **OK** to begin the fracturing process.

26. Delete the fragment from the **Temp** collection using the **Outliner** section. Select the fragment and then press *X* to delete it.

Figure 9.9 – Fracturing the statue model using the Cell Fracture add-on

Feel free to continue this process to create even smaller fragments. Be creative and have fun. Try breaking some parts into even smaller fragments as this will add realism to your simulation.

Congratulations – you have now fractured your statue model into smaller fragments. In the next section, we will focus on fracturing the impact point to create even smaller fractures where an object will hit the statue and break it apart. Please save your project now.

Fracturing the impact point using the Annotation Pencil

In this section, we're going to focus on the impact point, where an object will impact our statue and break it apart. First, decide where you want the object to hit your statue. Then, we will use the Annotation Pencil to indicate the point of contact and use the Cell Fracture add-on to generate fractures using the lines we drew with the Annotation Pencil.

Let's get started:

1. Decide where the impact point will be on the statue and zoom in closer to that specific fragment.

2. Click the **Annotation Pencil** tool in the **Tools** menu to the left of the 3D Viewport.

3. At the top of the 3D Viewport, you will see the **Placement** area of the Annotation Pencil. Click the drop-down menu and select **Surface** from the list. This means we will be drawing on the surface of our model using the Annotation Pencil.

4. Now, using **Annotation Pencil**, draw lines from the center of the impact area outward, as shown in the following screenshot:

Figure 9.10 – Drawing lines using the Annotation Pencil

5. With this fragment selected, press *M* to bring up the **Move to Collection** dialog box and select **Temp** from the drop-down menu to move this fragment into the **Temp** collection so that it's easy to delete later.

6. Now, with this fragment still selected, click the **Object** menu and select **Quick Effects | Cell Fracture** to bring up the **Cell Fracture** dialog box.

7. Under **Point Source**, click **Annotation Pencil** to specify that we're using the Annotation Pencil lines to indicate where the fractures should be generated.

8. Still under the **Point Source** section, change the **Noise** amount to 0.25. We're lowering this from 1 as we would like to make the shape of the fragments a bit less random and closer to the annotation lines that we drew.

9. Set **Source Limit** to 50 to break this fragment into 50 pieces.

10. Under the **Scene** section, make sure the collection is still set to Fracture as we would like to move these new fragments into the **Fracture** collection as well.

11. Click **OK** to begin the Cell Fracture process.

12. Once the process has been completed, delete the fragment from the **Temp** collection in the **Outliner** section. Select the fragment and click *X* to delete it.

    Notice how the statue has been fractured along the Annotation lines. Feel free to undo this step and experiment with different Annotation line shapes until you are happy with the results.

13. You can now erase the Annotation lines by selecting the **Annotate Eraser** tool from the **Tools** menu. Click and hold the **Annotation Pencil** icon and select the **Annotate Eraser** tool from the drop-down menu. Click and drag inside the 3D Viewport to erase the Annotation lines.

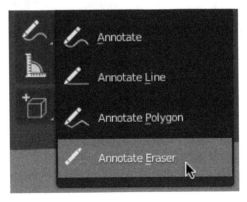

Figure 9.11 – Using the Annotate Eraser tool to erase the annotation lines from the 3D Viewport

With that, we have generated the fractured pieces for the impact point where an object will impact the statue. In the next section, we will apply Rigid Body physics to all the fragments. Please save your project now.

Rigid Body physics

In this section, we will apply Rigid Body physics to all the fragments of the statue. We will also look at the different physics parameters and what they do. You will also learn how to calculate the mass of each fragment to create a realistic-looking simulation.

Let's get started:

1. Let's begin by centering the origin (or pivot) of each fragment. Select all the fragments in the 3D Viewport (without selecting the ground plane). An easy way to do this is to right-click the **Fracture** collection in the **Outliner** section and click **Select Objects**. This is an easy way to select all the fragments or objects in that collection.

2. Click the **Object** menu at the top of the 3D Viewport, then click **Set Origin** and select **Origin to Center of Mass (Volume)**. This will position the origin of each fragment to the center of its mass by volume.

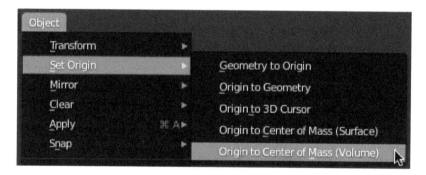

Figure 9.12 – Centering the origin of each fragment

3. Next, let's apply Rigid Body physics to each fragment. With all the fragments still selected, click the **Object** menu again, and then select **Rigid Body | Add Active**. Now, each fragment has physics properties.

4. With your mouse cursor over the 3D Viewport, press *Space* to play the animation. Notice how all the fragments fall, but they do not interact with the floor plane. The reason for this is that the floor plane has no physics properties yet.

5. Press *Space* again to stop the animation. Then, press *Shift* + left arrow to go back to frame 1.

6. Click the floor plane in the 3D Viewport to select it. Now, click the **Physics Properties** icon to the right of the 3D Viewport to open the **Physics Properties** panel.

7. Click **Rigid Body** in the **Physics Properties** panel to activate it for the floor plane.

8. Click the drop-down menu next to **Type** and select **Passive** from the list. This will set the floor to a **Passive Rigid Body** object instead of an **Active Rigid Body** object. This means it will not be affected by gravity, but it will still interact with other objects.

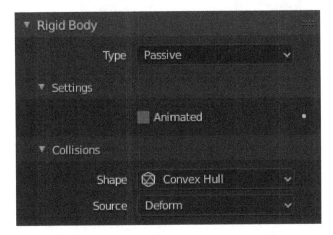

Figure 9.13 – Setting the floor as a Passive Rigid Body

9. Hover your mouse cursor over the 3D Viewport again and press *Space* to play the animation. See how the statue crumbles and interacts with the floor plane? Pretty cool, right?

Rigid Body physics properties

Let's have a look at the different Rigid Body physics properties. These parameters can change the way your simulation works, and they can change how objects interact with each other. Remember to save your project often since working with physics simulations can cause your computer to crash or become unstable. This way, you eliminate losing too much work. Save your project now.

Let's get started:

1. Click one of the statue's fragments in the 3D Viewport to select it. Then, click
    the **Physics Properties** icon to the right of the 3D Viewport to see the physics
    properties of this one fragment.

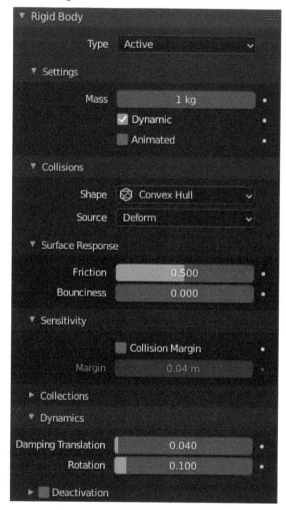

Figure 9.14 – The Rigid Body parameters

2. Under **Settings**, you will see the object's **Mass**. This is currently the default mass
    of **1 kg**, but we will calculate a more realistic value later in this section.

    Next, you will see **Dynamic** and **Animated**. **Dynamic** means that the object will
    be participating in the simulation, while **Animated** means that the object has
    animation keyframes applied to it.

3. Under **Collision**, you will see **Shape**, which is the shape of the object. We will leave this on **Convex Hull** as this works for most shapes. You can also use **Mesh** to make use of the actual mesh of the object, but this will slow down the simulation drastically, though it can make it more accurate.

    Next is **Source**. By default, this is set to **Deform**, which means the simulation will account for any deformation that's applied to the selected object. This is not required for our scene, but let's leave it as **Deform** for now.

4. Next is **Surface Response**. Here, you can set the **Friction** and **Bounciness** values of your object's surface. We will leave these values as-is for now. Feel free to experiment with these values and see how they affect the simulation.

5. Next is **Sensitivity**. Here, you can activate the **Collision Margin** area to change the distance or gap between the objects. I find that this can make your simulation slightly more stable, so let's click the tick box next to **Collision Margin** to activate it. Set **Margin** to 0.001 – I find that this value usually works well, but feel free to experiment with this value if you are working with very large or very small scenes. Simulations are all about experimenting and tweaking parameters until you are happy with the results.

6. Next is **Collections**. Here, you can group simulations into collections. We're not going to make use of simulation collections in this chapter as we will only run a single simulation. This can come in handy if you are working with larger scenes with multiple physics simulations running at the same time.

7. Next is **Dynamics**. Here, you can set your **Damping Translation** and **Rotation**. **Damping Translation** is the amount of linear velocity that's lost over time, while **Rotation** is the amount of angular velocity that's lost over time. Let's leave both these as-is. Feel free to experiment with these and see how they affect the simulation. These settings can come in handy when you're working with underwater simulations, for example.

8. Lastly, we have **Deactivation**. By default, this will be disabled. When enabled, the simulation will stop simulating when the object's linear or angular velocity goes below a set threshold. Here, you can also enable **Start Deactivated**, meaning that the simulation will start as *paused* and wait for a force before activating. Let's leave these as-is for now.

Transferring Rigid Body physics properties to other objects

Now that we have made changes to a fragment's **Sensitivity**, we need to copy these settings to all the other fragments. Remember which fragment you selected as this will become important in the next few steps. Let's get started:

1. Let's select all the fragments again – right-click the **Facture** collection in the **Outliner** section and click **Select Objects**.

2. Now, in the 3D Viewport, we need to select the object with the settings we want to copy, last. This is very important. To do this, press and hold *Shift* while clicking the fragment with the modified settings. You will notice a lighter outline around this fragment. This is also called the **active object**.

3. Click the **Object** menu at the top of the 3D Viewport, then click **Rigid Body** and select **Copy from Active**. This means that all the **Rigid Body** settings will be copied from the active object to all the other objects.

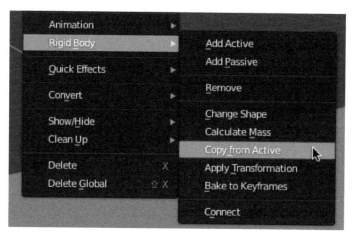

Figure 9.15 – Copying the Rigid Body settings from the active object to all the other selected objects

4. To verify that the copy was successful, click any of the fragments in the 3D Viewport and look at their physics properties. Confirm that **Collision Margin** is active and that **Margin** is set to 0.001.

5. Let's preview our simulation. Make sure you are on frame 1 by pressing *Shift* + left arrow and then press *Space* to play the simulation. The simulation should look very similar since we have only changed the margin settings.

6. Let's continue to make more changes to our simulation. Press *Space* to stop the simulation, and then press *Shift* + left arrow to return to frame 1.

Configuring mass, gravity, and speed

As we noticed earlier, all the fragments have the same mass of 1 kg. Luckily, it's very easy to calculate a more accurate mass in Blender. Let's do this now. Please save your project.

Let's get started:

1. Select all the fragments again by right-clicking the **Fracture** collection in the **Outliner** section and clicking **Select Objects**.

2. Click the **Object** menu at the top of the 3D Viewport, then click **Rigid Body** and select **Calculate Mass**. A list of different materials will be shown. Select **Stone** from the list.

3. Now, click on the different fragments in the 3D Viewport and see how their **mass value** changes in the **Physics Properties** side panel.

    Let's see how we can change the core physics properties of our simulation. The core physics properties contain parameters such as **Gravity**, **Speed**, **Substeps**, and **Solver Iterations**.

4. To access the core physics properties, click the **Scene Properties** icon to the right of the 3D Viewport.

5. Expand the **Gravity** section. Here, you will see that gravity is active on the **Z** axis and is set to **-9.8 m/s²**, which is the correct setting for planet Earth. Let's leave this as-is. This parameter can be handy for underwater scenes or if you are simulating a scene on another planet.

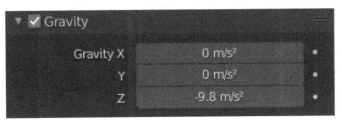

Figure 9.16 – The Gravity forces can be changed if required

6. Next, let's expand **Rigid Body World**. Here, you will see the **Speed** parameter, as well as the **Substeps Per Frame** and **Solver Iterations** parameters. By default, **Substeps Per Frame** and **Solver Iterations** are both set to **10**.

Both of these values are linked to the number of simulation steps that are taken per frame – the higher the value, the more accurate the simulation. However, higher values will slow down simulation times. **Substeps Per Frame** will affect the physics simulation, while **Solver Iterations** will affect the constraints calculations.

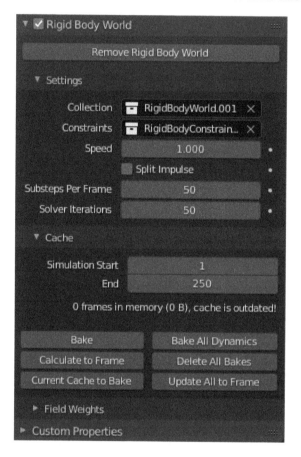

Figure 9.17 – Rigid Body World settings

Let's change both the **Substeps Per Frame** and **Solver Iterations** values to 50. This will increase the accuracy of the simulation and won't slow it down too much.

Further down, you will also see the **Cache** parameters, where you can specify the **Start** and **End** frames of your simulation. You will also find the baking controls here. We will talk about this more at the end of this chapter.

7. Press *Space* to play the simulation!

8. Press *Space* again to stop the simulation. Then, press *Shift* + left arrow to go back to frame 1.

Congratulations – you have created a Rigid Body physics simulation! In the next section, we will add Rigid Body constraints to link the fragments together. This is probably the most important step when you're breaking things apart as constraints can add realism to your destructions. Please save your project now.

Linking fractured pieces together using Rigid Body Constraints

Let's talk about **Rigid Body constraints**. At the moment, our whole statue crumbles at the same time when we start the simulation. While this is very exciting, we can make it a lot more realistic. Let's say we have an object that hits our statue – we want the statue to start breaking at the impact point. Then, the rest of the statue should start to crumble, piece by piece, and then it should collapse.

This is possible with constraints. **Constraints** are joints or the glue that's connecting the fragments. This is the secret sauce to any destruction simulation. Working with constraints involves a lot of tweaking, so please remember to save your project often. Before playing the simulation after each tweak, remember to hit that save button.

Let's get started:

1. Select all the fragments by right-clicking the **Fracture** collection in the **Outliner** section and clicking **Select Objects**.

2. Click the **Object** menu at the top of the 3D Viewport. Then, select **Rigid Body** followed by **Connect**.

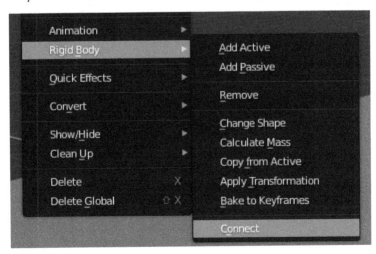

Figure 9.18 – Adding constraints to the selected fragments

3. In the bottom-left corner of the 3D Viewport, you should see a **Connect Rigid Bodies** dialog box. Make sure that **Type** is set to **Fixed**. This is the type of constraint we're going to use for this simulation. There are quite a few different types of constraints, so feel free to experiment with them all.

4. Set **Location** to **Selected**. This means the pivot of the constraint will be at the location of the selected object.

5. Lastly, set **Connection Pattern** to **Chain by Distance**. This means that the fragments will be linked to other fragments based on their distance from each other, forming a connected chain.

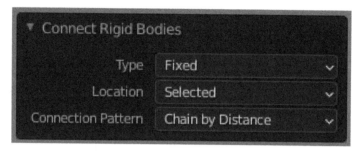

Figure 9.19 – Setting the constraint's parameters

6. Click anywhere in the 3D Viewport to confirm these parameters.

    You should now see interesting-looking black lines on the statue. These are the constraints. You will also see them in the **Outliner** section. Let's put them in their collection.

7. In the **Outliner** section. select the first constraint, and then scroll down to the last one. Hold *Shift* and click the last constraint to select them all.

8. Press *M* to bring up the **Move to Collection** dialog box. Click **New Collection** and rename it Constraints. Click **OK** to confirm this. Now, all our constraints are in a separate collection.

    Let's play our simulation to see the constraints in action! Remember to save your project. Press *Space* to begin the simulation. As you will notice, all the fragments have been glued together. The statue may move a bit, and if the pieces are big and heavy enough, they may even break off.

    Let's have a look at how we can change the constraint's parameters to create something more interesting. Stop the simulation and go back to frame 1.

9. Let's select all the constraints since we can change all their properties at the same time. An easy way to select them all is to use the **Outliner** section. Right-click the **Constraints** collection and click **Select Objects**.

10. Click the **Physics Properties** icon to the right of the 3D Viewport to see their properties.

11. At the top, we can see the **Type** property of the constraint. This should be set to **Fixed**, as we did when we created them.

12. Under **Settings**, you will see **Enabled**. Here, you can disable constraints if needed. Let's leave this set to **Enabled**.

13. Next is **Disable Collisions**. This means that collisions are disabled between Rigid Body objects. We need to enable collisions by unticking this box. Before unticking the box, note that there is a way to change a parameter for all the selected constraints. To do this, simply hold *Alt* and untick the box next to **Disable Collisions**.

    Let's confirm whether this parameter changed for all the constraints.

14. Click on random constraints in the 3D Viewport to select them individually and keep your eye on the **Physics Properties** panel. Note that the box for **Disable Collisions** is unticked. Select all the constraints again.

15. Next, you will see **Breakable**. This means that the constraints can be broken. This is good as we want our fragments to be able to break apart from each other! Let's enable this for all our constraints. Hold *Alt* and tick the box next to **Breakable**.

    Next, we have the **Threshold** value. This is the impulse threshold that the constraint must reach before breaking. You may spend a lot of time tweaking this parameter as the threshold depends on force, mass, gravity, and more and can change your simulation drastically. You can have different groups of constraints with different threshold values to create very interesting-looking destructions.

16. By default, the **Threshold** value is set to 10. Let's leave it as-is for now.

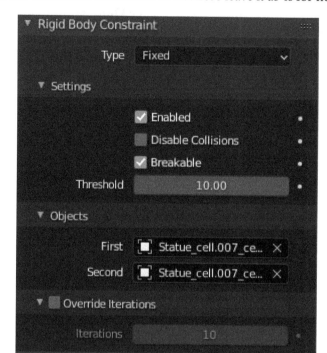

Figure 9.20 – Rigid Body Constraint parameters

Now, let's save our project and press *Space* to play the simulation. At this point, some of the fragments should start sticking together. This will depend on the mass of the fragments, so if you don't see anything different, you may need to change the **Threshold** value. I've set my threshold from anything as low as 0.1 up to 5000. You will need to experiment with this value to get the results you want.

Experiment with the **Threshold** value until you are happy with the way the fragments are sticking together. It's okay if the statue crumbles. We will start the simulation as deactivated, but we'll cover that in more detail later in this chapter. I'm setting my **Threshold** value to 50, which gives me good results. Some parts are sticking nicely together and breaking apart when they hit the floor.

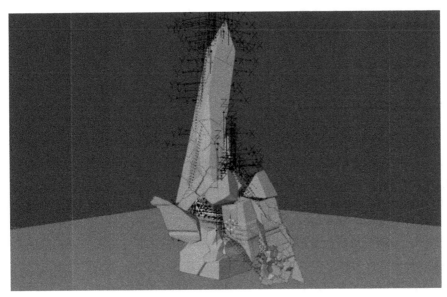

Figure 9.21 – Experiment with the Threshold value until you are happy with the results

17. You can hide the constraints from the 3D Viewport once you are happy with the results by clicking the eye icon next to the **Constraints** collection in the **Outliner** section.

18. Lastly, I would like to mention that if you don't see any changes in your simulation, even after you have made changes to the physics properties, you may need to enforce the simulation engine to update. An easy way to do this is to click the **Scene Properties** icon and make a slight change to the **Substeps per Frame** value. Change it to 51 and play the simulation – if it works, you can change the **Substeps per Frame** value back to 50. This is likely a bug and might be fixed in future versions.

Congratulations! You have created a Rigid Body physics simulation using Rigid Body constraints. The combination of using physics and constraints can be extremely powerful. Remember that you can have certain constraints with certain properties, while other parts of your simulations have constraints with different properties. The same goes for Rigid Body properties.

Different fragments can have different properties, so feel free to experiment and see how they affect your simulation. Remember that you can change the floor properties as well. Tweak the settings we have covered in this section until you are happy with the results. In the next section, we will animate an impact object that will crash into our statue! Please save your project now.

Animating a Rigid Body impact object

In this section, we will create a very basic impact object that will crash into our statue. We will also look at how to start the simulation as *deactivated*, thus waiting for the force from the impact object to trigger the physics simulation.

Let's see how we can do this:

1. Let's create a **Sphere** object by pressing *Shift + A* and selecting **Mesh | UV Sphere**.

2. Press *S* and scale it down to a reasonable size.

3. Move the sphere a short distance away from the impact position on the statue. I am choosing the area with the most and smallest fragments. Use *G* to move the sphere into its first position.

4. Make sure that you are on frame 1 by pressing *Shift* + left arrow.

5. Let's create a keyframe. With the sphere selected, press *I* and choose **Location** from the drop-down menu to create a **Location** keyframe on frame 1.

    Before we create the second keyframe for the sphere, let's change our fragments' physics properties so that they will wait for the impact before starting the simulation.

6. Click one of the fragments on your statue in the 3D Viewport. Remember which one you have selected.

7. Click the **Physics Properties** icon and scroll down until you see **Deactivation**. Tick the box next to **Deactivation**.

8. Tick the box next to **Start Deactivated**. This will wait for a force to occur before activating the simulation. Let's leave the threshold limits, **Velocity Linear** and **Angular**, as-is for now. Feel free to experiment with these values if your simulation starts without any impact.

    Next, we need to copy the physics properties from this one fragment to all the other fragments.

9. First, select all the fragments by right-clicking the **Fracture** collection in the **Outliner** section and clicking **Select Objects**.

10. Hold *Shift* and click the fragment that you have changed the physics properties of. That fragment should now have a lighter orange outline.

11. Click the **Object** menu at the top of the 3D Viewport. Then, select **Rigid Body** and click **Copy from Active** to copy the physics properties from the active object to all the other selected fragments.

Now that our simulation will wait for impact, let's continue creating keyframes for the impact object. You can preview the simulation but remember to save your project first. Playing the simulation should not break the statue; it should be waiting for impact.

12. Click the **Sphere** object to select it and then go to frame 20 by clicking the **Timeline** area below the 3D Viewport.

13. Press *G* and move the sphere to the other side of the statue so that it will fly through the statue.

14. With the sphere selected, press *I* to bring up the **Insert Keyframe** menu, and then click **Location** from the drop-down menu to create a new **Location** keyframe on frame 20.

15. Go back to frame 1 and save your project! Press *Space* to play the simulation.

16. Let's make the simulation much more dramatic by slowing it down! Click the **Scene Properties** icon to access the core physics properties.

17. Change the **Speed** parameter to 0.2.

18. Save your project and press *Space* to play the simulations! Amazing, right?

Figure 9.22 – The impacting object interacts with the statue

Before we end this chapter, let's bake our simulation. Baking means we're saving the simulation data to disk so that we can replay the simulation without calculating the physics.

Baking the final physics simulation

Baking will also save your simulation so that you don't have to recalculate it the next time you open this project file. Let's get started:

1. Make sure you are on frame 1.

2. Still under the **Scene Properties** panel, scroll down until you see **Cache**.

3. Click the **Bake** button. It's as simple as that:

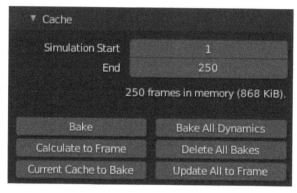

Figure 9.23 – Clicking the Bake button to bake your simulation

4. You can always delete your bake if you want to change any of the simulation parameters by clicking the **Delete All Bakes** button. Then, you can make the required changes and bake the simulation again once you are happy with the results.

Summary

Congratulations! With that, you have created an amazing physics simulation using Rigid Body physics and constraints! You have learned how to install the required Blender add-ons, **Cell Fracture** and **Import-Export STL**, and how to use them. You should now be familiar with the **Cell Fracture** add-on and how to use it to break objects into smaller fragments by using automatic fracturing or making use of the Annotation Pencil to specify where to fracture objects.

You also learned how to apply Rigid Body physics to the fractured pieces and how to tweak the parameters to adjust your simulation. We also looked at how you can link the fractured pieces together using Rigid Body constraints to create a more realistic simulation. After that, we added an animated object to our scene that will interact with your simulation. Lastly, we learned how to bake the final simulation to cache.

Simulations are all about experimenting and tweaking parameters one at a time to see how they affect the overall simulation.

Understanding the basic workflow of Rigid Body simulations is a powerful skill to have as you can create amazing simulations that are used in many VFX-heavy movies and commercials.

Have lots of fun and see what other simulations you can create!

In the next chapter, we will take a look at cloth simulations. Please save your project now.

10
Dynamic Cloth Simulations

In this exciting chapter, we will create clothing for an animated character and add a cloth simulation to simulate the way the clothing interacts with a rigged character. We will also add forces to enhance the realism of the cloth simulation. Cloth simulations are extremely versatile as you can use them for a few different things, such as curtains, flags, duvets, and clothing. Let's get started!

The main topics we'll cover in this chapter are as follows:

- Importing our character and walk cycle
- Creating a rest pose to assist with the cloth simulation
- Modeling the clothing for our character
- Cloth simulation physics
- Using forces to enhance the simulation
- Baking the cloth simulation
- Adding final modifiers to our cloth simulation

Importing our character and walk cycle

In this section, we will append our rigged Alien character with its walk cycle animation from *Chapter 8*, *Rigging and Animating Your 3D Cartoon Character*, into a new Blender project. Appending is an easy way to import objects, materials, and animations from one Blender project into another. Feel free to use a different character if you have one available:

1. Create a new Blender project, and then select all the default objects in the scene by pressing *A*. Then, press *X* and click **Delete** to delete these objects.

2. Click **File | Append** to open the **Append** dialog box.

3. Browse to the Blender project file that you created in *Chapter 8*, *Rigging and Animating Your 3D Cartoon Character*.

4. Double-click the Blender project file to display its contents.

5. Double-click the Object folder to display its contents.

6. Select both the Alien character model and the rig from this list, and then click **Append**.

7. You will see that both the character and the rig have been imported into your new project. Please save your project now.

8. In the Outliner, you will see a list of WGT objects, or widgets if you used **Rigify** to create the rig.

    Let's clean this up by moving the WGT objects into a new collection.

9. Select all the WGT objects by clicking the first one in the Outliner, then scroll down, hold *Shift*, and click the last WGT object in the list:

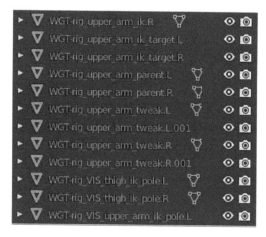

Figure 10.1 – Selecting all the WGT objects in the Outliner

10. Press *M* to open the **Move to Collection** dialog box and click **New Collection**.

11. Let's give this new collection a name by entering WGT into the **Name** field, and then click **OK** to confirm:

Figure 10.2 – Creating a new collection for the WGT objects

12. Hide this new collection from the Viewport and render by unticking the box next to its name in the Outliner, as well as the Viewport (eye) and Render (camera) icons:

Figure 10.3 – Hide the WGT collection using the Outliner

Great! You should now see your character with its walk cycle animation in the 3D Viewport. In the next section, we will create a rest pose for our character to assist with the cloth simulation later in this chapter. Please save your project now:

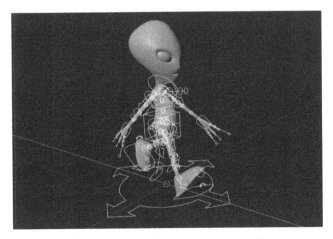

Figure 10.4 – The imported character and rig

Adding a rest pose

In this section, we will create a rest pose for our character using the Rigify rig that we appended in the *Importing our character and walk cycle* section. A rest pose is similar to a T-pose, and it will greatly assist with the cloth simulation later in this chapter. The rest post will also assist us when we model the clothing later in this chapter in the *Creating clothing for our character* section. Let's get started!

1. First, we need to see all the keyframes on the rig that we have created for the walk cycle. Click the rig in the 3D Viewport to select it.

2. Enter **Pose Mode** by pressing *Ctrl + Tab*.

3. In **Pose Mode**, press *A* to select all the rig components. This will ensure that all the keyframes are shown in the timeline:

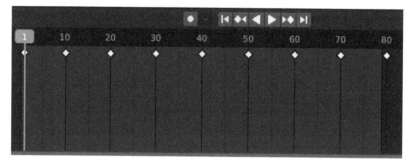

Figure 10.5 – The keyframes for the walk cycle are displayed in the timeline

4. Move these keyframes to the right to make space for the rest pose. Hover the mouse cursor over the timeline at the bottom of the interface and press *A* to select all the keyframes.

5. With all the keyframes selected, press *G* and move them to the right so that the first keyframe is sitting on frame number **30**. This will give us 30 frames from the rest pose, which we will create on frame number **1**, to the first pose of our walk cycle:

Figure 10.6 – Moving the walk cycle keyframes to the right to make space for the rest pose

Let's create the rest pose.

6. Make sure you are on frame number **1** by clicking on the timeline. Hover your mouse cursor over the 3D Viewport and press *A* to select all the rig controls.

7. With all the rig controls selected, press *Alt + R* to reset the rotation values. Then, press *Alt + G* to reset the position values. This will reset the rig back to the rest pose. You might notice that the overall position of your character has changed as well – we will fix this soon.

8. With the rig controls still selected, press *I* (*I* for *India*) to insert a new keyframe on frame number **1**. Select **Whole Character** from the **Insert Keyframe** menu:

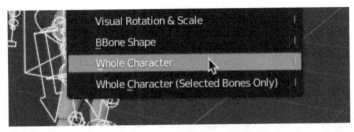

Figure 10.7 – Choosing Whole Character to insert a new keyframe for all the rig controls

9. To fix the overall position of your character, select the Root control of the rig, as shown in the following screenshot:

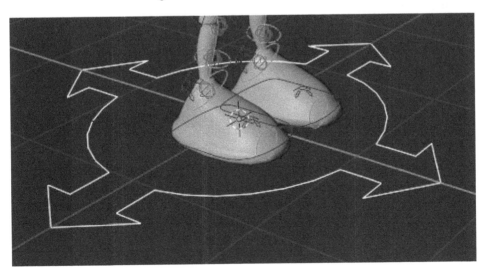

Figure 10.8 – Select the Root control of the rig

10. With the Root control selected, hover your mouse cursor over the timeline at the bottom of the interface. Press *A* to select all the keyframes for the Root control, press *X*, and select **Delete Keyframes** from the menu to delete all the keyframes on the Root control.

11. Next, let's set the *start* and *end* frames of our animation. My walk cycle is 80 frames in duration, and it starts at frame number **30**.

    My total animation duration is 110 frames, but I am excluding frame **110** because it's the same as the keyframe on frame **30**. Please note that your frame numbers might be different than mine. You want your animation to loop from the rest post to the last frame of your walk cycle, as shown in the following screenshot:

Figure 10.9 – My walk cycle starts at frame 30 and ends at frame 110

12. Set your *start* and *end* frame numbers to the right of the timeline at the bottom of the interface:

Figure 10.10 – Setting the start and end frame numbers to include the full animation

13. We can now switch back to **Object Mode**, but before doing so, ensure that you select all the rig controls so that we see all the keyframes in **Object Mode**. Hover your mouse cursor over the 3D Viewport and press *A* to select all the rig controls.

14. Press *Ctrl + Tab* to switch to **Object Mode**.

Congratulations! You have now created a rest pose for your character, which will make the cloth simulation work a lot better! In the next section, we will create clothing for our Alien character. Please save your project now.

Creating clothing for our character

In this section, we will model a basic clothing item for our character that we will later use for the cloth simulation. Feel free to follow along or try to create something completely different. It's time to be creative!

Let's get started!

1. Let's begin by hiding the rig from the 3D Viewport – this will make modeling the clothing item easier. In **Object Mode**, click the rig in the 3D Viewport to select it and press *H* to hide it.

2. Click the character in the 3D Viewport to select it, and then press *Tab* to enter **Edit Mode**.

3. Press *3* for **Face Select Mode**.

4. For the next part, I prefer to use **Circle Select Mode** to easily select certain faces of our character. Press *W* to toggle between the different select modes until your cursor changes into a circle.

Next, we're going to select the faces from which we will create the clothing item. We will be creating a basic shirt item. Feel free to create your own design:

1. Click and drag to highlight the faces you want to select. You can also hold *Shift* while clicking and dragging to add more faces to your selection:

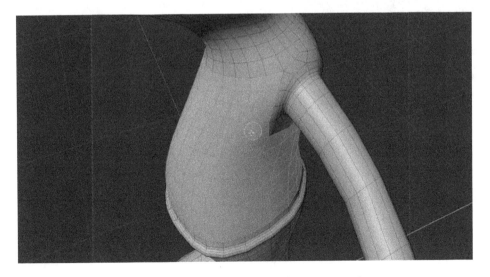

Figure 10.11 – Highlight the faces for creating a shirt

2.   Continue selecting faces around the character:

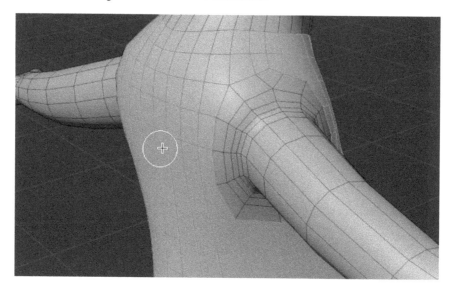

Figure 10.12 – Selecting more faces to create the shirt clothing item

3.   Continue selecting faces from which the shirt will be created:

Figure 10.13 – All the faces for the shirt item have been highlighted

4. Once you have selected all the required faces, press *Shift + D* to duplicate the selected faces. Press *Esc* to reset their position.

5. Right-click in the 3D Viewport and select **Separate | Selection** from the drop-down menu. This will separate the selected faces from our character mesh.

6. Press *Tab* to exit **Edit Mode**.

7. Rename this new mesh Shirt in the Outliner. Note that this new mesh will be located under the rig in the Outliner. The reason for this is that we have duplicated these faces from the character mesh, thus keeping the **Armature** modifier that is currently applied to it:

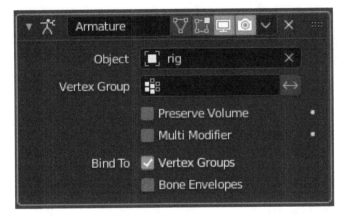

Figure 10.14 – The Armature modifier is automatically applied to the shirt
because of the duplicate command

Note that if you are creating the clothing separately from your character, you will have to manually parent the clothing mesh to the rig.

8. To do this, select your clothing mesh first, and then hold *Shift* and select the rig. Right-click in the 3D Viewport and select **Parent | With Automatic Weights** from the drop-down menu:

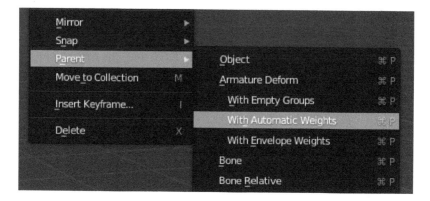

Figure 10.15 – Manually parenting the clothing to the rig

9. Click the shirt mesh to select it in the 3D Viewport. Then, right-click and select **Set Origin | Origin to Geometry** from the drop-down menu. This will set the shirt's origin to the center of the mesh.

Next, we need to scale the shirt so that it's slightly bigger than our character:

1. Select the shirt in the 3D Viewport and press *S* to scale it so that it's only slightly bigger than the character:

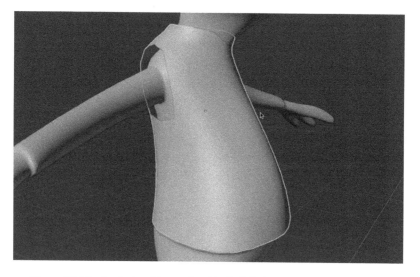

Figure 10.16 – Scale the shirt so that it's slightly bigger than the character

2. Switch to the front view by pressing *1* on the numpad.

3. With the shirt still selected, press *S* and then press *X* to scale it only slightly on the *X* axis.

4. Switch to the side view by pressing *3* on the numpad.

5. With the shirt still selected, press *S* and then press *Y* to scale it slightly on the *Y* axis.

6. You can also scale it on the *Z* axis if needed. Select the shirt, and then press *S* and *Z* to scale it slightly on the *Z* axis.

7. Ensure that the shirt is not overlapping with your character. Move and rotate the shirt mesh if required.

8. Switch to **Wireframe Mode** by holding *Z* and selecting **Wireframe** from the **Radial** menu. Click the character to select it – this makes it easier to see whether the clothing overlaps with your character. Make adjustments to the shirt if needed.

9. Switch back to the solid view by holding *Z* and selecting **Solid** from the **Radial** menu.

10. Press *spacebar* to play your animation. Note that the shirt is following the basic movement of the rig. This is a great start, but we will add a cloth simulation to the shirt later in this chapter to make it more realistic.

11. Let's add some more interesting features to our shirt mesh. Click the shirt in the 3D Viewport to select it and press *Tab* to enter **Edit Mode**.

12. Press *2* to switch to **Edge Select Mode**.

13. Select the bottom edges at the back of the shirt:

Figure 10.17 – Selecting the bottom edges at the back of the shirt

14. Press *E* and then *Z* to extrude these edges downward to just above the floor grid.

15. With these edges still selected, press *G* and then *Y* to move them backward, away from the character. Make sure that the shirt mesh does not overlap with your character:

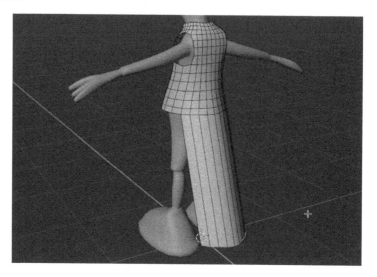

Figure 10.18 – Extruding the edges at the back of the shirt

16. Press *Ctrl* + *R* and hover your mouse cursor over the extruded part of the shirt to insert a loop cut. Roll the mouse wheel to increase the amount of loop cuts. Try and match the size of the new faces with the rest of the shirt mesh:

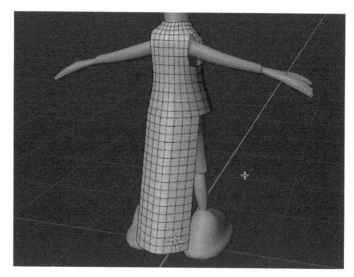

Figure 10.19 – Adding loop cuts to the extruded part of the shirt

17. Next, let's add something interesting to the front of the shirt. Select a few edges at the bottom at the front of the shirt. Press *E* and then *Z* to extrude them downward, as shown in the following screenshot:

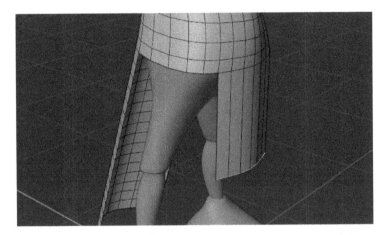

Figure 10.20 – Extrude the bottom edges at the front of the shirt

18. Now, let's add some loop cuts! Press *Ctrl + R* and hover your mouse over the extruded part of the shirt. Roll the mouse wheel to increase the number of loop cuts. Again, try to match the size of the faces to the rest of the shirt mesh:

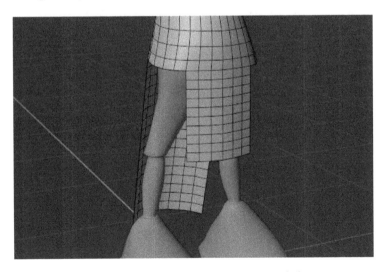

Figure 10.21 – Adding loop cuts to the extruded part

19. Press *Tab* to exit **Edit Mode**.

20. Next, we need to apply the scale of our shirt mesh. This step is very important, especially when doing any type of simulation. Select the shirt mesh in the 3D Viewport, press *Ctrl + A*, and select **Scale** from the drop-down menu.

21. Switch back to **Wireframe Mode** by holding *Z* and selecting **Wireframe** from the **Radial Menu**. Orbit around your character and ensure that your clothing mesh is not overlapping with any parts of the character. Make adjustments to the clothing mesh in **Edit Mode** if required.

22. Finally, switch back to Solid View by holding *Z* and selecting **Solid** from the **Radial** menu.

Congratulations! You have now created the clothing mesh for your character! As always, feel free to change the design and make it your own. In the next section, we will do the cloth simulation. Please save your project now.

The cloth simulation

In this section, we will focus on the actual cloth simulation and all the parameters that go with it. Running any kind of simulation in Blender can produce interesting and sometimes unpredictable results, so it's very important that you save your project often.

Simulations are also about experimenting – making small tweaks to certain parameters can sometimes give amazing results, so feel free to make changes to different parameters to see how they affect the simulation. Most importantly, have fun! Simulations are definitely one of my favorite areas of the 3D world. Let's get started!

First, let's give our cloth mesh a material so that we can easily see it in the 3D Viewport, and it just looks better!

1. Select the shirt mesh in the 3D Viewport.

2. Click on the **Material Properties** tab to the right of the 3D Viewport.

3. Click **New** to create a new default material.

4. Scroll all the way down until you see **Viewport Display**.

5. Click the color box next to **Color** and choose a viewport material color for the shirt. I went with a light teal:

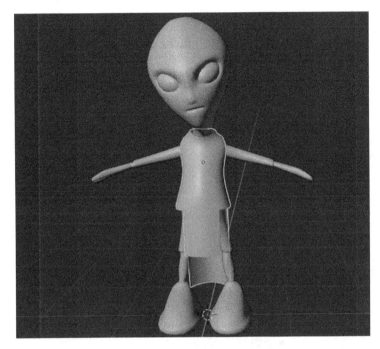

Figure 10.22 – Set the viewport material color to something bright

Let's make sure our shirt mesh is set to **Shade Smooth**.

6. Click the shirt mesh to select it, and then right-click in the 3D Viewport and select **Shade Smooth** from the drop-down menu. This will render the mesh as smooth.

7. Click the **Physics Properties** tab to the right of the 3D Viewport.

8. Here, we will enable the cloth simulation for our shirt mesh. Click the **Cloth** button at the top of this properties panel. Our shirt mesh will now act like a cloth object.

9. Press the *spacebar* to run the simulation. Always remember to be on frame **1** when running the simulation. A handy shortcut to remember is *Shift* + the left arrow.

See how the shirt falls through everything in the scene? This is because there is nothing for the shirt mesh to interact with. We need a collision object. Let's create one now:

1. Click the Alien character in the 3D viewport to select it.

2. In the **Physics Properties** panel, click **Collision**. This will set our Alien character as a collision mesh. Let's see how it works.

3. Press *Shift* + the left arrow to jump to frame **1**, and press the *spacebar* to run the simulation. It's as easy as that!

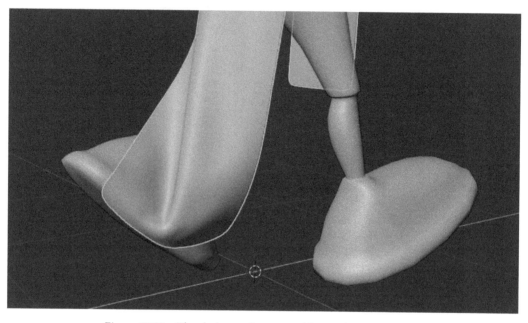

Figure 10.23 – The cloth now interacts with our character model

See how the shirt object interacts with the character? Amazing, right? The cloth still looks very stiff. This is because our cloth mesh does not have many faces, or a high-poly count, as well as many other factors we will get to shortly. Remember, the higher the poly count, the better the cloth simulation – most of the time. But this will also slow down the simulation time.

It's a perfect balance between quality and speed, so always remember to experiment until you have the best results that time will allow. Let the animation loop through to cache the simulation so that it plays back smoothly in the 3D Viewport. There will be more on caching later in this chapter. Let's tweak some parameters to create a more realistic cloth simulation!

Let's begin by looking at the collision object's properties:

1. Click the Alien character mesh in the 3D Viewport to select it.

2. In the **Physics Properties** panel, scroll to the bottom until you see the **Softbody & Cloth** section. These are the properties that will affect how the cloth will interact with this collision object.

    Damping is the amount of bounce that the surface will have. I usually get good results with the default value, but feel free to experiment. Setting this to 0 will produce a lot of bounce whereas 1 will give no bounce at all.

    Thickness Outer is the outer thickness of each face. This is where the cloth will interact with the surface of the collision object. I usually get good results with the default value of 0.02.

    Inner is the inner face thickness. I like to change this to 0.02, but it won't really affect our simulation, as nothing should interact with the inside of our character mesh.

    Friction is the amount of friction the cloth has on the collision mesh, or how slippery the cloth is when interacting with the mesh. The lower the value, the more slippery the cloth will be when colliding with the mesh. Let's leave this at the default value of 5 for now, but feel free to try different values.

    Next, we have **Single Sided**. I always leave this *on*. When enabled, the collider mesh is considered to represent a boundary of a solid object rather than a thin surface around it.

    Override Normals I also always keep *off*. When enabled, cloth collisions will act in the direction of the collider mesh normals.

    Next, let's take a look at the cloth simulation parameters. I will not cover every single parameter, but I will try to cover the most important ones. Again, feel free to experiment, and always refer to the online Blender documentation for the most up-to-date information regarding simulation parameters in newer versions of Blender.

3. Click the shirt mesh in the 3D Viewport to select it.

4. Let's look at the parameters in the **Physics Properties** panel:

    *   **Quality Steps**: This is the overall quality of the cloth simulation. The higher the value, the better the simulation but also the slowest simulation speed. Let's set this to 10 for now, which is quite a high value.

    *   **Speed Multiplier**: We will leave this at 1. Lowering this value will give you a great slow-motion effect.

    *   **Vertex Mass**: This is the mass of the cloth object. Let's set this value to 0.1 to make our cloth a bit lighter to create more bounce.

    *   **Air Viscosity**: This is the amount of air thickness, which slows things falling down. Let's leave this at the default value of 1.

    *   Leave **Bending Model** as **Angular**, as this is the new model that the cloth simulation uses.

    *   Under **Stiffness**, you will see the **Tension** parameter. This is how much the material resists stretching. Change this value to 5 to make the cloth more stretchable and bouncier.

    *   **Compression**: This is how much the cloth resists compressing. Let's set this value to 5 as well.

    *   Remember to often save your project. Also, press the *spacebar* every now and then to run the simulation to see how the different parameters affect your cloth simulation. I recommend running the simulation every time you change a parameter to see how it affects it.

    *   **Shear**: This is how much the cloth resists shearing. Leave this value at 5.

    *   Next, we have **Bending**, which shows how much the cloth resists wrinkling. Higher values create larger folds in the cloth. Let's leave this value at 0.5 for now.

5. Under the **Physical Properties** section, you will see a **Damping** section with similar parameters underneath. You can use these parameters to adjust the damping parameters if required. I usually leave this as default, but feel free to experiment and see how it affects your simulation.

6. Next, you will see the **Internal Springs** section. This section won't be covered in this chapter. **Internal Springs** make the cloth behave similar to a soft body object. I would personally rather make use of a soft body simulation than **Internal Springs**, but feel free to experiment with the **Internal Springs** parameters and see what you can create.

7. Below **Internal Springs**, you will see the **Pressure** section. This will not be covered in this chapter, as it relates more to a mesh that behaves like a pillow instead of clothing or cloth. Feel free to experiment with the **Pressure** parameters to see what types of objects you can create.

8. There is a section called *Baking the cloth simulation* later in this chapter that is dedicated to **Cache**.

9. Under **Shape**, you will see the **Pin Group** parameter. We won't use this in our clothing simulation, but it's good to understand how it works. We can use **Pin Group** to pin certain vertices so that they are not affected by the cloth simulation. Let's see how this works.

10. With the shirt mesh selected in the 3D Viewport, press *Tab* to enter **Edit Mode**.

11. Press *3* to select **Face Select Mode**.

12. Press *W* until you see the **Select Circle** cursor.

13. Select all the front faces at the bottom section of the shirt, as shown in the following screenshot:

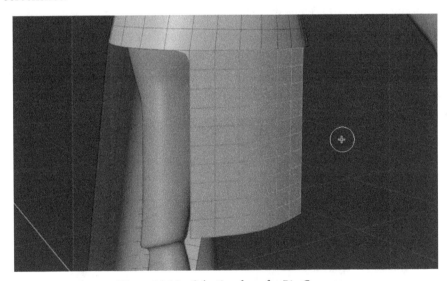

Figure 10.24 – Selecting faces for Pin Group

14. With the faces selected, click the **Object Data Properties** tab to the right of the 3D Viewport.

15. Click the plus (+) icon in the top area of the properties panel to create a new vertex group.

16. Double-click the **Group** entry and rename it `Pin`.

17. Click the **Assign** button to assign the selected faces to this new vertex group.

18. Hover the mouse cursor over the 3D Viewport and press *Tab* to exit **Edit Mode**.

19. With the cloth mesh still selected, click the **Physics Properties** tab.

20. Scroll down to the **Shape** section.

21. Click the box next to **Pin Group** and select our newly created vertex group called **Pin** from the list. This will tell the simulation to pin all the vertices in this vertex group and exclude them from the cloth simulation.

22. Go to frame **1** and press the *spacebar* to run the simulation.

    Note that these faces are now excluded from the cloth simulation. They still move with the character because they are parented to the rig, but they won't interact with gravity or the character mesh. The **Pin Group** parameter is most commonly used when doing a *flag-in-the-wind* simulation and pinning the flag to the flagpole.

23. **Stiffness** just below the **Pin Group** parameter controls the influence of the **Pin Group** parameter.

24. Let's disable the **Pin Group** parameter for now, as we want that section of our shirt to be simulated. Click **X** next to **Pin** to remove it from the **Pin Group** parameter:

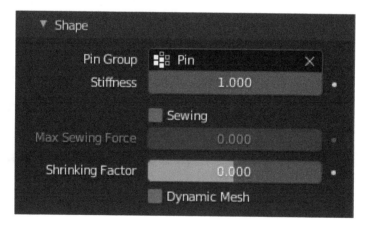

Figure 10.25 – Pinning a vertex group to exclude it from the simulation

Next, let's look at the **Collision** section. Here, you will see both the **Object Collisions** and **Self Collisions** settings. **Object Collisions** will enable the cloth to interact with other objects, such as our character, while **Self Collisions** will allow the cloth to interact with itself:

1. Under **Object Collisions**, you will see a **Quality** parameter. This is the quality of the simulation when calculating collisions. The higher the value, the better the simulation, but this will also slow down the simulation time. I usually leave this value at 5.

2. **Distance** is the minimum distance between the cloth and other objects before they will start to collide. Let's leave this at the default, 0.015.

3. Tick the box next to the **Self Collisions** settings to enable the cloth to interact with itself. This will greatly improve the realism of the simulation.

4. If your cloth simulation acts strangely at this point, it's probably to do with the **Self Collisions** parameters. I usually change the **Distance** setting to 0.002 to get good results. This is the distance between the faces of the cloth that will interact with each other. Experiment with this value until you see good results.

5. You can also set the **Friction** amount here, which is how much friction the cloth has on itself. Let's leave this on the default value of 5.

6. Go to frame **1** and press the *spacebar* to run the simulation. You should now see good results. Note how the cloth is interacting with the legs and feet of our character and the cloth itself:

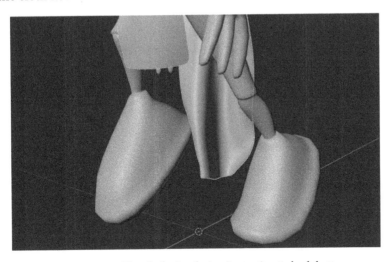

Figure 10.26 – The cloth simulation is starting to look better

7. You can also switch to **Wireframe mode** by holding *Z* and selecting **Wireframe** from the **Radial** menu to see the cloth interactions better:

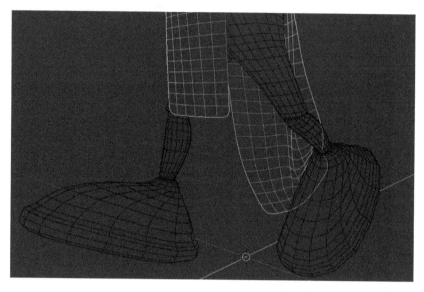

Figure 10.27 – Switch to Wireframe mode to see the interactions between the cloth and the character

Once you are happy with the overall cloth simulation, we can increase the quality of the simulation drastically by applying a Subdivision Surface modifier to our cloth mesh. The important thing to remember is where in the modifier stack to place the Subdivision Surface modifier.

We need to place it above (or before) the armature and cloth modifiers so that they can both benefit from the extra geometry generated by the Subdivision Surface modifier. It's a lot easier than it sounds:

1. Switch back to Solid View by holding *Z* and selecting **Solid** from the **Radial** menu.
2. Click the shirt mesh in the 3D Viewport to select it.
3. Click the **Modifier Properties** tab to the right of the 3D Viewport.
4. Click the **Add Modifier** button and select **Subdivision Surface** from the drop-down menu.

5. By default, the modifier will be placed at the bottom of the stack. Use the handles on the right side of the modifier and drag it above both the **Armature** and **Cloth** modifiers, as shown in the following screenshot:

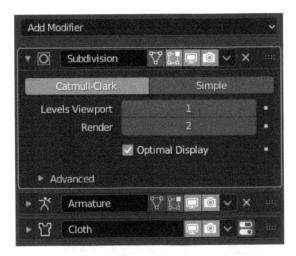

Figure 10.28 – Position the Subdivision Surface modifier above the Armature and Cloth modifiers

I usually get good results with a **Subdivision Viewport** level of 1 and a **Render** level of 2, but as always, feel free to experiment with these values. Remember that the higher the subdivision levels, the better the simulation will look, but it will also slow down the simulation time drastically. Please save your project now.

6. Go to frame **1** and press the *spacebar* to run the simulation.

Your simulation is looking great so far! Experiment with these parameters until you are happy with the results. See how the different parameters change the way the cloth interacts with other objects as well as itself. In the next section, we will add forces, such as wind, to our scene to enhance our simulation.

Using forces to enhance the simulation

In this section, we will focus our attention on forces and how to use them with our cloth simulation. Using forces such as wind or turbulence can add realism as well as randomness to our simulations. Let's get started!

1. Let's begin by adding a **Wind** force to our scene. Hover your mouse cursor over the 3D Viewport and press *Shift + A* to show the **Add** menu.

2. Mouse over the **Force** fields and select **Wind** from the list:

Figure 10.29 – You can create many different forces in Blender

3. The **Wind** force field will be created at the location of the 3D cursor. By default, the direction of the wind will point upward on the *Z* axis. Note the yellow arrow showing the direction of the force:

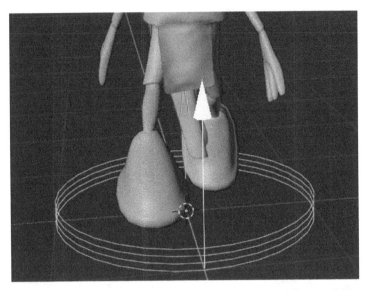

Figure 10.30 – The yellow arrow indicates the direction of the Wind force

4. Let's reposition the **Wind** force. Select the **Force** widget in the 3D Viewport, press G, and then X to move it to the right of the character.

5. With the **Force** widget still selected, press R and then Y, and then type -90 to rotate the force -90 degrees around the Y axis:

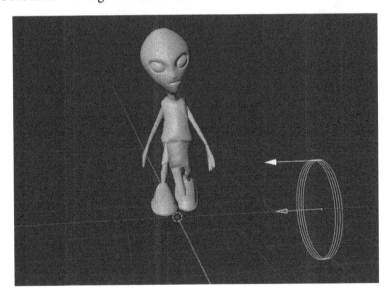

Figure 10.31 – Position the Wind force to the right of the character

6. Save your project now. Then, press the *spacebar* to run the simulation.

Note that the **Wind** force does not really have any effect on the current simulation. The reason for this is that the **Wind** force strength is not powerful enough. Let's see how we can increase its strength:

1. Click the wind force widget in the 3D Viewport to select it.

2. Click the **Physics Properties** tab to the right of the 3D Viewport to view its properties.

3. At the top of the properties panel, you will see the type of force. Here, you can easily change the force type by using the drop-down menu. Let's leave it on **Wind** for now.

4. Below the **Type** section, you will see **Settings**. Here, you can change the properties of the force. Let's increase the **Strength** parameter to 500.

5. Go to frame **1** and press the *spacebar* to run the simulation. The wind should now affect the cloth simulation!

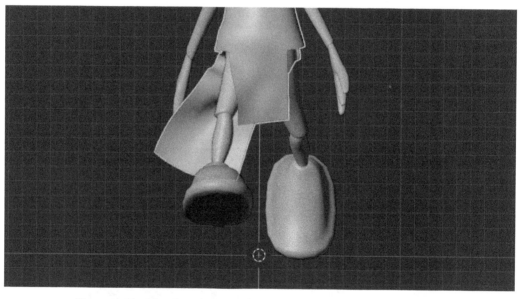

Figure 10.32 – Note how the Wind force is pushing the cloth toward the left

Note that the strength of the force is directly linked to the mass and scale of your cloth object, so it's best to experiment with different strength values to see how it affects the simulation.

6. We can also increase **Noise Amount** to make the wind behave more naturally and erratically. Set **Noise Amount** to 10.

7. Go to frame **1** and press the *spacebar* to run the simulation. Note that the cloth simulation looks a lot more natural now.

Experiment with the wind strength and noise amount until you are happy with the results. Feel free to move and rotate the **Wind** force widget to see how it affects the cloth simulation from different angles:

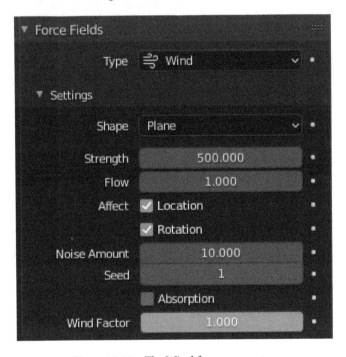

Figure 10.33 – The Wind force parameters

Let's have a look at some of the other forces available in Blender:

1. With the **Wind** force field widget still selected, click the **Type** drop-down menu at the top of the **Physics Properties** panel and select **Vortex** from the list. This will change the selected force from **Wind** to **Vortex**.

2. Set **Vortex Strength** to 100 and run the simulation again – see how it affects the cloth differently than the wind?

Figure 10.34 – See how the Vortex force affects the cloth simulation

Next, let's have a look at the **Turbulence** force. This adds random air turbulence, which is great for static cloth simulations when you need slight movement in the cloth:

1. With the **Force** widget still selected, click the **Type** drop-down menu in the **Physics Properties** panel and select **Turbulence** from the list.

2. Set the **Strength** to 1000.

3. The **Size** parameter will change the size of the turbulence. A bigger value will generate bigger ripples in the cloth while a smaller value will create smaller ripples. Experiment with values ranging from 0.1 to 10 to see how it affects the simulation:

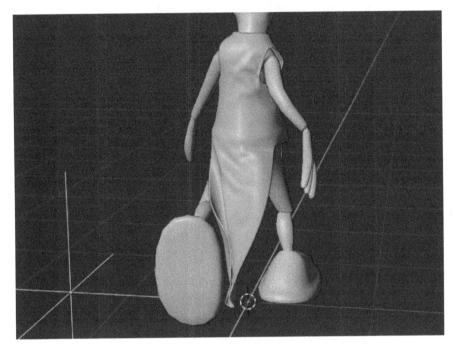

Figure 10.35 – Turbulence adds random ripples and movement to the cloth

You can also control how much effect a certain force will have on a specific cloth object by using the **Field Weights** section. Let's see how we can use this.

4. Click the shirt mesh in the 3D Viewport to select it.

5. Click the **Physics Properties** tab to view the cloth parameters.

6. Scroll down until you see **Field Weights**. Here, you will see a list of weight sliders where you can control how much effect each force has on the cloth simulation:

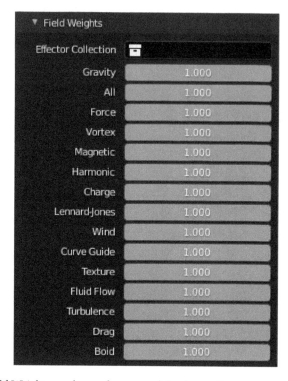

Figure 10.36 – Field Weights can be used to control the force effect on a certain cloth simulation

7. For example, if you have a **Wind** force in your scene, you can set the field weight for **Wind** to 0.5, which will give you a strength of 50%.

Experiment with the different forces and their settings to see how they affect the simulation. In the next section, we will focus on baking the cloth simulation. Please save your project now.

Baking the cloth simulation

In this section, we will learn how to bake our simulation. **Baking** refers to the process of saving or caching the results of a simulation to memory or disk. The result of the simulation is automatically cached in memory when the animation is played. If you bake the simulation, the cache data is protected, and you will be unable to make any changes to the simulation until you delete or free the baked frames.

Let's see how we can bake our cloth simulation:

1. Click the shirt object in the 3D Viewport to select it.

2. Click the **Physics Properties** tab to view the cloth simulation parameters.

3. Scroll down until you see the **Cache** section:

Figure 10.37 – The Cache parameters

4. Set the **Simulation Start** and **End** frames to your animation length. This means that only frames in this range will be baked into cache.

5. Make sure you are on frame **1** in the timeline.

6. Click **Bake** to start the baking process.

You will notice the baking progress bar at the bottom of the timeline. Once the baking process is complete, you can freely scrub the timeline to view your cloth simulation. You won't be able to make any changes to the simulation until you delete the current bake.

Let's see how we can do that.

7. In the **Physics Properties** tab, note that the **Bake** button has changed to **Delete Bake**. Click this button to delete the baked cache data.

8. You can now make changes to your cloth simulation settings and re-bake the simulation by clicking the **Bake** button again.

   You can also convert the cloth simulation to a static mesh if needed. Let's see how we can do this. Please save your project now, as you might want to revert to this state.

9. Scrub the timeline until you find a frame where the cloth simulation looks interesting.

10. Click the cloth mesh in the 3D Viewport to select it.

11. Right-click in the 3D Viewport and select **Convert To | Mesh** from the drop-down menu:

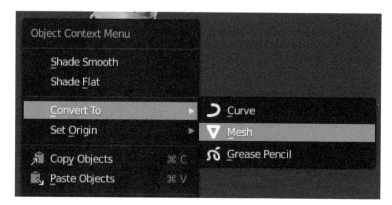

Figure 10.38 – Converting the cloth mesh to a static object

Once you have converted the cloth object to a mesh object, the cloth will no longer be simulated. It will be a static mesh that you can use in your scene. Undo this step or revert to the previously saved project to keep the cloth simulation active for now.

In the next section, we will add some final modifiers to our cloth mesh to make it look even better. Please save your project now.

Adding final modifiers

In this section, we will add two modifiers to our shirt mesh to make it look better and more realistic. The first modifier is the Solidify modifier, which will give the cloth some thickness. The second modifier will be another Subdivision Surface modifier, which will create a smooth and final look for our cloth.

Let's get started!

1. Select the shirt object in the 3D Viewport.

2. Click the **Modifier Properties** tab to the right of the 3D Viewport.

3. Click the **Add Modifier** button at the top and select **Solidify** from the drop-down menu.

4. Make sure that the **Solidify** modifier is below all the other modifiers. This will ensure that the cloth simulation won't take this modifier into consideration when running the simulation.

5. The default **Solidify** settings work great. Feel free to adjust the **Thickness** value to increase or decrease the thickness of the cloth.

6. The **Offset** value is set to -1 by default. This means that the cloth will expand inward when increasing the **Thickness** value. If you prefer, you can change the **Offset** value to 1, which means that the cloth will expand outward when increasing the **Thickness** value. I usually prefer to use an **Offset** value of -1, as this doesn't affect the look of the cloth simulation from the outside.

7. Finally, let's add another Subdivision Surface modifier to our stack. Click the **Add Modifier** button and select **Subdivision Surface** from the drop-down menu.

8. Make sure that this modifier is positioned at the bottom of the modifier stack. This means that the modifier will only be applied to the mesh after the cloth simulation is calculated. Set both the **Viewport** and **Render** levels to 2, which should give you good results. Note how smooth your shirt object looks now:

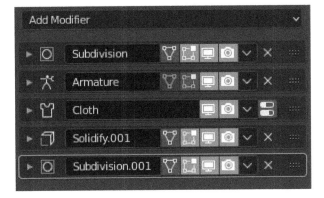

Figure 10.9 – The final modifier stack

Summary

Congratulations! You have now created a dynamic cloth simulation that interacts with your character's animation. You now have the skills to create amazing cloth-like objects to add realism to your scenes.

You have learned how to append a character model with its walk cycle from another Blender project. You should now also be familiar with creating a rest pose that assists with the cloth simulation and modeling of the clothing item. We also looked at how you can easily model clothing using the faces of your character mesh.

You also learned how to customize the cloth simulation using the physics parameters, as well as using forces that interact with the cloth simulation. Finally, we looked at baking and how to cache our simulation, as well as adding the final modifiers that provide thickness and smooth geometry to our cloth.

Remember that physics simulations are all about experimenting and changing the different parameters until you see good results. Experiment with different forces to see how they change the overall look of your cloth simulations. Most importantly, have loads of fun!

In the next chapter, we will create hair using particles and have them interact with physics. Please save your project now!

11
Creating Dynamic Hair Using Particles

In this very exciting chapter, we will create hair for our alien character and simulate the hair dynamically using physics! Additionally, you will learn how to groom your character's hair using specific tools in Blender, making it really easy. Finally, we will create a basic hair shader to add color and texture for amazing-looking hair renders. Being able to create hair, in any 3D application, will give you the ability to create your own unique and amazing characters.

When it comes to animating hair, that's a whole different story. For most artists, animating hair can be extremely time-consuming and even frustrating. However, using physics to automatically do most of the work for you will save you loads of time. And simulations are fun, right?

In this chapter, the main topics that we'll cover are as follows:

- Reusing our alien character and walk cycle animation
- Creating a Vertex Group for the hair particles
- Creating hair particles that interact with physics
- Grooming and styling the hair particles
- Baking the hair simulation to cache
- Setting up a hair shader for rendering

Reusing our alien character and walk cycle animation

In this section, we will reuse our alien character with its walk cycle animation from *Chapter 8, Rigging and Animating Your 3D Cartoon Character,* and save the project to a new file. Yes, I know – aliens, as we know them, usually don't have much hair if any, but this alien is different. However, as always, feel free to use a different character or animation – it's all up to you.

Let's get started and create some amazing-looking hair! Perform the following steps:

1. Open the Blender project that we saved in *Chapter 8, Rigging and Animating Your 3D Cartoon Character.*

2. Now, click on **File | Save As** and save this project as Chapter 11 - Create Dynamic Hair Using Particles.

3. Let's clean up this project by deleting any unnecessary objects such as lights and cameras. We only want to keep our character and the rig that controls the character animation. Click on any lights or unwanted objects in the 3D Viewport. Then, press *X* and click on **Delete** to confirm.

4. Let's hide the rig from the 3D Viewport so that it's easier to see our character. Click on the rig in the 3D Viewport and then press *H* to hide it from the 3D Viewport.

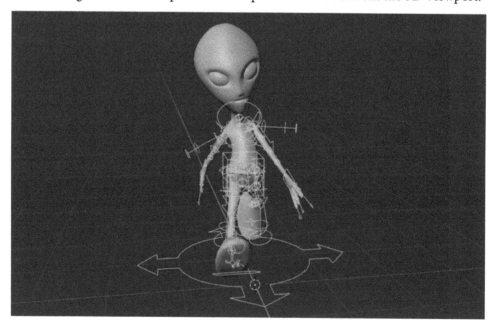

Figure 11.1 – Selecting the rig and hiding it from the 3D Viewport

5. With the rig now hidden from view, press *Spacebar* and preview your character's walk cycle animation.

6. Select the character in the 3D Viewport.

7. With the character selected, press *N* to open the side menu.

8. Click on the **Item** tab in the side menu.

9. Ensure that the character's **Scale** setting has been set to 1 – 1 – 1. It's always good practice to ensure your object scale is set to 1 when doing any type of simulation work in Blender, as the scale of an object will change the way the simulation works.

10. If the scale is not set to 1 – 1 – 1, select the character in the 3D Viewport and press *Ctrl + A*. Then, select **Scale** from the drop-down menu. This will set your character's scale to 1 on all axes.

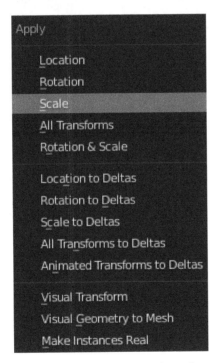

Figure 11.2 – Applying the scale of our character

11. Press *N* to hide the side menu from the 3D Viewport.

Great! Now we have a new, clean project containing our character and the walk cycle animation. In the next section, we will create a new Vertex Group for our hair particles. Please save your project now!

Creating a Vertex Group

In this section, we will create a new Vertex Group for our hair particles. You can make use of Vertex Groups to control where hair particles will be created on your character.

Let's begin! Perform the following steps:

1. Select your character in the 3D Viewport.
2. Press *Tab* to enter **Edit Mode**.
3. Press *3* to activate the **Face Select** mode.
4. Zoom into the top area of your character's head.
5. Select the upper-middle faces of the head.

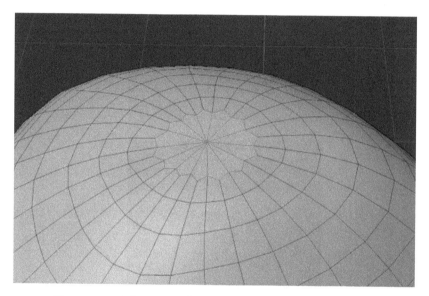

Figure 11.3 – Selecting the faces at the top of the character's head

6. Hold *Ctrl* and tap the + button on the numpad to grow the selection of faces until you have enough faces where the hair will grow from, as shown in the following screenshot:

Figure 11.4 – Growing the selection of faces where hair particles will be created

7. Click on the **Object Data Properties** tab on the right-hand side of the 3D Viewport.

8. At the top of the **Object Data Properties** panel, under **Vertex Groups**, click on the plus symbol to create a new Vertex Group.

9. A new Vertex Group called **Group** will be created. You will see many other Vertex Groups listed that are used by the rig.

10. Double-click on this new Vertex Group and rename it to Hair.

11. With the faces still selected in the 3D Viewport, click on the **Assign** button under the list of Vertex Groups to assign the selected faces to this new **Hair** Vertex Group.

12. Hover your mouse cursor over the 3D Viewport and press *Tab* to exit **Edit Mode**.

You have now successfully created a new Vertex Group called **Hair** and you have assigned the selected faces to this Vertex Group. Remember that you can always add or remove faces to this Vertex Group later and, therefore, change the area where hair will grow on your character.

In the next section, we will add the hair particle system and see how they interact with physics. Please save your project now.

Creating hair particles that interact with physics

In this section, we will focus on creating hair particles and animating our character's hair using physics! Additionally, you will learn how to make other objects in your scene interact with the hair simulation. There are many different parameters when it comes to hair particle simulations, and we will probably not cover every single parameter in this book. But I will try my best to explain the most important parameters so that you will be able to create amazing-looking hair animations for your characters.

Try not to get overwhelmed with all the settings – focus on one parameter at a time and see how it affects your hair simulation. Please remember to save your project frequently, as working with physics simulations can quickly produce interesting or unwanted results. So, save often to prevent losing any work.

Let's get started! Perform the following steps:

1. Click on the character in the 3D Viewport to select it.

2. Then, click on the **Particle Properties** tab on the right-hand side of the 3D Viewport.

3. Now, click on the + symbol at the top to create a new particle system.

4. Double-click on the particle system name to rename it to Hair to keep things nice and tidy.

5. Click on the **Hair** button beneath this section to switch from **Emitter** to **Hair**.

Figure 11.5 – Clicking on Hair to change from Emitter to Hair

You will notice that something has happened in 3D Viewport. Your character has hair growing from everywhere! We will fix this soon.

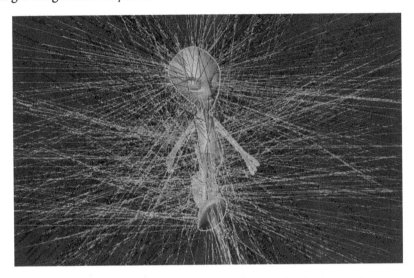

Figure 11.6 – Our character is emitting hair particles from every face

6. First, let's change the number of hair particles. Under the **Emission** section, set the **Number** value to 150. This will create 150 parent hair particles.

> **Quick Tip**
> Minimize the different sections under this properties panel when you are not using it. There are many sections and subsections, and it can quickly become overwhelming! Keep it clean and simple.

7. Minimize the **Emission** section and expand the **Vertex Group** section close to the bottom of the list.

    Here, you will see a list of parameters that you can assign to different Vertex Groups. We want to influence the **Density** setting of our hair particles.

8. Click on the box next to **Density** and choose **Hair** from the list. Additionally, you can type in the name to filter if you have multiple Vertex Groups.

    Things should now look slightly better in the 3D Viewport. Hair particles should only emit from the faces in the **Hair** Vertex Group. This is good!

9. Let's go back to the **Emission** section. Remember to minimize the **Vertex Group** section to keep things tidy. Note that we might jump between sections!

10. Under the **Emission** section, change the **Hair Length** setting to something a bit more realistic. I used 1 m, but it all depends on the size of your character.

11. Next, let's increase the number of **Segments** to 10. This will add more *subdivisions* to your hair particles, making them bend more naturally.

12. Expand the **Source** section. If you click on the drop-down menu next to **Emit From**, you can choose where to emit hair particles from – **Vertices, Faces,** or **Volume.** Let's keep this on **Faces.**

13. Let's minimize the **Emission** section and expand the **Render** section. Here, we can change some of the render settings.

14. Under **Path,** tick the box next to **B-Spline.** This will interpolate the hair particles as B-splines, which I find looks more realistic.

15. Increase the number of **Steps** to 5. This will add more subdivisions to the B-spline curve, making it bend more naturally.

16. Minimize the **Render** section and expand the **Viewport Display** section.

17. Increase the number of **Strand Steps** to 5.

This will make the hair look more natural in the 3D Viewport by adding subdivisions. This will not influence your final render. You can set this number to a lower value if you experience any slowing down when we run the physics simulation.

Now for the exciting part – let's run our first hair simulation to see how the hair interacts with our character's animation. Please save your project now. Then, perform the following steps:

1. Minimize the **Viewport Display** section, and tick the box next to the **Hair Dynamics** section to activate it. Now expand the **Hair Dynamics** section.

2. First, let's increase the number of **Quality Steps** to 10. This will give us a better simulation, but it will also slow down the simulation time. You can increase or decrease this number later, depending on your computer's speed.

3. Expand **Collisions** and set the **Quality** setting to 4. This will increase the quality of hair collisions but also slow down the simulation time.

4. Here, you can also set the **Distance** value of when a collision is detected. For now, let's leave this in its default setting. You can increase this number if some hair strands go through your collision objects during the simulation.

5. Hover your mouse cursor over the 3D Viewport and press *Spacebar* to run the simulation.

Amazing, right? Well, not yet. As you can see, the hair particles are going through your character and are not interacting with it. This is because we have not set our character as a collision object.

Let's do this now:

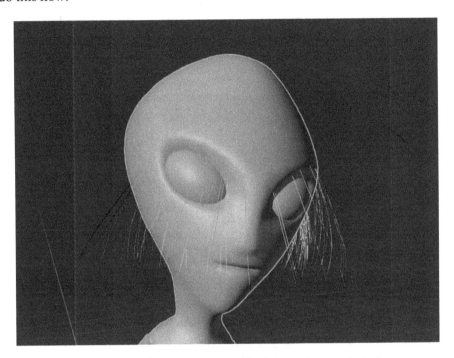

Figure 11.7 – Hair particles going through our character's mesh

1. Press *Spacebar* to stop the simulation. Then, press *Shift* + the left arrow to go back to frame number 1.

2. Click on the character in the 3D Viewport to select it. Then, click on the **Physics Properties** tab on the right-hand side of the 3D Viewport.

3. Click on **Collision** at the top to make our character a collision object.

   Here, you can change the collision object's parameters such as **Friction** and **Damping**, but let's leave these at their default settings for now. Please feel free to experiment with these values to see how they affect your simulation.

4. Press *Spacebar* to run the simulation again.

   Do you notice how the hair particles are now colliding with your character? That's great! Let's see what other parameters we can change to improve our simulation. Please save your project now.

5. Click on the **Particles Properties** tab and expand the **Hair Dynamics** section.

6. Then, expand the **Structure** section under **Hair Dynamics**.

Here, you can specify the structural properties of your hair particles such as the **Vertex Mass** property, which is the mass of the hair. The **Stiffness** property controls how much the hair particle resists bending. This is in addition to **Randomness** and **Damping**, which will slow down the fall of a hair particle. Usually, the default values give good results, but feel free to change them to see how they will affect the simulation.

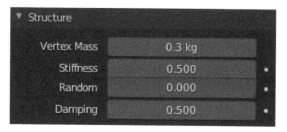

Figure 11.8 – The hair particle's Structure parameters

7. Minimize the **Structure** section and expand the **Volume** section.

Here, you will find the volume properties. Usually, I only change the **Air Drag** parameter, which will make the air thicker, resulting in slower falling hair particles. This is in addition to the **Internal Friction** parameter, which sets the amount of friction between individual hair particles. Feel free to experiment with these values.

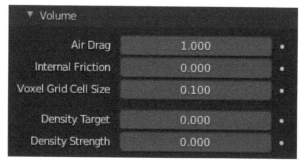

Figure 11.9 – The hair's Volume parameters

Remember to run the simulation each time you make adjustments to see how it affects your simulation. And save often!

8. Minimize the **Hair Dynamics** section and expand **Children**.

9. Click on the **Interpolated** button to create child particles.

You will instantly see a difference in the 3D Viewport. Each parent hair particle now has 10 child particles, as you can see in the following screenshot. I have given my character and hair particles a basic color material so that it's easier to see the hair particles. You don't have to do this as we will cover materials later in this chapter.

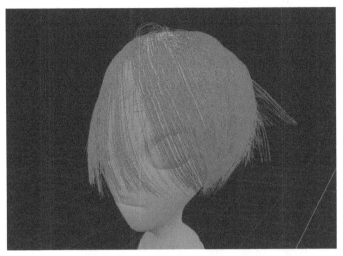

Figure 11.10 – Each parent hair particle now has multiple child hair particles

10. Set the **Display Amount** setting and the **Render Amount** setting to 3 0. This will create 30 child hair particles for every one parent hair particle.

   You can adjust this number as needed. Remember, you can only display a few child particles in the 3D Viewport by lowering the **Display Amount** setting while rendering many more. This will speed up your 3D Viewport drastically.

11. Additionally, you can change the **Length** parameter of your hair particles here. I'm going to leave the **Length** parameter at the default setting of 1, but feel free to adjust this if required.

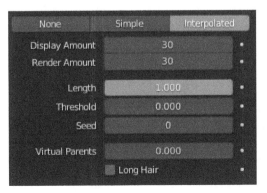

Figure 11.11 – The child particle parameters

12. Expand the **Parting** section.

13. Increase the **Parting** parameter and see how the hair particles move away from each other. I prefer to use **Clumping** rather than **Parting**, so let's leave this value at 0.

14. Expand the **Clumping** section.

15. Tick the box next to **Use Clump Curve** to enable this parameter. It's much easier to visualize clumping by using this curve.

16. Pull the upper-right vertex of the curve down to the lower-right corner.

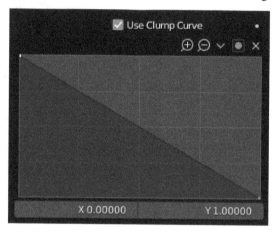

Figure 11.12 – Using the curve to adjust the clumping parameters

See how the hair clumps together at the tip.

Figure 11.13 – The hair particles clumping together at the tip

17. Let's make it a bit more realistic – try and match the curve in the following screenshot to create more natural-looking clumps.

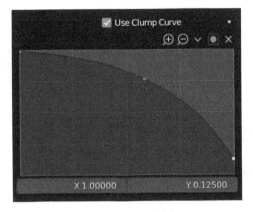

Figure 11.14 – Creating a more natural clump curve

Run the simulation again and see how the clumping affects the overall look of your hair simulation.

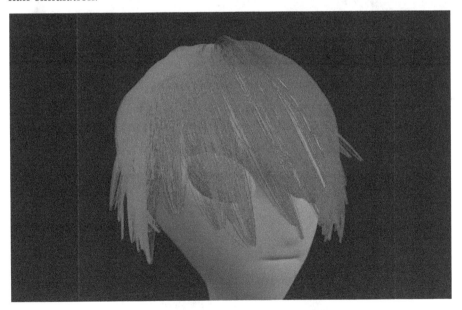

Figure 11.15 – The hair clumping in a more natural way

18. Click on the **Render Properties** tab on the right-hand side of the 3D Viewport.

19. For now, make sure the **Render Engine** option is set to **Eevee**. We will change this to **Cycles** when doing our final render.

20. Expand the **Hair** section and then click on **Strip**.

    This parameter will also change the hair type from **Strand** to **Strip** for the 3D Viewport when rendering with **Eevee**. Notice how you can see the individual hair strands in the 3D Viewport.

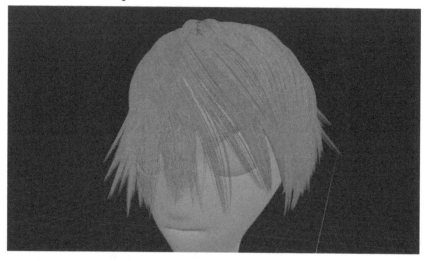

Figure 11.16 – Changing the hair type to Strip makes it much easier to visualize the final look

Let's go back to the **Particle Properties** tab.

21. Expand the **Roughness** section underneath **Clumping**.

22. Increase the **Uniform** parameter and see how it affects the look of the hair particles. You can tweak all of these parameters to add **Roughness** to your hair. Set these parameters as you wish.

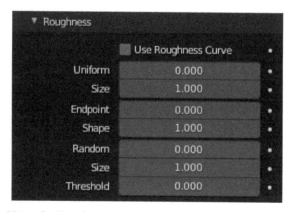

Figure 11.17 – Using the Roughness parameters to add roughness to your hair particles

23. Next, let's expand the **Kink** section.

24. Here, you can choose between the following different **Kink Type** options by clicking on the drop-down menu next to **Kink Type** – **Curl**, **Radial**, **Wave**, **Braid**, **Spiral**, and **Nothing**.

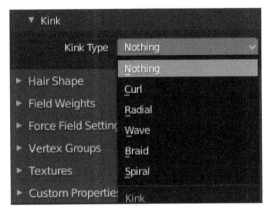

Figure 11.18 – Different kink types

25. Experiment with the different **Kink Type** options and see how they can dramatically change the look of your character's hair.

26. Next, let's minimize the **Children** section and expand the **Hair Shape** section.

27. The **Strand Shape** slider will change the overall shape of the hair strand. Adjust the **Strand Shape** slider to see how it affects the thickness of the hair strands in the 3D Viewport.

28. Next, you have the **Diameter Root** value. This value will increase or decrease the diameter of the root of each hair strand. Adjust this value as required.

29. The **Tip** value controls the diameter of the tip of each hair strand. Set this value as required.

30. Finally, we have the **Diameter Scale** parameter. This will increase or decrease the overall diameter of each hair strand. This can be very useful when creating stylized hair.

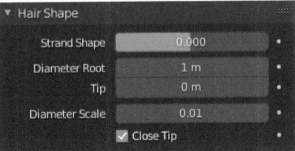

Figure 11.19 – The Hair Shape parameters changing the overall thickness of each hair strand

Congratulations! You have now created the look and feel of your hair particles along with the physics parameters. Experiment with all of these parameters until you are happy with the way your character's hair looks and how it interacts with the character and the animation.

In the next section, we will groom and style the hair! Save your project once you are happy with your hair simulation.

Grooming and styling

In this section, we will focus on grooming and styling your character's hair. It is good practice to only start the grooming process once you are happy with the basic hair parameters. This is because once you start the grooming and styling processes, some of the particle parameters will be locked, and you won't be able to make any changes to them until you delete your grooming edits.

Grooming and styling the character's hair can be a lot of fun, so get ready to experiment and be creative to see what interesting styles you can create.

Let's get started! Perform the following steps:

1. Click on your character in the 3D Viewport to select it.

2. We need to switch to the **Particle Edit** mode to edit or style the hair particles. There are a few ways you can do this:

    - Click on the drop-down menu from the upper-left corner of the 3D Viewport and select **Particle Edit** from the list.

    - Alternatively, you can use the *Ctrl + Tab* shortcut and select **Particle Edit** from the radial menu.

In the **Particle Edit** mode, you can change or style your hair particles as a group or even individual hair particles one at a time. The **Particle Edit** mode is extremely powerful and fun to use. On the left-hand side of the 3D Viewport, you will see the available tools to groom and style the hair particles.

Let's see how we can use them to create amazing character hairstyles. Let's begin at the top.

Figure 11.20 – The different style and groom brushes

- **Comb Tool**: With this tool, you can brush or comb the hair particles. Click on this tool to select it. Then, click and drag across the hair particles in the 3D Viewport. You will quickly get a feel for it, and it can be a lot of fun! Press *F* to increase or decrease the **Radius** setting of the brush. *Shift + F* controls the **Strength** setting.

We can use the comb tool to style the hair particles, as shown in the following screenshot:

Figure 11.21 – Using the comb tool

Also, you can use the sliders at the top of the 3D Viewport to set the **Radius** and **Strength** settings of your brush. Let's look at the next tool in the side menu.

- **Smooth Tool**: This tool will make the hair particles smooth and straight. You can use the same shortcuts to change the **Radius** and **Strength** settings.

  We can use the smooth tool to straighten the hair particles, as shown in the following screenshot:

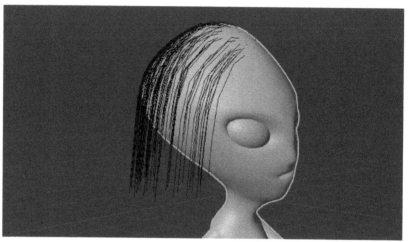

Figure 11.22 – Using the smooth tool

3. **Add Tool**: With this tool, you can add hair particles to the surface of your character.

   With the add tool, you can add more hair particles to your mesh, as shown in the following screenshot:

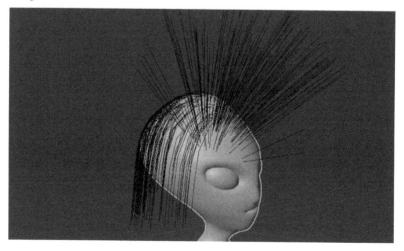

Figure 11.23 – Using the add tool

- **Length Tool**: With this tool, you can increase or decrease the length of the hair particles. Click and drag over a few hair particles to see how they grow. Note, at the top of the 3D Viewport, you can switch between **Grow** and **Shrink**.

You can use the length tool to shorten or lengthen certain hair particles, as shown in the following screenshot:

Figure 11.24 – Using the length tool

- **Puff Tool**: This tool will puff the hair particles away from the character mesh. Note, at the top of the 3D Viewport, you can select between **Add** and **Sub**, which will give different results. Experiment and have fun styling your character's hair!

We can use the puff tool to easily create an instant Karen effect, as shown in the following screenshot:

Figure 11.25 – Using the puff tool

- **Cut Tool**: A classic! Click and drag to cut the hair particles, as shown in the following screenshot:

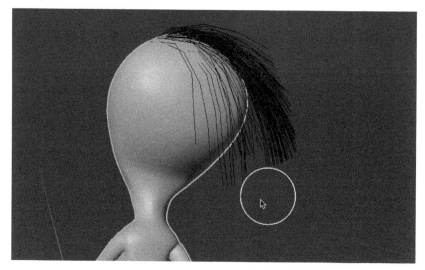

Figure 11.26 – Using the cut tool to cut hair particles

- **Weight Tool**: You can use this tool to manually weight paint the hair particles, as shown in the following screenshot. Let's leave it at its default setting, but feel free to experiment with this.

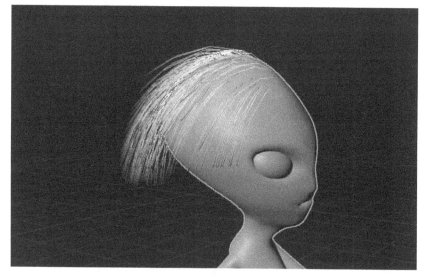

Figure 11.27 – You can use the weight tool to apply custom weight attributes to the hair particles

Play around with the different styling tools and see what amazing styles you can create! Go wild and have fun! Once you are happy with your basic style, move on to the next step.

Let's run the simulation to see how the hair interacts with the character and movement. Perform the following steps:

1. Let's go back to **Object Mode**. You can use the drop-down menu in the upper-left corner of the 3D Viewport or press the *Ctrl + Tab* shortcut to select **Object Mode** from the radial menu.

2. Let's run the simulation by pressing *Spacebar*. Amazing, right?

    See how your character's newly created hairstyle interacts with its movement. There is a parameter that will assist you if the hair particles move around too much and you end up losing the style that you have created. Let's see how we can use it to keep our style in place.

3. Stop the simulation by pressing *Spacebar* and go back to frame **1** by pressing *Shift* + the left arrow key.

4. Open the **Particle Properties** tab on the right-hand side of the 3D Viewport.

5. Expand the **Hair Dynamics** section.

6. Here, you will see a parameter called **Pin Goal Strength**. Increase its value slightly to keep the hairstyle in place. I set mine to 0 . 5, but as always, feel free to experiment.

7. Run the simulation again by pressing *Spacebar*. Notice how the hair sticks to its position a bit better. Great! Take a look at the following screenshot:

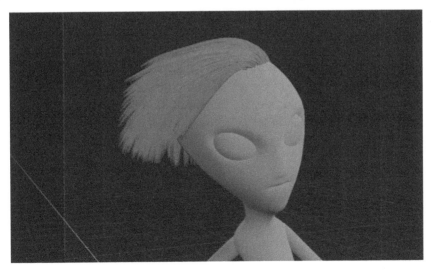

Figure 11.28 – The final hair simulation look

You have now created a custom hairstyle for your character and simulated it using physics. Well done! Feel free to click on the **Delete Edit** button under the **Particles Properties** panel to reset the style back to its default settings. Then, you can go back into **Particle Edit Mode** to create a new style. Once you are happy with your hair simulation, you can move on to the next section.

Figure 11.29 – Reset the style back by clicking on the Delete Edit button

In the next section, we will bake our simulation to cache. Please save your project now!

Baking the hair simulation to cache

Once you are happy with your hair simulation, it's time to bake it to cache. Baking your hair simulation to cache will save the animation data so that it won't calculate the simulation every time you play the animation. This will also speed up the viewport animation drastically, so you can preview your animation in close to real time.

Let's get to baking! Perform the following steps:

1. Select your character in the 3D Viewport.

2. Click on the **Particle Properties** tab on the right-hand side of the 3D Viewport.

3. Expand the **Cache** section.

    Here, you will find all the **Cache** parameters. It's extremely easy to bake the simulation to cache. We can set the **Simulation Start** and **End** frame numbers. Note that you can set a negative number for the **Simulation Start** frame, which is great if you want your hair to start simulating before the first frame of your animation.

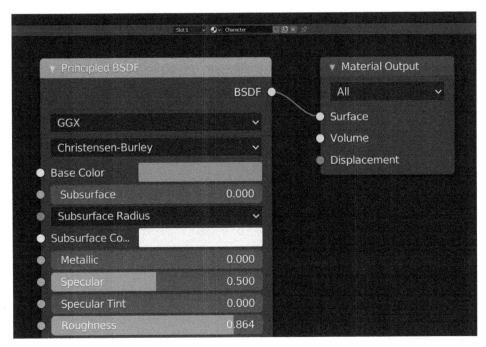

Figure 11.30 – The Cache parameters

4. Set the **Simulation Start** value to -30. This means our simulation will start at frame -30 and will allow the hair to settle into a rest position before the animation starts. Experiment with this number as it will depend on many different factors.

5. Set the **End** value to the length of your animation. My animation ends at frame **79**, so I will set the **End** value to 79.

6. Tick the box next to **Disk Cache**. This means the cached data for your simulation will be saved to your hard drive.

7. Save your project now.

8. Click on the **Bake** button to bake your simulation to cache.

Notice that the play indicator on the timeline, underneath the 3D Viewport, starts caching from frame -**30**. Allow it to run through the length of your animation. This might take a while depending on the complexity of the simulation and the speed of your computer. Once the bake is complete, you can play the animation back by pressing *Spacebar*. Notice how the playback speed has increased? This is because the simulation has been cached, so no physics calculations are being processed. Additionally, you can scrub the timeline freely.

If you want to make any changes to your simulation, you have to delete the current bake by clicking on the **Delete Bake** button. You can then make changes to your simulation and rebake the cache once you are happy with the simulation.

In the next section, we will create a basic hair shader to add some color and texture to your character's hair. Please save your project now.

Setting up a hair shader for rendering

Once you have baked your hair simulation to cache, and you are happy with the way the simulation looks, it's time to add color and texture! In this section, we will focus on setting up a simple but effective hair shader to create realistic-looking hair renders.

Let's get started! Perform the following steps:

1. Click on your character in the 3D Viewport to select it.

2. Then, click on the **Shading** tab at the top of the 3D Viewport to switch to the Shading workspace section.

    We need to create two shaders: one for the character and one for our hair particles. First, let's create a placeholder character shader that we can modify at a later stage.

3. Just underneath the 3D Viewport in the **Shading Workspace** section, click on the **New** button to create a new shader.

4. Give the shader a name by clicking on the default name at the top of the **Shader Editor** window. Let's call it Character.

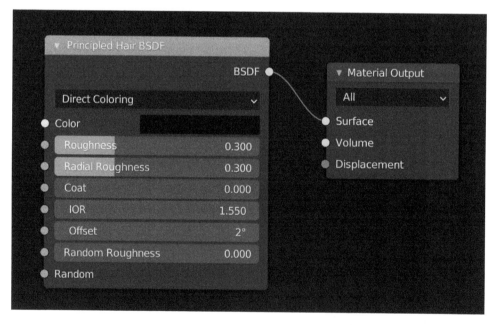

Figure 11.31 – Creating a new shader for the character

5. Click on the **Slot 1** drop-down menu at the top of the **Shader Editor** window.

6. Now, click on the + symbol to create a second shader.

7. Click on the **New** button again and rename this shader to Hair.

   Now we have created two new shaders: one for our character and one for the hair. We need to specify which shader the hair particle system will use. Let's do this next.

8. Click on the **Particle Properties** tab next to the 3D Viewport.

9. Expand the **Render** section.

10. Click on the drop-down menu next to **Material** and select the **Hair** shader we have just created.

    To make use of the **Principled Hair BSDF** shader, we need to switch to the **Cycles Render Engine** section. Let's do this next.

11. Click on the **Render Properties** tab next to the 3D Viewport.

12. At the top of the **Render Properties** panel, click on the drop-down menu next to **Render Engine** and select **Cycles** from the list.

    We are now ready to create our hair shader! Please save your project now.

13. Click on the **Principled BSDF** shader node in the **Shader Editor** window. Then, press *X* to delete it.

14. Hover your mouse cursor over the **Shader Editor** window and press *Shift + A* to display the **Add** menu.

15. Using the search function at the top, type in Hair and select **Principled Hair BSDF** from the list.

16. Position this node on the left-hand side of the **Material Output** node.

17. Connect the **BSDF** output of the **Principled Hair BSDF** node to the **Surface** input of the **Material Output** node.

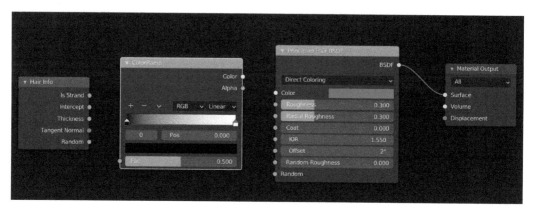

Figure 11.32 – Your node tree should now look like this

18. Click on the color box next to **Color** and choose a bright color. I'm going with a nice bright red.

    You can adjust the parameters of the **Principled Hair BSDF** node, such as the **Roughness, IOR,** and more. Experiment with these values and see how the look of the hair changes in the 3D Viewport. Feel free to switch to **Render View** if you want to see a **Cycles** preview render.

19. Switch to **Render View** by hovering your mouse cursor over the 3D Viewport. Press *Z* and then select **Rendered** from the radial menu.

    You might need to add a light to your scene if required. Let's see how we can make the hair more interesting. Let's blend different colors together and see how that looks.

20. Create a new material node by pressing *Shift* + *A* and using the search function. Type in color, and select **ColorRamp** from the list.

21. Position the **ColorRamp** node to the left-hand side of the **Principled Hair BSDF** node.

22. Create a new material node by pressing *Shift* + *A* and using the search function. Type in `hair`, and select **Hair Info** from the list.

23. Position the **Hair Info** node to the left-hand side of the **ColorRamp** node, as shown in the following screenshot:

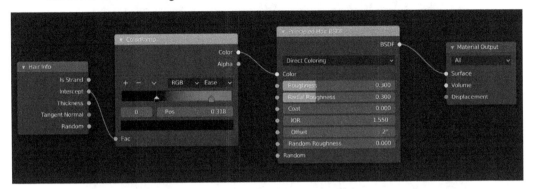

Figure 11.33 – Your node tree should now look something like this

24. Connect the **Intercept** output of the **Hair Info** node to the **Fac** input of the **ColorRamp** node.

25. Connect the **Color** output of the **ColorRamp** node to the **Color** input of the **Principled Hair BSDF** node.

26. Let's modify the **ColorRamp** node – drag the black and white sliders closer to each other and change the white color to red.

27. Click on the linear drop-down menu in the **ColorRamp** node and select **Ease** from the list. This will smooth out the gradient between the two colors.

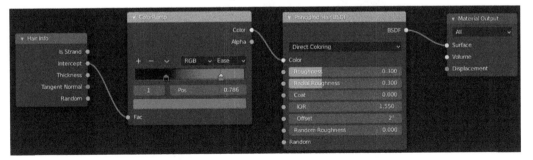

Figure 11.34 – Your node tree should now look like this

Notice how the hair looks in the 3D Viewport. See how the color gradient flows from black, which is closer to the hair roots, to red, which is closer to the hair tips. Let's add one more color to our gradient.

Figure 11.35 – The gradient runs from the hair root to the hair tip

28. Click on the + symbol in the **ColorRamp** node in the **Shader Editor** window to create a new color slot.

29. Drag this new color slider all the way to the right-hand side of the **ColorRamp** node.

30. Set this new color to white, as shown in the following screenshot:

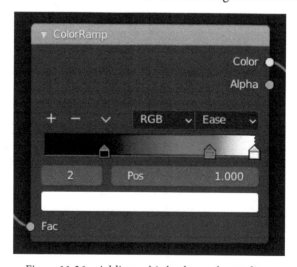

Figure 11.36 – Adding a third color to the gradient

Notice how the hair shader has been updated in the 3D Viewport. Now the gradient goes from black to red, to white. See what other interesting hair shaders you can create.

Figure 11.37 – The final look showing the three-color gradient

Summary

Congratulations! You have created an amazing-looking hair simulation for your character with a great-looking shader! You should now have a good understanding of hair particles and how they interact with physics. Additionally, you have learned how to groom and style your character's hair to create interesting and custom looks for your characters. We have also looked at how you can bake your simulation to cache, which will save the simulation to memory. Finally, you learned how to create interesting-looking shaders for your character's hair.

Remember, the hair particle system can be used for so much more than just a character's hairstyle. You can use it to create grass, animal fur, facial hair, and more. You can even render objects instead of hair paths to create water droplets on glass, spikes on a shield, or even use it to scatter rocks and trees across a landscape.

In the next chapter, we will explore the exciting world of camera tracking or match moving. Please save your project now.

Part 3: Match Moving and Compositing

In this part we will be focusing on Match Moving or Camera Tracking as well as Compositing in Blender.

We will cover the following chapters in this section:

12
Matching Blender's Camera Movement to Live Action Footage

In this exciting chapter, we're going to focus on camera tracking in Blender. Camera tracking or match moving, as many call it in the film and visual effects (VFX) industry, is the process of matching the movement of a real-world camera with a virtual camera in your 3D software. One of the main reasons you would do camera tracking is to insert 3D objects such as characters, props, buildings, explosions, particles, or anything you can imagine into a live-action scene where a moving camera is being used.

This process is also used extensively with scenes that make use of a green screen, where the full background behind the actors needs to be replaced. Tracking markers are often placed on the floor or the green screen if no high-contrast objects are visible, which will make the tracking process much easier. Once you have a matching virtual camera, it is fairly easy to add 3D elements to your scene as the 3D camera will match the exact movement of the real camera.

In this chapter, we will cover the following topics:

- Creating an image sequence from a video
- Importing the image sequence into Blender
- Camera tracking or match moving
- Solving and refining the track and orienting the scene
- Testing the camera track with test objects

Creating an image sequence from a video

In this section, we will create a PNG image sequence from a video file using Blender. It's always good practice to use an image sequence rather than a video file when doing VFX work because using an image sequence will ensure that you are using the correct number of frames. An image sequence is also not linked to a **Frames Per Second** (**FPS**) value, eliminating possible issues. Many applications can convert a video file into an image sequence, such as DaVinci Resolve, Adobe Premiere, and After Effects, to name a few, but Blender can do it even better!

Let me show you how easy it is to convert a video into a PNG image sequence using Blender. Let's get started:

1. You can download the video I will be using from `https://github.com/PacktPublishing/Taking-Blender-to-the-Next-Level/blob/main/Chapter12/Chapter%2012%20-%20Footage_5sec.mp4`, but feel free to use your own footage:

Figure 12.1 – You can download the clip I'll be using from the URL mentioned previously

2.   Create a new Blender project.

3.   Click the + symbol to the right of the workspace tabs, above the 3D Viewport:

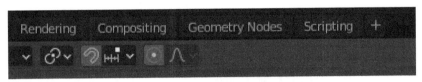

Figure 12.2 – The workspace tabs

4.   From the drop-down menu, select **Video Editing**, then click **Video Editing** to switch over to the Video Editing workspace:

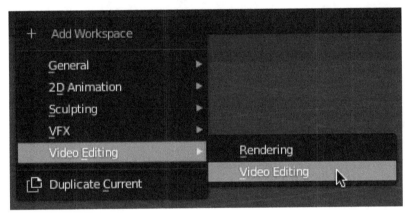

Figure 12.3 – Changing over to the Video Editing workspace

5.   At the bottom of the Video Editing workspace, you will see the **Sequencer** window. Drag and drop the video file you want to convert into an image sequence onto the **Sequencer** window to import the video:

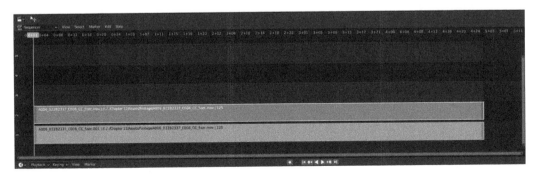

Figure 12.4 – Importing the video into Blender

6.   Now, press *Spacebar* to play the video. Press *Spacebar* again to stop the playback.

Next, let's set the number of frames, resolution, and output settings for our image sequence. If you look at the video clip on the timeline, you will see the total number of frames to the right of the video clip. The video clip I'm using is 5 seconds in duration and my camera was set to record at 25 FPS. As you can see, the total number of frames in the clip I'm using is 125:

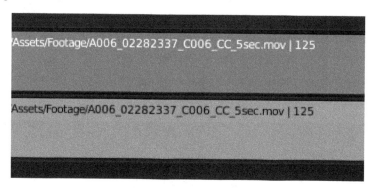

Figure 12.5 – The total number of frames is displayed on the clip in the timeline

7. To set the number of frames, resolution, and output settings, we need to open the **Output Properties** tab. Click the **Output Properties** icon to the right of the viewport. It's the icon that looks like a printer.

8. Under **Dimensions**, set the **Resolution** property of your image sequence. Ensure this is the same as the video clip that you are using. I'm using an HD video, so I will set my resolution to 1920 X 1080.

9. Next, set the total number of frames to match the video clip that you're using. Leave **Frame Start** on 1 but set the **End** parameter to the number of frames in your video clip.

10. Now, we can set the **Frame Rate** property of the video. Click the dropdown and choose the frame rate that matches the video clip:

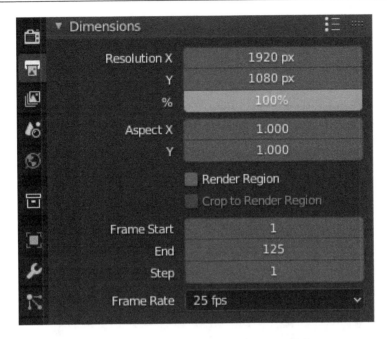

Figure 12.6 – Setting the resolution, total frames, and frame rate

11. Under the **Output** section, click the **Folder** icon and browse to a location where you want to save the image sequence.

12. Give your image sequence a name and add an _ (underscore) to the end of the filename. This will ensure that the frame number is separate from the filename and is easier to interoperate by an application such as Blender.

13. Click **Accept** to save the file path.

14. Click the drop-down menu next to **File Format** and select **PNG**. This is a good image type to use when you're doing camera tracking as it is not compressed. You can experiment with other formats if required.

15. Next to **Color**, select **RGB**. This means we are saving an RGB image without an alpha channel, which is perfect for a video.

16. Set **Color Depth** to **16** as this will preserve more details. For camera tracking, you want as much detail as possible to ensure you have a good track.

17. Finally, set **Compression** to 0%. This will ensure that the images are not compressed, again retaining all the details we can:

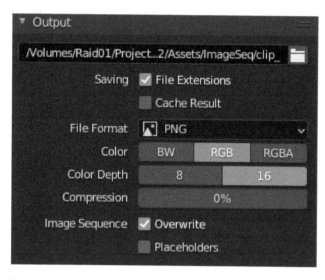

Figure 12.7 – Setting the Output settings of the image sequence

Before we export the image sequence, let's ensure that our **Color Management** has been configured correctly. This can change the way the image sequence is rendered.

18. Click the **Render Properties** icon (the camera icon) next to the Viewport.

19. Scroll down and expand **Color Management**.

20. Ensure that **View Transform** is set to **Standard**. This will ensure that the image is rendered using the correct exposure and contrast settings.

21. If you want to adjust the contrast of the image sequence, you can click the dropdown next to **Look** and select one of the options. This is useful if your video does not have enough contrast:

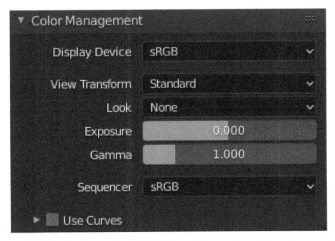

Figure 12.8 – Ensuring that Color Management is configured correctly

22. You can even make further adjustments to your image sequence by clicking the box next to **Use Curves**.

Now, we are ready to export our image sequence.

23. Click **Render** at the top of the Blender UI and select **Render Animation** from the drop-down menu to begin rendering your image sequence:

Figure 12.9 – Using Render Animation to start exporting the image sequence

Great – your image sequence is now being rendered! If you browse to the location you chose, you will see the frames being exported. Each frame has a filename followed by an underscore, then the frame number – for example, Clip_0001.png. Allow a few minutes, depending on the number of frames, for the render to complete.

In the next section, you will learn how to import this image sequence back into Blender, ready for the camera tracking process. Please save your project now.

Importing the image sequence into Blender

In this section, we will import the image sequence that we have created back into Blender. Let's get started:

1. Create a new Blender project.

2. Select all the default objects in the scene by pressing *A*, then *X*. Click **Delete** to confirm.

3. Click the + symbol at the top, to the right of the workspace tabs, and select **VFX | Motion Tracking**. This will open the **Motion Tracking** workspace:

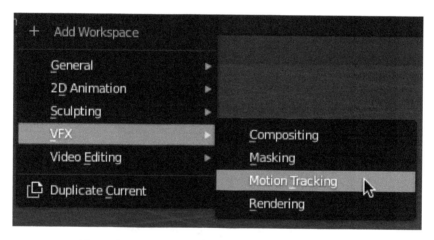

Figure 12.10 – Opening the Motion Tracking workspace

4. At the top of the main viewport, you will see the **Movie Clip** editor. Click **Open**.

5. Browse to the folder where you exported the image sequence.

6. Press *A* to select all the images in the folder.

7. Click **Open Clip** to import the image sequence.

    The image sequence will now be imported into Blender. You will see the video displayed in the main viewport. You can zoom in and out by scrolling the mouse wheel and pan around by holding the mouse wheel. You can play/stop the sequence by pressing *Spacebar*.

8. To the left of the main viewport, click **Set Scene Frames**. This will set the frame duration of the project so that it matches the number of frames in your image sequence.

9. Click the **Prefetch** button under **Set Scene Frames**. This will load the image sequence into the cache or memory for faster playback in the viewport. You should see a progress bar at the bottom of the UI labeled **Prefetching**. Once it's complete, press *Spacebar* to see the video playback in the viewport:

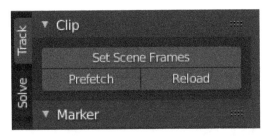

Figure 12.11 – Using Set Scene Frames and Prefetch to load the image sequence into memory

10. Let's also set the frame rate of our project. Click the **Output Properties** tab to the right of the main viewport.

11. Click the drop-down menu next to **Frame Rate** and choose the required frame rate for your project. I'm using a frame rate of 25, but feel free to use any frame rate you need.

Congratulations – you have successfully imported the image sequence that you have created and are ready to start the camera tracking process! Please go ahead and save your project now. In the next section, we will place trackers and track our camera's movement. Let's go!

Camera tracking or match moving

In this section, we will begin the process of tracking the real-world camera by creating trackers on high-contrast features in the scene. We need to try and track features that are close to the camera as well as far away from the camera. This will provide parallax and will also help Blender create a better track.

If you have control over the filming of the footage, always try to use a high shutter speed as this will reduce the amount of motion blur in the footage. Motion blur is a camera tracker's worst nightmare. It is possible to track footage with lots of motion blur, but it requires a lot of manual input and will take much longer.

First, let's configure our scene and look at some of the tracking parameters. Let's get started:

1. Hover your mouse cursor over the main viewport and press *N* to bring up the side menu.

2. Click the **Track** tab.

3. Expand the **Objects** section.

4. Here, you will see the object that will be tracked. Leave this set to **Camera** as we're going to track the movement of the camera:

Figure 12.12 – The Camera object

5. Expand the **Camera** section.

6. Here, you can set the **Sensor Width** property of the camera, which is used to capture the footage to get a more accurate track. Leave this as is if you don't know the sensor width of the camera. You can also use the **Preset** drop-down menu (the three dots and three lines) to choose a preset from the list.

7. Next, expand the **Lens** section.

8. Here, you can also specify the **Focal Length** property of the lens, which is used to capture the scene. Again, leave this as is if you don't know what lens was used. These settings will assist in getting a better track if you have access to that information:

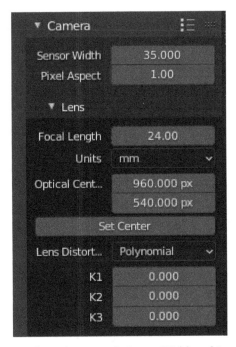

Figure 12.13 – Specifying the camera's Sensor Width and Lens Focal Length

Let's have a look at the main **Tracking Settings** to the left of the main viewport. Ensure that the **Track** tab is active. This is where we will configure our trackers and set how they track the pixels in the viewport:

Figure 12.14 – The main Tracking Settings to the left of the Viewport

The following settings can be adjusted for each track, so it's usually best to try different settings if you experience any tracking issues:

- **Pattern Size**: This parameter specifies the size of the area that Blender will try to track. I usually leave this as is (21), but it can be increased or decreased if you experience tracking problems or the track jumps off the tracked feature.

- **Search Size**: This parameter specifies the search area around the pattern. This is where Blender will look for the pattern that's being tracked. If you have a fast-moving camera, you may need to increase the search size, but the default value of 71 should be fine for normal camera movement.

- **Motion Model**: There are a few different motion models you can use when you're tracking a feature. **Motion Model** defines which motions a tracking feature has. This option should be set based on which motion a particular feature has; it will make tracking more accurate for such a motion. Here, we have **Location, Location & Rotation, Location & Scale, Location, Rotation & Scale, Affine**, and **Perspective**. I usually start a new track using **Location** but if that does not track well, I experiment with other motion models. For now, let's leave this set to **Location**.

- **Match**: Here, you can specify whether a tracker will try to match the tracked feature from **Keyframe** or **Previous frame**. I usually get better results when using **Previous frame** but feel free to experiment with both.

- **Prepass**: This setting enables two-pass tracking, where the first pass is a brute-force tracking of location only, while the second pass will use tracking of the full motion model to refine the first pass. I usually leave this option ticked.

- **Normalize**: With this setting active, patterns will be normalized by their average brightness intensity while tracking is taking place. An example where this is useful is in a scene where a marker moves into the shadow of another object. I usually leave this off by default and only activate it when required.

Next, let's expand **Tracking Settings Extra** and have a look at the available parameters:

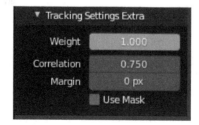

Figure 12.15 – Tracking Settings Extra

Here, we can change some advanced tracker settings, such as the weight of each tracker. The following concern the overall camera track, as well as the minimum tracker quality:

- **Weight**: Here, you can specify the influence of newly created trackers on the final solution. I usually leave this set to 1.000.

- **Correlation**: This value defines the minimum correlation between a matched pattern and a reference to be considered a successful track. A value of 0.750 will require a 75% match for a track to be successful. If the tracker stops too early, decrease this value; when a track is slipping too much, increase this value. I usually leave this on the default value of 0.750.

- **Margin**: Here, you can set the distance from the boundary or edge of the video where a marker will stop tracking. I usually leave this set to 0, which means that the tracker will stop when it gets to the edge of the frame.

When tracking, you need to consider a few things, as follows:

- Look for high-contrast features that will help Blender track the feature better.

- Track static objects! You don't want to track anything that moves – watch out for shadows of trees and so on.

- Try tracking features that stay inside the frame from the beginning of the shot until the end. This is not always possible but will make the tracking process a bit easier.

- You can either track forward or backward, depending on the feature you are tracking.

- The following are some useful shortcuts to know for tracking:

  - **Place new tracker**: Hold *Ctrl* + left click

  - **Track forward**: *Ctrl* + *T*

  - **Track backward**: *Shift* + *Ctrl* + *T*

  - **Track one frame forward**: *Alt* + right arrow

  - **Track one frame backward**: *Alt* + left arrow

- You can also make use of the tracking icons above the timeline if you don't know a specific shortcut:

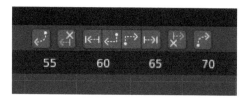

Figure 12.16 – Tracking icons are located above the timeline

Now that we have looked at the main tracking settings, we are ready to begin tracking our camera. Let's create our first tracker!

Placing trackers in the viewport

In this section, we will start tracking high-contrast features in our scene by placing trackers in the viewport. Let's get started:

1. Press *Shift* + left arrow to go to frame **1**.

2. Zoom into the ground area of the shot and look for a high-contrast point. For this example, I will track the cracked area on the floor.

3. Hover the mouse cursor over the feature you want to track, then hold *Ctrl* + left click to place your first tracker:

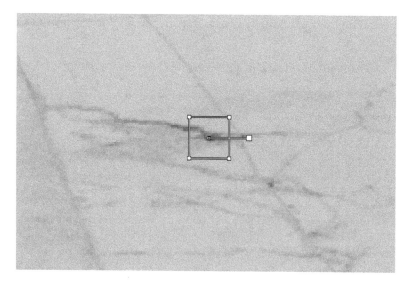

Figure 12.17 – Placing our first tracker on the cracks of the ground

You should now see a close-up of the feature you are tracking, in the side menu to the right of the viewport, as shown in the following screenshot. This close-up view is extremely handy when you're tracking as you can quickly see whether a tracker is slipping or jumping to another feature. Always keep your eye on this close-up view when you're running a track:

Figure 12.18 – Close-up view of the tracked feature

4. To start the track, press *Ctrl + T* or click the **Track Markers** icon with the arrow pointing to the right, located above the timeline.

    The feature will now be tracked from the first frame to the last frame. Keep an eye on the close-up tracker view to see whether the tracker sticks to the feature. The tracking process will be very quick, so I find it easier to scrub the timeline by clicking and dragging over the frame numbers above the timeline.

    You can also click and drag the frame number right below the viewport. Keep an eye on the close-up view of the tracker to see whether it's sticking to the feature you are tracking.

If you have any tracking issues, you can always delete the tracker by clicking next to it in the viewport and pressing *X*. Try not to click directly on the tracker when you're selecting it as this may move the tracker's points.

If you want to make any adjustments to **Tracker Settings**, first, make the adjustments, then place the tracker into the scene by holding *Ctrl* and clicking on a feature. This new tracker will then inherit the new tracker settings you have specified.

Once the tracking process has been completed, you should see a blue and red line connected to the tracker in the viewport, as shown in the following screenshot – this is the path of the tracker:

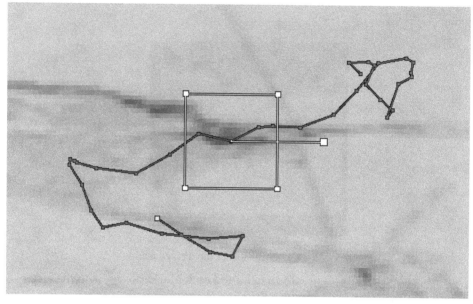

Figure 12.19 – The tracker's path is displayed in the viewport

You should also see position keyframes in the timeline connected by green and red lines, as shown in the following screenshot. These values show the tracker's position in the viewport. This is called the **graph view**:

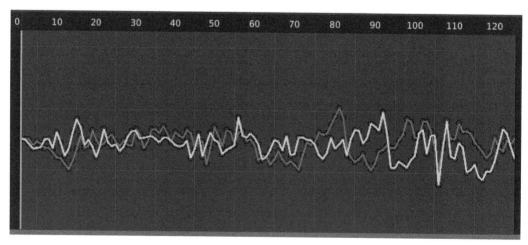

Figure 12.20 – The tracker's position keyframes are shown in the graph view/timeline

In the window to the top left of the interface, called **Dopesheet,** you will see your first tracker, as well as its keyframes. If the tracker successfully tracked through the whole clip, you should see a keyframe on the first and last frames, as shown in the following screenshot:

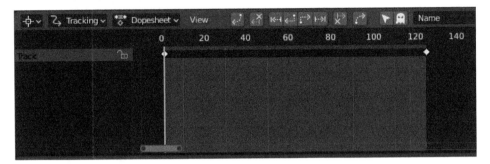

Figure 12.21 – All the trackers will be listed with their keyframes in the window to the top left of the interface

Once you are happy with your first tracker, it's time to create our second tracker. The total number of trackers depends on the shot, but I usually try to have at least 10-20 good trackers that overlap at any given time in the clip. Let's get started:

1. Press *Shift* + left arrow to go back to frame **1**.

2. Zoom in and pan around the viewport and find another high-contrast point on the floor area. Look for shadow corners or any feature that has high contrast.

3. Hover your mouse cursor over the feature and hold *Ctrl* + click to place a new tracker:

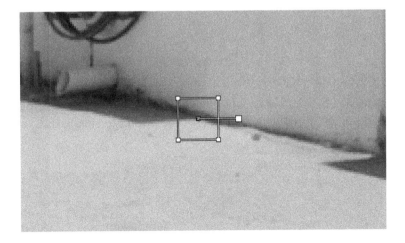

Figure 12.22 – Placing the second tracker in our scene

4.   Press *Ctrl + T* to track forward.

If the feature you are tracking goes off-screen, you can simply scrub the timeline to the last good keyframe, then click the **Clear Track Path** icon (the icon with an *X* and direction arrows) above the timeline to delete the remaining path of that track. You can either clear the track path forward (using the icon with an *X* and forward arrows) or backward (using the icon with an *X* and back arrows). We'll cover this in more detail later in this chapter.

Once you are happy with the second tracker, we can move on to the next!

5.   Press *Shift* + left arrow to go back to frame **1**.

6.   Let's find another tracking feature on the ground, then hold *Ctrl* + click to place the tracker:

Figure 12.23 – Placing our third tracker

7.   Press *Ctrl + T* to track forward.

8.   Scrub the timeline by clicking and dragging the frame numbers above the timeline while keeping an eye on the close-up view of the tracker to ensure that you have a good track.

Now, let's try tracking backward.

9. Press *Shift* + right arrow to go to the last frame of the clip.

10. Zoom in and pan around the viewport and find another high-contrast point on the floor. I am going to track the edge of this long crack, as shown in the following screenshot.

11. Hold *Ctrl* + click to place the tracker on the feature:

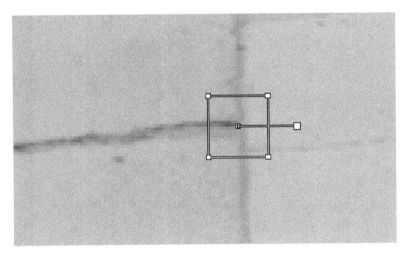

Figure 12.24 – Placing our fourth tracker

12. To track backward, press *Shift* + *Ctrl* + *T*.

13. Scrub the timeline while keeping an eye on the close-up view of the tracker to ensure that it's sticking to the tracked feature.

> **Tip**
> Remember, it's always better to have fewer good trackers than more bad trackers. One bad track can cause a bad overall camera track, so always ensure that each tracker is sticking well to its tracked feature. If a track is not sticking well, delete it and try adjusting the tracking settings or find a different feature to track in the scene.

Let's create our next tracker.

14. Press *Shift* + left arrow to go to frame **1**.

15. Pan and zoom around the viewport to find a new feature to track. This time, let's find a feature on the ground that's further away from the camera:

Figure 12.25 – Placing our fifth tracker

16. Hold *Ctrl* + click to place the tracker.

17. Press *Ctrl* + *T* to track forward.

18. Scrub the timeline to ensure you have a good track. Please save your project now!

Tracking features that go off-screen

For the next tracker, we're going to track a feature that will go off-screen. This is sometimes unavoidable, so let me show you how to do this. Let's get started:

1. Press *Shift* + left arrow to go to the first frame.

2. Pan and zoom around the viewport and look for a feature that goes off-screen during the clip.

   If you are using the clip provided, look for the rock to the right-hand side of the scene, on the edge of the shadow. This rock goes off the screen at around frame **80**:

Figure 12.26 – Tracking something that goes off-screen

3.   Hold *Ctrl* + click to place a tracker on the rock:

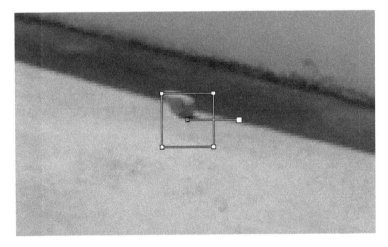

Figure 12.27 – Placing our sixth tracker

4.   Press *Ctrl* + *T* to track forward.

Notice that the track will stop as soon as the tracker gets close to the edge of the frame. My tracker stopped at frame **60**, but your tracker may stop at a different frame, depending on the **Pattern Size** parameter, as well as the **Margin** parameter under **Tracking Settings Extra**.

5.   Press the left and right arrow keys to find the last good, tracked frame. Keep your eye on the close-up view of the tracker while pressing the arrow keys.

6.   Click the **Clear Track Path** icon (the icon with the *X* and forward arrows, right above the timeline) to delete the tracker's path after the current frame. This will tell Blender that this is the final keyframe for this tracker.

Looking at **Dopesheet**, you will see all your trackers and their keyframes. Notice how the sixth tracker has a different end keyframe than the rest. To get good tracking results, have at least eight trackers overlapping at any given time:

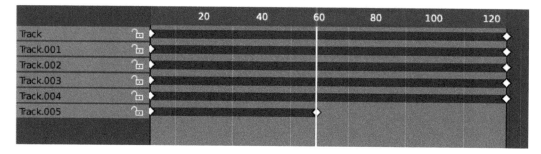

Figure 12.28 – The sixth tracker is only tracked halfway through the shot

For our next tracker, let's find something far toward the back of the scene. I'm going to track the corner of the small rectangular sign on the building in the far background. Let's get started:

1. Press *Shift* + left arrow to go to frame **1**.

2. Zoom in on the building in the background.

3. Hold *Ctrl* + click the corner of the sign on the building to place our seventh tracker:

Figure 12.29 – Placing our seventh tracker

4.   Press *Ctrl* + *T* to track forward.

5.   Ensure you have a good track by scrubbing the timeline.

Let's create a few more good trackers in our scene. I'm going to move a bit quicker now but follow the same process that we used previously – place a tracker, track forward or backward, and confirm that it's a good track by scrubbing the timeline. Let's get started:

1.   Go to frame **1** and track the yellow sign in the background:

Figure 12.30 – Tracking our eighth feature

2.   Go to frame **1** and track the small window on the building in the background:

Figure 12.31 – Tracking our ninth feature

3. Go to frame **1** and track the base of the furthest telephone pole:

Figure 12.32 – Tracking our tenth feature

4. Go to frame **1** and track the base of the other telephone pole:

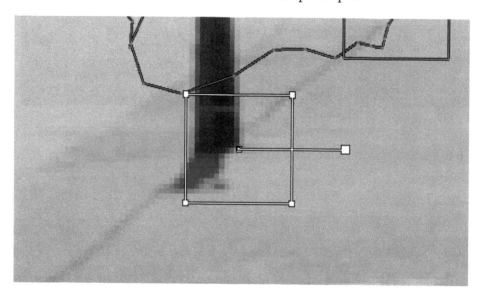

Figure 12.33 – Tracking our eleventh feature

5. Go to frame **1** and track the cross shadow/line on the ground:

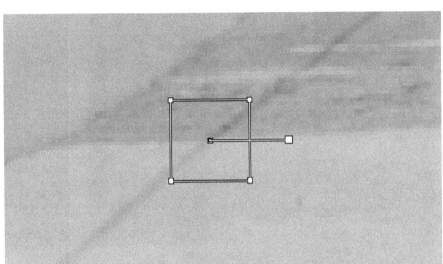

Figure 12.34 – Tracking our twelfth feature

This might be a tricky feature to track as it's not very high contrast. See whether you can get a successful track from this feature. I got a good track by using a **Pattern Size** value of 50 and a **Search Size** value of 100. Remember to set these values back to their defaults once you have tracked this feature (**Pattern Size**: 21/**Search Size**: 71).

6. Go to frame **1** and track the bottom corner of the door, to the right of the scene:

Figure 12.35 – Tracking our thirteenth feature

7. Go to frame **1** and track the switch next to the door, to the right of the scene:

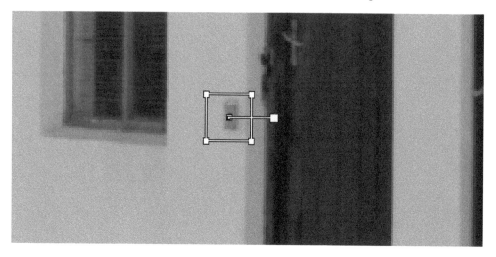

Figure 12.36 – Tracking our fourteenth feature

8. Go to frame **1** and track the corner of the sign above the steel gate:

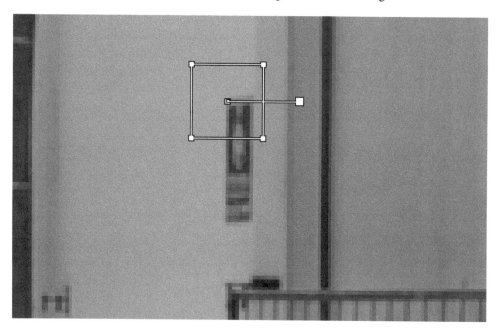

Figure 12.37 – Tracking our fifteenth feature

9. Go to frame **1** and track the corner shadow below the door, to the right of the scene:

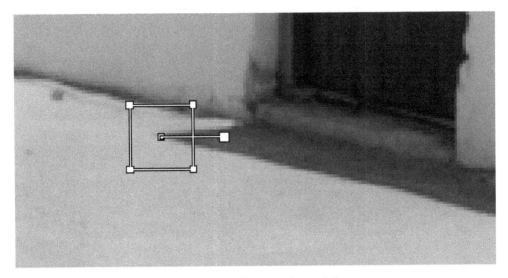

Figure 12.38 – Tracking our sixteenth feature

10. Go to frame **1** and track the red stop sign in the background:

Figure 12.39 – Tracking our seventeenth feature

How do you know when you have enough trackers in your scene? You need at least eight good trackers overlapping at any point in time. Make use of the **Dopesheet** view at the top left of the tracking workspace. Here, you can easily visualize all the trackers in your scene, over time. Make sure at least eight trackers are overlapping at any given time.

You may get an error message when you're solving the track if you have less than eight overlapping trackers. Please add more trackers to your scene if you do not have enough. Look at the following screenshot for a reference:

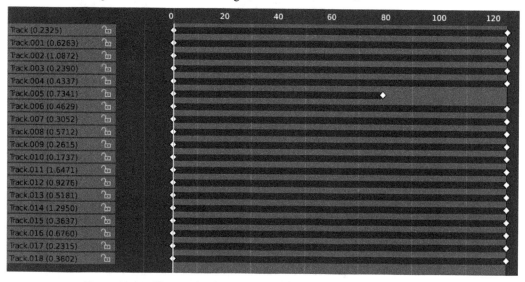

Figure 12.40 – You need at least eight tracks to be overlapping at any time

Congratulations! You should now have enough good trackers in the scene to create a good camera solution:

Figure 12.41 – All the trackers in our scene

Looking at the graph view, you will see each tracker's movement plotted on a graph:

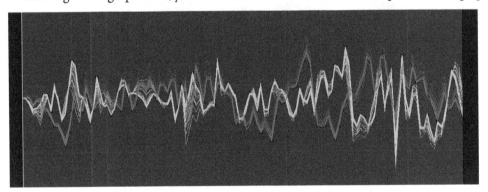

Figure 12.42 – The graph view showing each tracker's position over time

Finally, let's lock our trackers so that we don't accidentally move them around.

11. Hover your mouse cursor over the viewport and press *A* to select all the trackers in the scene.

12. Right-click in the viewport and click **Lock Tracks** from the drop-down menu. This will lock the trackers so that you can't move them.

Great – you have successfully created 18 good trackers in your scene. In the next section, you will learn how to solve the track, how to refine the track, as well as how to orient the scene. Please save your project now.

Solving and refining the track and orienting the scene

In this section, we will solve our camera track using the trackers from the previous section to create a tracked camera in our scene. Then, we will refine the track by making some adjustments and deleting any problematic trackers. This is an important step to ensure that the camera track is as accurate as possible.

Tracking errors or bad trackers can cause 3D objects to *slide* and not *stick* to the track – this will break the illusion that the 3D objects are really in the scene. Finally, we will orient our tracked scene so that it aligns with our grid.

Let's get started:

1. Click the **Solve** tab to the right of the viewport to open the **Solve** settings:

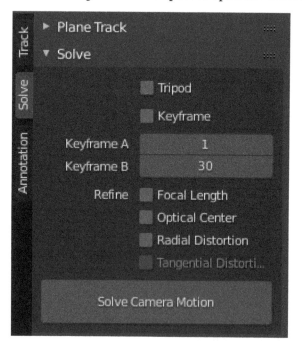

Figure 12.43 – The Solve settings to the right of the viewport

2. Click the **Solve Camera Motion** button to solve our camera track.

    You should now see the **Solve Error** value to the top right of the viewport. The lower this number is, the better. This value is measured in pixels. You should always try and aim for a value lower than 1, which means you have a great track! My **Solve error** is currently at 242.41, which is not good at all. Let's see how we can refine our camera solve and lower the **Solve error** value so that it's below 1:

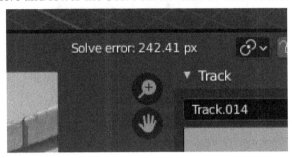

Figure 12.44 – The Solve error value is displayed above the viewport

    Looking at the graph below the viewport, you should see a blue line. This is our camera solve:

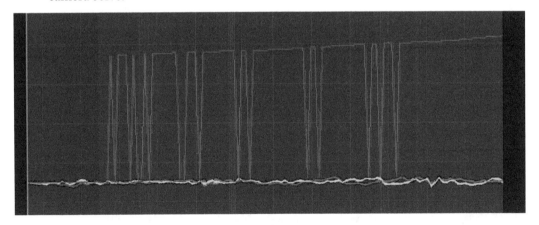

Figure 12.45 – The graph is displaying the camera solve in blue

    The closer the blue line is to the 0 value of the graph, the better the solve. Let's refine our camera solve to get a much better result.

    Let's adjust the **Keyframe A** and **Keyframe B** values under **Solve Settings** to the left of the viewport. These keyframes are used when we're solving the camera movement and it's usually a best practice to specify a section of the video clip where parallax is most noticeable. There should also be at least eight common trackers on both of the selected keyframes.

3. Set **Keyframe A** to 22 and **Keyframe B** to 96:

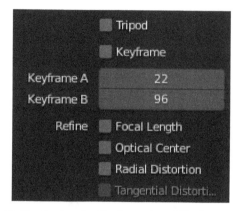

Figure 12.46 – Setting the Keyframe A and Keyframe B values

4. Let's click **Solve Camera Motion** again to re-solve our camera.

I am now getting a **Solve error** value of **0.58,** which is a great solve! Feel free to make adjustments to the **Keyframe A** and **Keyframe B** values until you get a good **Solve error** value:

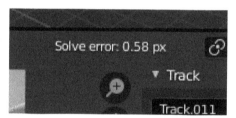

Figure 12.47 – A Solve error value of less than 1 means you have a great track

You will also notice that the blue line in the graph view is much closer to 0, which is great:

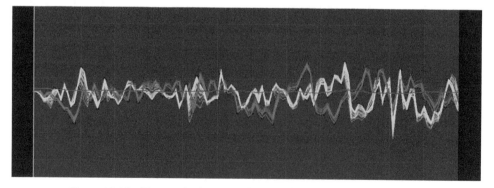

Figure 12.48 – The graph view now shows a blue line close to the 0 value

We can try to refine our track even more by letting Blender estimate the **focal length** that's used to film the scene.

5.   Tick the box next to **Focal Length** under the **Solve** settings:

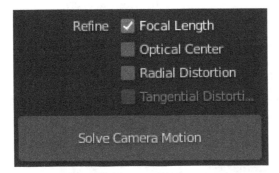

Figure 12.49 – Letting Blender estimate the focal length that's used to film the scene

6.   Click the **Solve Camera Motion** button again to re-solve our camera movement.

I'm now getting a **Solve error** value of 0.30, which is great:

Figure 12.50 – A low Solve error of 0.30 means you have a very good camera solve

To see the new focal length estimation, click the **Track** tab to the right of the viewport and expand the **Camera** section, then expand the **Lens** section. Here, you will see the new focal length that Blender estimated:

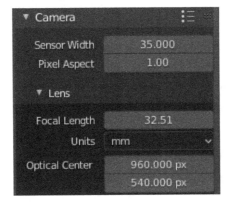

Figure 12.51 – Blender has estimated a new Focal Length value of 32.51

We can refine our camera solve more to get an even better result by deleting any bad trackers. Looking at Dopesheet (at the top left of the UI), you will see a list of all the trackers in your scene. Next to the name of each tracker is the **average error value** for that specific track. As you can see, the highest average error tracker is **Track.005** with a value of **0.6451**:

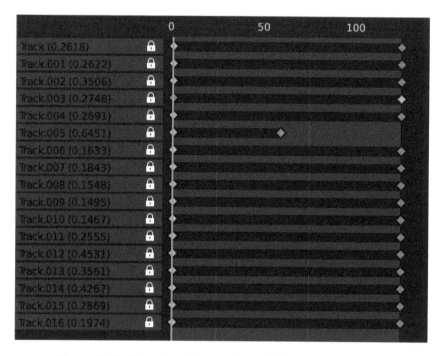

Figure 12.52 – Dopesheet shows each tracker's average error value

Let's see how we can delete the bad trackers from our scene:

1. First, let's unlock all our trackers so that Blender can delete the bad trackers. Hover your mouse over the viewport, then press *A* to select all the trackers in the scene.

2. Right-click anywhere in the viewport and select **Unlock Tracks** from the drop-down menu to unlock all the trackers.

3. Next, expand the **Clean Up** section under the **Solve** tab to the left of the viewport.

4. Click the **Clean Tracks** button.

5. Expand the **Clean Tracks** dialog box in the bottom corner of the viewport.

6. Set **Action** to **Select**. This means that the **Clean Tracks** process will only select the bad trackers in the scene and not automatically delete them.

7. Now, slowly increase the **Reprojection Error** value in the **Clean Tracks** dialog box to around 0.5. Hold *Shift* while dragging the value to increase it slowly:

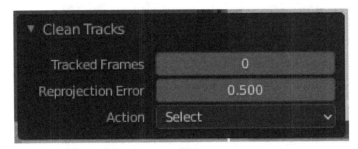

Figure 12.53 – The Clean Tracks dialog box

Notice that trackers with a higher error value will be automatically selected in the viewport. Setting the **Reprojection Error** value to 0.5 will only select trackers with an error value of 0.5 or higher. Let's delete these bad trackers.

8. With the bad trackers selected in the viewport, press *X* and select **Delete Track** to delete these trackers from our scene.

9. Now, click the **Solve Camera Motion** button again to re-solve the scene without the bad trackers.

    I am now getting a **Solve error** value of 0.23, which is amazing. As you can see, it's always better to have fewer, good trackers in the scene than more trackers with a higher error value. You can always add more trackers to the scene if needed and re-solve the camera motion until you have a good **Solve error** value.

Let's lock our trackers again so that we don't accidentally move them around:

1. Hover your mouse cursor over the viewport and press *A* to select all the trackers in the scene.

2. Right-click anywhere in the viewport and select **Lock Tracks** from the drop-down menu.

    Next, we're going to set the **Orientation** property of our scene so that the floor plane aligns with the grid.

3. Expand the **Orientation** section under the **Solve** tab to the left of the viewport:

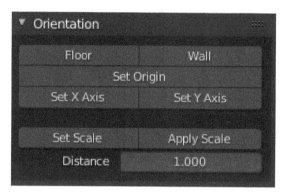

Figure 12.54 – The Orientation parameters

4. Select the three trackers in the viewport that are on the ground plane by holding *Shift* and clicking on the trackers.

5. Now, click the **Floor** button in the **Orientation** section. This will set the ground plane so that it aligns with the three trackers that you have selected.

6. Next, we're going to specify the middle or **Origin** of our scene. Select one tracker in the viewport that's on the ground plane, but also in the middle of the scene.

7. Click the **Set Origin** button so that it aligns this tracker with the world origin.

8. Next, let's specify the axis of our scene. Select one tracker that is on the ground, but further away from the **Origin** tracker, on the *Y* axis. This will align the selected tracker on the *Y* axis with the origin tracker.

9. Click **Set Y Axis** to align the selected tracker to the *Y* axis of our scene. The following screenshot shows my **Origin** and **Set Y Axis** trackers:

Figure 12.55 – The Origin and Set Y Axis trackers in the scene

10. Next, let's set the scale of our scene. Select two trackers in the scene by holding *Shift* and clicking them.

11. Set the **Distance** parameter (in meters) under the **Orientation** section to the left of the viewport. You can estimate the distance between the two trackers if you don't know the exact value:

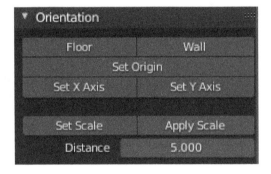

Figure 12.56 – Setting the Distance parameter between the selected trackers to a value of 5 meters

12. Click the **Set Scale** button to apply the scale value of the scene.

13. Expand the **Scene Setup** section under the **Solve** tab to the left of the viewport.

14. Finally, click the **Setup Tracking Scene** button to create the tracked scene:

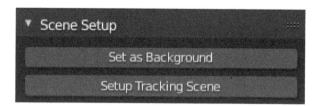

Figure 12.57 – Using Setup Tracking Scene to create the tracked scene

Now, we can go back to the **Layout** workspace and make some final adjustments to our scene's orientation by moving and rotating our camera to align the trackers to the grid as best as possible.

15. Click the **Layout** workspace at the top of the Blender interface.

You will notice that a cube, plane, and light were created in our scene. Let's delete the cube and the light as we don't need them:

Figure 12.58 – The tracked scene has been set up

1. Click the cube to select it in the 3D Viewport and press *X*. Click **Delete** to confirm this selection.

2. Click the light to select it in the 3D Viewport and press *X*. Click **Delete** to confirm this selection.

3. Click the **Overlays** drop-down at the top right of the 3D Viewport:

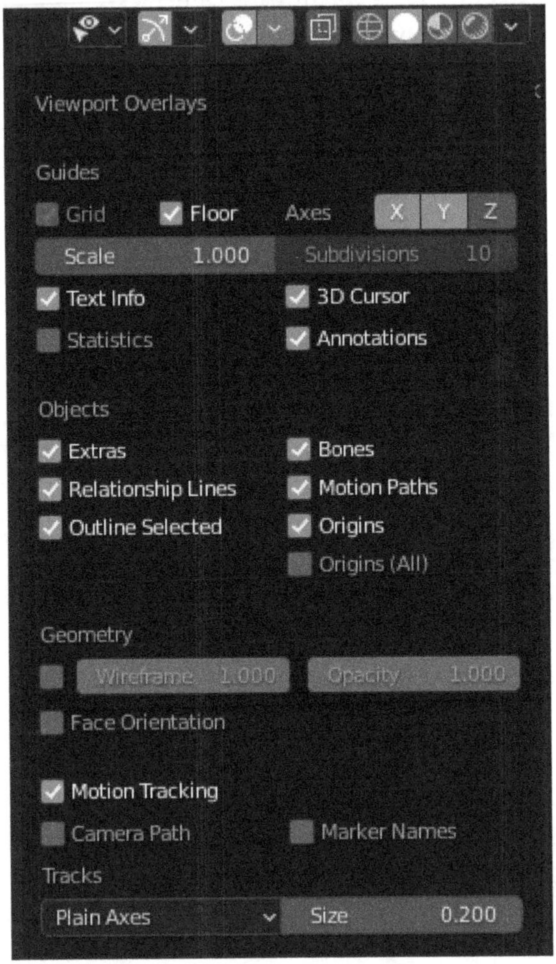

Figure 12.59 – The Overlay drop-down menu

4. Tick **Motion Tracking** at the bottom of the drop-down menu to show the trackers in the 3D Viewport.

You should now see the trackers in the 3D Viewport. Now, we can use these trackers and align them perfectly to our grid by rotating the camera. We want to ensure that the trackers on the ground are aligned with our floor grid:

Figure 12.60 – You should now see the trackers displayed in the 3D Viewport

Let's learn how to do this:

1. Press *1* on the numpad to switch to the **Front View** area:

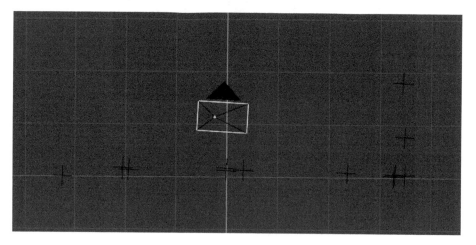

Figure 12.61 – Viewing the trackers from the Front View area

2. Click the camera to select it, then press *R* to rotate. Rotate the camera slightly until the trackers are best aligned to the red axis line.

3. Press *3* on the numpad to switch to the **Side View** area:

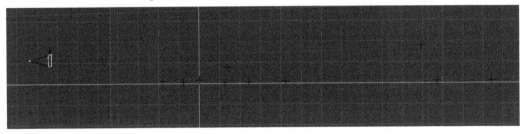

Figure 12.62 – Viewing the trackers from the Side View area

4. Click the camera to select it, then press *R* to rotate. Rotate the camera slightly until the trackers are best aligned to the green axis line.

    Next, let's align the *Z* position or height of the camera so that the floor plane aligns with our scene.

5. Press *0* on the numpad to look through the camera.

6. Click the frame of the 3D Viewport to select the camera – or select the camera in the **Outliner** section.

7. Press *G* then press *Z* and move your mouse slowly to adjust the height of the camera.

8. Try to align the floor plane with the ground and a wall in the scene so that the plane object is perfectly aligned with our scene:

Figure 12.63 – Adjusting the height of the camera to align the floor with our scene

9. Now, press *Spacebar* to play the sequence and see how the floor is moving with our scene.

Congratulations – you have successfully created a tracked camera in Blender! If the floor plane is not sticking to the scene, go back to the front and side views and make slight adjustments to the camera's rotation. Then, go back into the camera view and adjust the height of the camera. Do this until the plane aligns perfectly with the scene.

In the next section, we will add a few test objects into the scene to test our track. Please save your project now!

Testing the camera track with test objects

Once you are happy with the track, you can add test objects to your scene to test the camera track. This will ensure that any 3D objects that have been added to your scene will stick to the scene and be tracked with the moving camera. Let's get started:

1. First, let's hide the trackers from the 3D Viewport by clicking the **Overlays** drop-down menu at the top of the 3D Viewport.

2. Untick the box next to **Motion Tracking** to hide the trackers from the 3D Viewport.

3. Press *Shift + A*, then select **Mesh** and click **Cone** to add a cone object to our scene.

4. With the cone object selected, press *G* and then press *Z* and move the cone up so that its base is on the floor plane.

5. Duplicate the cone object a few times by pressing *Shift + D*. Then, move the copies around the scene. Ensure the bases of the cones are sitting on the floor plane.

6. Select the floor plane and press *H* to hide it from the 3D Viewport.

7. Now, press *Spacebar* to play the sequence. Notice how the cones are sticking to our scene:

Figure 12.64 – The cone test objects are moving with our scene

The scene will now play in the viewport and the 3D test objects should *stick* to the track and move with our camera.

Summary

Congratulations! You have successfully created a camera track in Blender. Camera tracking is one of the most powerful processes in the world of VFX. Once you have mastered the art of camera tracking, you will be able to add anything to your scene that you can imagine – think of Jurassic Park! As always, you need to practice this skill because every shot is different, and you will only get better with experience and lots of practice. Have fun creating amazing scenes!

In the next chapter, we will look at **compositing**. This is the process of making our 3D objects fit better into our real-world scene by adding shadows, lighting, and color grading effects. Please save your project now.

13
Compositing the Alien Cartoon Character onto the Live Action Footage

In this chapter, we're going to focus on **compositing**. Compositing is the process of combining different parts of your render into one final image or video. Compositing is extremely powerful because it gives you the ability to make adjustments to these different layers of your render without re-rendering the full image, which can save a lot of time. For instance, you can add image effects—such as color grading, hue and saturation, blur, and much more—to a certain object in your scene, such as a character or prop. You can even adjust the look of individual shadows.

In this chapter, we're going to composite our alien character with its walk-cycle animation from *Chapter 8, Rigging and Animating Your 3D Cartoon Character,* into the live-action scene that we tracked in *Chapter 12, Matching Blender's Camera Movement to Live Action Footage.*

These are the main topics we'll cover in this chapter:

- Importing our alien character and tracked camera into a new Blender project
- Matching the lighting to our live-action scene

- Configuring View Layers
- Compositing using nodes

Importing our alien character and tracked camera into a new Blender project

In this section, we will import our character with its walk-cycle animation, as well as the tracked camera, into a new Blender project. We will reuse the walk cycle and tracked camera to composite our character onto the live-action footage. Let's get started! Proceed as follows:

1. Create a new Blender project.
2. Delete everything in the scene by pressing *A* and then pressing *X* and clicking **Delete** to confirm.
3. Click **File | Append**.
4. Browse to the location where you have saved the Blender project we created in *Chapter 8, Rigging and Animating Your 3D Cartoon Character*.
5. Double-click on the .blend file to see its contents.
6. Double-click the Object folder.
7. Select the character from the list. I named my character Alien, but yours might be called something else.
8. Click **Append** to import the character into the new project. You can see a screenshot of this here:

Figure 13.1 – Importing your character into the new Blender project

9. In the **Outliner**, select all objects starting with **WGT**. Make sure you don't select the
    rig object because we want to keep the rig in the current collection.

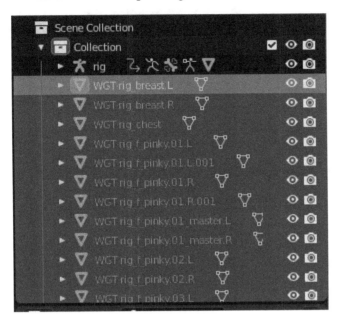

Figure 13.2 – Selecting all WGT objects in the Outliner

10. With all **WGT** objects selected, press *M* and click **New Collection**.

11. Name this new collection WGT and click **OK** to confirm.

12. Untick the box next to the new WGT collection in the **Outliner** to hide them from
    the viewport.

13. Now, save your project as Chapter13.blend.

Converting the tracked camera to keyframes

Before we can import the tracked camera from *Chapter 12, Matching Blender's Camera
Movement to Live Action Footage*, we need to convert the tracked camera to keyframes.
Let's do that now, as follows:

1. Open the Blender project that you saved at the end of *Chapter 12, Matching
    Blender's Camera Movement to Live Action Footage*.

2. Select **Camera** in the **Outliner**.

3. Click the **Object Constraint Properties** icon to the right of 3D Viewport.

4. Click the **Constraint to F-Curve** button to convert the camera's motion
    into keyframes.

You should now see the camera's keyframes in the timeline below 3D Viewport, as illustrated in the following screenshot:

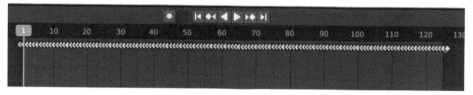

Figure 13.3 – The Camera keyframes are now shown in the timeline

5. Save this project as a new project and call it `Tracked_Camera`.

Importing the tracked camera into our new project

We are now ready to import this tracked camera into our new Blender project. Let's do that now, as follows:

1. Open the previous Blender project called `Chapter13.blend` that we created at the beginning of this section.
2. Click **File | Append**.
3. Browse to the `Tracked_Camera` project file that you saved in *Step 5* of the previous section.
4. Double-click the `Tracked_Camera.blend` file to view its contents.
5. Double-click the `Object` folder to view its contents.
6. Select the **Camera** object and click **Append**.

You can see the resultant output here:

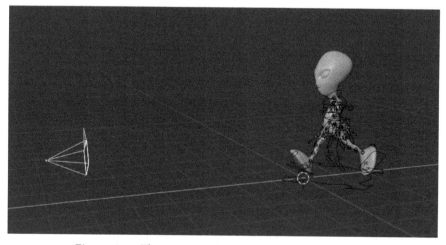

Figure 13.4 – The camera and character have been imported

The tracked camera has now been imported into the new Blender project. Press the *Spacebar* to preview the tracked camera's motion. Let's set our scene's frame duration to match our camera's animation of 125 frames. Proceed as follows:

1. Click the **Output Properties** icon to the right of 3D Viewport.

2. Set the **End** parameter to 125 to match the camera's animation duration, as illustrated in the following screenshot:

Frame Start	1
End	125
Step	1

Figure 13.5 – Setting the scene-frame duration to match the camera's animation

You will notice that the walk cycle of the character is shorter than the camera's animation of 125 frames. Let's loop our character's walk cycle to match our scene frame duration.

3. Select the character rig in 3D Viewport.

4. Press *Ctrl + Tab* to enter **Pose Mode.**

5. Press *A* to select all the rig controls.

6. Press *Ctrl + Tab* again to exit **Pose Mode.**

   With all the rig controls selected in **Pose Mode,** you will be able to see all of the keyframes in the timeline once you are back in **Object Mode.**

7. With the rig still selected in 3D Viewport, hover your mouse cursor over the timeline area where you see the keyframes.

8. Press *A* to select all the keyframes.

9. Press *Shift + D* to duplicate all the keyframes. Now, move the mouse to the right until the first duplicated keyframe is on top of the last keyframe.

10. Click to confirm the position of the duplicated keyframes. Your screen should now look like this:

Figure 13.6 – Duplicating the keyframes to loop the walk-cycle animation

11. Press *Spacebar* to preview the animation. The walk cycle should now run seamlessly until frame 125.

Importing the live-action image sequence

Next, we need to load the live-action image sequence so that we can position our character in the scene. Proceed as follows:

1. Select the **Camera** object in 3D Viewport.

2. Click the **Object Data Properties** icon to the right of 3D Viewport.

3. Tick **Background Images** if it's not ticked already.

4. Expand **Background Images** and click the **Movie Clip** button.

5. Click **Open**.

6. Browse to the **Image Sequence** live action that we used in *Chapter 12, Matching Blender's Camera Movement to Live Action Footage.*

7. Press *A* to select all the image-sequence files, then click **Open Clip**.

8. Under the **Background Images** section, increase the **Opacity** parameter to 1. This will set the opacity of the live-action footage in 3D Viewport to 100%. You can see this parameter in the following screenshot:

Figure 13.7 – Importing the live-action footage image sequence and setting the opacity to 1

9. Press *0* on the numpad to look through the camera. You should now see the live-action footage.

10. Press *Spacebar* to view the animation.

Positioning our character in the scene

Notice how our character's movement is matching the live-action footage using our tracked camera. Let's position our character in the scene, as follows:

Figure 13.8 – Our character should now match the live-action footage using our tracked camera

Next, proceed as follows:

1. Select the rig in 3D Viewport.
2. Press *Ctrl + Tab* to enter **Pose Mode**.
3. Select **Root Control** only (the circle with four arrows below the character).
4. Press *Ctrl + Tab* again to exit **Pose Mode**.

   We should now only see the keyframes of the **Root Control** in the timeline.

5. With the rig still selected, hover your mouse cursor over the timeline window and press *A* to select all keyframes if any are visible.
6. Press *X* and select **Delete Keyframes** to delete all keyframes on the root control.
7. Select the character rig in 3D Viewport and press *S* to scale the character down so that it matches the scene better.
8. With the rig still selected, press *G* and then *X* to move the character closer to the building on the right of the scene.

9. Now, press *G* and then *Y* to move the character back further away from the camera. Position the character next to the power box on the wall. Your scene should now look like this:

Figure 13.9 – Positioning the character in the scene

10. Go to frame 1 by pressing *Shift* + left arrow.

11. With the rig still selected, press *I* (for India) and select **Location** from the drop-down menu to create a location keyframe.

12. Go to frame 125 by pressing *Shift* + right arrow.

13. With the rig still selected, press *G* and then *Y* to move the character closer to the camera. Position the character next to the closest door to the camera.

14. With the rig selected, press *I* (for India) and select **Location** from the drop-down menu to create another location keyframe.

15. Hover your mouse cursor over the timeline and press *A* to select both keyframes.

16. Right-click in the timeline area, then select **Interpolation Mode** and click **Linear**. This will ensure that the motion of our character is constant. These settings are shown in the following screenshot:

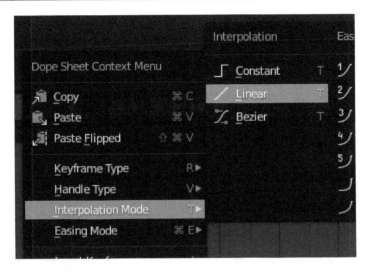

Figure 13.10 – Setting the keyframe interpolation mode to Linear

17. Select the rig in 3D Viewport and press *H* to hide it.

18. Press *Spacebar* to view the animation. The character should now walk from the power box on the wall toward the camera and stop at the door, as demonstrated in the following screenshot:

Figure 13.11 – Setting our character's walking start and end positions

19. Save your project now!

In the next section, we will match our scene's lighting with the lighting in the live-action footage. Feel free to add some materials to your character now. This won't be covered in this chapter as we have looked at adding materials in an earlier chapter, *Chapter 5, PBR Materials – Texturing our Mushroom Scene*. Be creative and add some color to your character. In the following screenshot, you can see an example of how your character could look:

Figure 13.12 – Adding materials to your character

Save your project once you are happy with the materials.

Matching the lighting to our live-action scene

In this section, we are going to set up lighting for our scene. It's important to try to match the lighting in your scene as best as you can with the lighting from the live-action footage to ensure that the shadows of your characters or props match the shadows in the live-action footage to create a realistic composite. Let's get started!

Let's first create a floor plane so that we can try to match the direction of the shadows of our character with the shadows from the live-action footage. We will later also use this plane as a **shadow catcher**. Follow these next steps:

1. Press *Shift + A* and select **Mesh | Plane** to create a new plane object.
2. Scale and move the plane on the *x* axis and align its edge to the wall of the building. Your scene should now look like this:

Figure 13.13 – Aligning the plane with the side of the building

3. Scale and move the plane object on the y axis until it fits the length of the building where our character will walk. You can see how this should look in the following screenshot:

Figure 13.14 – Scaling the plane object along the building

4. With the plane object selected, press *Tab* to enter **Edit Mode**.

5. Select the edge closest to the building and press *E* and then *Z* to extrude it up to the edge of the building's roof.

This plane object will allow us to cast a shadow—from the character—on the floor and the side of the building, as illustrated in the following screenshot:

Figure 13.15 – Extruding the plane's edge upward

6. Press *Tab* to exit **Edit Mode**.

7. With the floor object selected, press *Ctrl* + *A* and select **Scale** to apply the scale of the plane. Always good practice!

Great! We now have a plane object that we will use to cast shadows from our character onto the live-action footage.

Adding an HDRI image to light our scene

Let's set up our environment lighting. We will use a **High Dynamic Range Imaging** (**HDRI**) image to provide the ambient lighting in our scene. Proceed as follows:

1. Click the **Shading** workspace tab at the top of the interface.

2. Click the **Object** drop-down menu in the top-left corner of the **Shader Editor** and select **World**.

3. Select the **Background** node in the **Shader Editor** and press *Ctrl + T* to create an **Environment Texture** node as well as a **Mapping** node and **Texture Coordinate** node. For this shortcut to work, you need to enable the **Node Wrangler** add-on using **Blender Preferences**. You should then see a **World** shader tree, as follows:

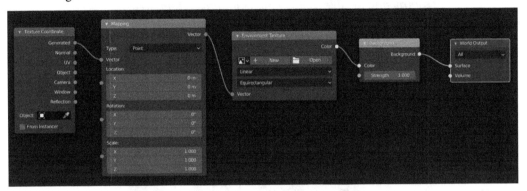

Figure 13.16 – The World shader tree should look like this

4. On the **Environment Texture** node, click **Open** and browse to an HDRI image that matches the scene.

There are many websites that offer free HDRI images for you to use. Simply google `Free HDRI`. I personally use `https://polyhaven.com/hdris`, which has a great selection of high-quality, free HDRI images. I'm going to use an HDRI called **Ulmer Muenster** that you can find on Polyhaven's website.

To see the HDRI image and lighting in our scene, we need to switch over to the **Cycles Render** view. Let's do that now, as follows:

1. At the top of 3D Viewport, click the sphere icon to the right to switch to **Render View**. You can also use the *Z* shortcut and select **Rendered** from the radial menu.

2. Click the **Render Properties** icon to the right of 3D Viewport.

3. Set **Render Engine** to **Cycles**.

Here is Blender's official description of the **Cycles** render engine:

> *"Cycles is Blender's physically-based path tracer for production rendering. It is designed to provide physically based results out-of-the-box, with artistic control and flexible shading nodes for production needs."*

> *–https://docs.blender.org*

Let's enable Viewport denoising so that we get a cleaner, noise-free render in 3D Viewport. Proceed as follows:

1. Expand the **Sampling** section, then expand **Denoising**.

2. Tick the boxes next to **Render** and **Viewport** to enable denoising for both the Viewport and when we do a render. You can see an illustration of this here:

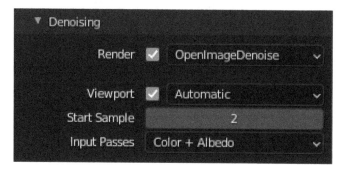

Figure 13.17 – Enabling Render and Viewport denoising

There are three different denoising algorithms in Blender 2.9—**NLM, OptiX,** and **OpenImageDenoise. NLM** is the **Cycles** native denoiser that can run on most hardware. **OptiX** uses **graphics processing unit (GPU)** acceleration but is only available on supported Nvidia GPUs. **OpenImageDenoise** uses Intel's Open Image Denoise, an **artificial intelligence (AI)** denoiser that runs on the **central processing unit (CPU)**.

1. Press *0* on the numpad to look through the camera.

2. Press *Spacebar* to play the animation, then press *Spacebar* again to stop when the character is closer to the camera.

You should now see the HDRI image lighting our scene, as illustrated in the following screenshot. Let's try to match the sun's direction to that of our live-action footage:

Figure 13.18 – The HDRI image is now lighting our scene

To see the live-action footage in 3D Viewport, instead of the HDRI image, we need to enable the **Transparent** setting under **Render Properties**. Proceed as follows:

3. Expand **Film**.

4. Tick the box next to **Transparent**, and you should now see the live-action footage in 3D Viewport, as illustrated in the following screenshot:

Figure 13.19 – Enabling Transparent to see the live-action footage

Look at the shadows in the live-action scene. Notice that the sun is directly above and in front of the camera. The shadow of the telephone pole is directly in line with the *y* axis of our scene. Let's try to match our HDRI's sun to the real sun in the scene.

5. Back in the **Shader Editor**, focus on the **Mapping** node. We're going to adjust the **Z Rotation** value of our HDRI to rotate it around our scene, changing the direction of the sun.

6. Click and drag the **Z Rotation** value until the character's shadow is in front of him. I used a **Z Rotation** value of 205 degrees to get his shadow in front of him and slightly on the side of the building. Your **Z Rotation** value might be completely different. Try to match the following reference screenshot:

Figure 13.20 – Matching the direction of the HDRI's sun to the real-world sun

7. Once you are happy with the HDRI's rotation, click the **Layout** tab at the top of the interface to return to the **Layout** workspace.

8. Switch to **Rendered** view by pressing *Z* and selecting **Rendered** from the radial menu.

    You can easily adjust the strength of the HDRI from the **World Properties** panel.

9. Click the **World Properties** icon to the right of 3D Viewport and expand **Surface**.

10. Adjust the **Strength** parameter to increase or decrease the brightness or strength of the HDRI. I found that a value of 1 works well.

Experiment with the **Strength** value and try to match the brightness of your scene. You can always change this value later. Our lighting setup is basically complete! Feel free to add more lights to the scene if required, but for this specific scene, an HDRI might be all that we need.

If your live-action scene has more lights, try to add lights that match their position, color, and intensity. Have fun matching your **three-dimensional (3D)** lights to real-world lights. In the next section, we will configure our **View Layers**. Please save your project now!

Configuring View Layers

In this section, we're going to set up View Layers. View Layers are used to split your scene into different render layers so that we have access to different parts of our scene, such as our character and shadows. Rendering separate layers allows you to make adjustments to individual objects when doing compositing. This can be extremely powerful. Let's get started!

First, we're going to create our **shadow catcher**. A shadow catcher will allow us to overlay the shadows of our 3D objects onto the live-action footage. Proceed as follows:

1. Select the **Plane** object in 3D Viewport.

2. Click the **Object Properties** icon to the right of 3D Viewport.

3. Scroll down and expand **Visibility**.

4. Tick the box next to **Shadow Catcher**.

   Immediately, you should see a change in 3D Viewport. The **Plane** object is now transparent, and you can see the character's shadows being cast onto the live-action footage. Notice how the character's shadow is also visible on the side of the building! You can see this here:

Figure 13.21 – Setting the Plane object as a shadow catcher

There are a few more settings we can adjust here. We can choose if our **Shadow Catcher** object will bounce diffuse light back onto our character. We can also control if the **Shadow Catcher** object will reflect onto our character if we have any glossy materials applied to our character.

5. Expand the **Ray Visibility** section.

Here, you will see a list of different rays you can enable or disable, as illustrated in the following screenshot. Disabling **Diffuse** will stop indirect light from bouncing back onto your character. Disabling **Glossy** will prevent the **Shadow Catcher** object from reflecting onto our character. For this scene, I will leave all these rays enabled. Experiment and see how these rays affect the look of your character model:

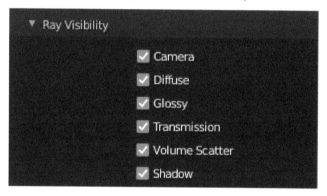

Figure 13.22 – The different Ray Visibility parameters

Using collections to separate render elements

Let's create separate **collections** for the elements we want to render separately. This will make it easier to group different objects together and keep the **Outliner** neat and tidy. Proceed as follows:

1. In the **Outliner**, expand the character's **rig** object.

2. Click the **rig** object, then press *Shift*, and click the last object under the **rig** object. You can see an illustration of this process in the following screenshot:

Figure 13.23 – Selecting the rig object and everything under it

3. Press *M* to move these objects to their own collection.

4. Name this new collection `Character` and click **OK** to confirm.

5. Select the **Plane** object in the **Outliner**.

6. Press *M* to move it to its own collection.

7. Name this new collection `Floor`, as illustrated in the following screenshot, and click **OK** to confirm:

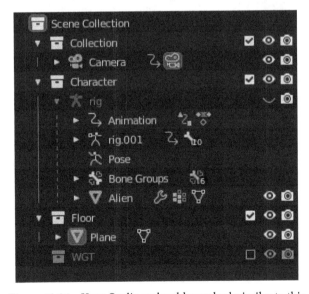

Figure 13.24 – Your Outliner should now look similar to this

Now, we can set up the **View Layers** so that we can render our scene in different layers. We want to render our character on one layer while rendering the shadows on their own layer. This will allow us to adjust these elements individually when we begin compositing. You will find the **View Layer** drop-down menu at the top right of the interface, as illustrated in the following screenshot:

Figure 13.25 – The View Layer drop-down menu

8. Click the **Add View Layer** button to the right of **View Layer** and select **New** from the drop-down menu.

9. Click **View Layer.001** to rename this View Layer. Let's call it Character as this layer will only render our character.

10. Click the **Filter** icon at the top of the **Outliner** and enable **Indirect Only**. This is the bounce-arrow icon to the right, as shown in the following screenshot. This will allow us to toggle **Indirect Lighting** only on certain collections in our scene:

Figure 13.26 – Enabling the Indirect Only toggle from the Filter drop-down menu

11. In the **Outliner,** click the **Indirect Only** icon next to the Floor collection to exclude it from the render but still allow indirect lighting from the floor object. This will render only the character on the current View Layer.

12. Untick the box next to the WGT collection to hide it from 3D Viewport.

13. You can also hide the **rig** object inside the Character collection, as illustrated in the following screenshot:

Figure 13.27 – The Character View Layer

14. Click the **Add View Layer** button again to add our second View Layer. Select **New** from the drop-down menu.

15. Rename this View Layer Shadow as this layer will only render the shadow of our character.

16. Now, enable the **Indirect Only** icon next to the Character collection to exclude it from this View Layer.

17. Untick the box next to the WGT collection to hide it from 3D Viewport.

18. You can also hide the **rig** object inside the Character collection, as illustrated in the following screenshot:

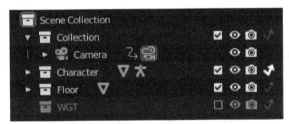

Figure 13.28 – The Shadow View Layer

19. Click the drop-down menu at the top of the **Outliner**, next to the **Shadow View Layer**, to see a list of all our View Layers. The following screenshot shows the list we have so far:

Figure 13.29 – We have three View Layers in our scene

As you can see, we now have a total of three View Layers: **View Layer**, which will render everything in our scene. **Character**, which will only render our character, and **Shadow**, which will only render our shadows.

20. Select **View Layer** from the drop-down menu.

21. Rename this **View Layer** All as it contains everything in our scene. You can see this View Layer in the following screenshot:

Figure 13.30 – Renaming the View Layer All

Let's take a moment to look at the different render passes that you can output for each View Layer. **Render passes** are individual elements or layers that make up a final render, such as direct and indirect lighting, and much more! You can specify different render passes for each of the View Layers we have created. Here's how you can do this:

1. Click the **View Layer Properties** icon to the right of 3D Viewport.

2. Expand the **Passes** section.

   Here, you will see a list of all the available **render passes** that the **Cycles** renderer offers, as illustrated in the following screenshot. We're not going to cover most of these passes in this chapter, but feel free to enable them to experiment once we do compositing:

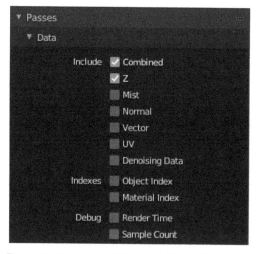

Figure 13.31 – Some of the available render passes

3. With the **All** View Layer active, scroll down and tick the box next to the **Ambient Occlusion** render pass under the **Light / Other** section. This will enable the **Ambient Occlusion** render pass only for the **All** View Layer.

The reason we're enabling the **Ambient Occlusion** pass is that we're going to make use of the overall scene ambient occlusion when we do compositing in the next section.

4. Click the **Output Properties** icon to the right of 3D Viewport.

5. Expand the **Output** section.

6. Set the **File Format** parameter to **PNG**.

7. Set the **Color** parameter to **RGBA**. This will ensure that we render an alpha channel for transparency.

We can now do a render test to see if our View Layers are working correctly. We're going to render a single frame, so scrub through the timeline and find a frame that you like. Please save your project now, then proceed as follows:

1. Click **Render** at the top of the interface and select **Render Image** from the drop-down menu.

The renderer will now render each View Layer as a separate render or layer. Allow a few moments for the renders to complete.

2. You can view different View Layers by clicking the drop-down menu at the top of the render window, as illustrated in the following screenshot:

Figure 13.32 – The View Layer drop-down menu shows the different View Layers available

3. Select each of the View Layers from the drop-down menu and see how the render changes. The **All** option should show the character and its shadow, the **Character** option should only show the character with no shadow, and the **Shadow** option should only show the character's shadow. You can see some screenshot examples of these three View Layers here:

Figure 13.33 – The three View Layers

4. Press *Esc* to exit the Render View and return to the **Layout** workspace.

Congratulations! You have now configured three different View Layers so that you have access to the individual elements when doing compositing. In the next section, we will begin the compositing process to combine the different elements into a final rendered image or video. Please save your project now!

Compositing using nodes

In this section, we're going to composite the different View Layers of our character's render back into a single image or video. We're also going to import the image sequence of our live-action footage and overlay our character onto that footage. We're going to add color effects and adjustments to the individual parts of our render to create our final render. Let's get started!

Rendering out one frame

First, we need to render out one frame. This can be any frame, so choose wisely. This will load the different View Layers into memory so that we can use them in the Compositor node tree. Proceed as follows:

1. Choose a frame where the character is well in frame. Scrub the timeline and position the play head on that frame.

2. Click the **Render Properties** tab to the right of 3D Viewport.

3. Expand the **Sampling** section.

4. Set the **Render** parameter to at least 128 samples. You can increase this value if required, but for now, you just want enough samples for a nice, clean render.

5. Expand the **Denoising** section.

6. Tick the box next to **Render** and choose a denoiser from the list. If you are not sure which denoiser to choose, select **OpenImageDenoise** from the list. If you have an Nvidia GPU, then choose **OptiX**. In the following screenshot, **OpenImageDenoise** has been selected:

Figure 13.34 – Setting the render samples

7. Click the **Output Properties** tab to the right of 3D Viewport.

8. Expand the **Output** section.

9. Set the **File Format** parameter to **PNG**.

10. Set the **Color** parameter to **RGBA** to ensure we render an alpha channel, as illustrated in the following screenshot:

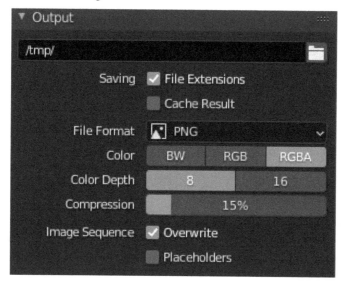

Figure 13.35 – Output parameters

Note that we do not have to specify an output file path as we are rendering to memory only.

11. Save your project.

12. Now, click **Render** at the top of the interface and select **Render Image** from the drop-down menu to render each of our **View Layers**.

Wait a moment for the render to complete—notice that each View Layer will render after the other.

13. Once the render is complete, click the **View Layers** drop-down menu at the top of the render window to see a list of all the View Layers, as illustrated in the following screenshot:

Figure 13.36 – The View Layers drop-down menu at the top of the render window

14. Toggle through all three View Layers to see each of the renders.

The **All** View Layer contains the alien character with its shadow, as illustrated here:

Figure 13.37 – The All View Layer

The **Character** View Layer contains the character only without any shadows, as illustrated here:

Figure 13.38 – The Character View Layer

The **Shadow** View Layer contains shadows only, as we can see here:

Figure 13.39 – The Shadow View Layer

15. Press *Esc* to close the render window.

16. Save your project now.

Now that we have rendered our View Layers, we can jump over to the **Compositing** workspace and start the compositing process.

Initiating the compositing process

In this section, we'll switch over to the **Compositing** workspace and start configuring the compositing nodes. Proceed as follows:

1. Click the **Compositing** tab at the top of the interface to open the **Compositing** workspace.

2. Tick **Use Nodes** at the top of the **Compositor** window, which appears in the middle of the workspace.

   The compositor window is where we will add nodes to create our final composition. By default, you should see two nodes: a **Render Layers** node and a **Composite** node. The **Render Layers** node is the input, where we can choose our different View Layers, while the **Composite** node is the final output. Let's see how we can use the different View Layers to create a final image.

   First, let's create a **Viewer** node so that we can see the final results as we work.

3. Hover your mouse cursor over the **Compositor** window and press *Shift + A* to display the **Add** window. Here, you can either browse or search for nodes, similar to the Shader Editor.

4. Click **Search** and search for a **Viewer** node. Position this node below the **Composite** node, as illustrated in the following screenshot:

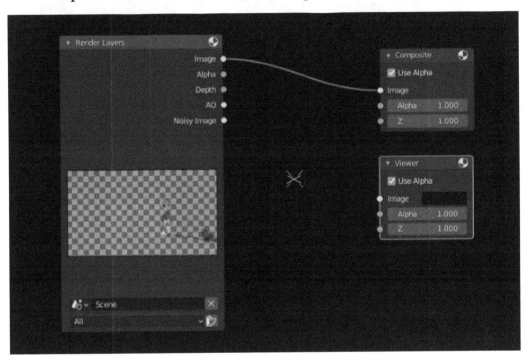

Figure 13.40 – Adding a Viewer node

5. Press *Shift + A* and search for `Reroute`.

6. Position this **Reroute** connector on the line between the **Render Layers** node and the **Composite** node.

7. Now, *connect* the **Reroute** connector to the **Image** input on the **Viewer** node, as illustrated in the following screenshot:

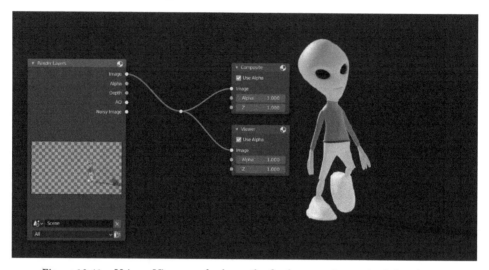

Figure 13.41 – Using a Viewer node shows the final composite as a backdrop image

You will now see the final output that the **Composite** node receives in the **Compositor** window behind the nodes.

Changing the backdrop image

Let's change the way our backdrop image is displayed. By default, Blender uses **Filmic**. Let's change this to **Standard** to get a more accurate result. Then, proceed as follows:

1. Click the **Render Properties** tab to the right of the **Compositor** window.

2. Scroll down and expand **Color Management**.

3. Change the **View Transform** parameter to **Standard**, as illustrated in the following screenshot:

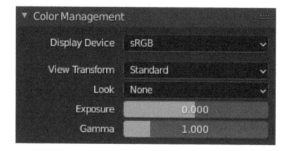

Figure 13.42 – Setting the View Transform parameter to Standard

4. To zoom in/out on or reposition the backdrop image, make use of the side menu (*N* shortcut key) and click the **View** tab. You will find all the controls needed to move and zoom in/out on the backdrop image, as illustrated in the following screenshot:

Figure 13.43 – The side menu has controls for zooming and moving the backdrop image

5. At the bottom of the **Render Layers** node is a drop-down menu where you can choose between different View Layers. Select **Character** from the list.

You will see the composite backdrop image has updated, showing our character without any shadows, as illustrated here:

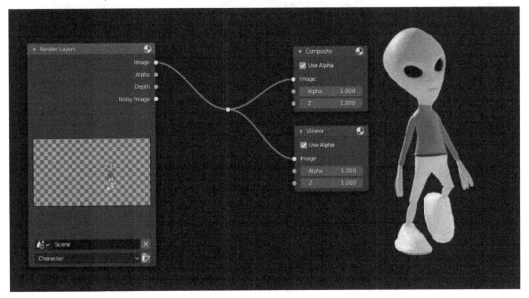

Figure 13.44 – The Character View Layer is now being rendered

Let's see how we can place the **Shadow** View Layer below our character. Proceed as follows:

1. Select the **Render Layers** node and press *Shift + D* to duplicate the node. Position the new node under the current **Render Layers** node.

2. On the new duplicated **Render Layers** node, click the drop-down menu at the bottom of the node and select the **Shadow** View Layer from the list, as illustrated in the following screenshot:

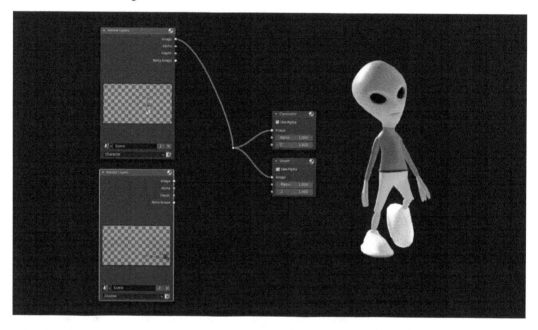

Figure 13.45 – We now have two Render Layers nodes in our tree

Now, we need to merge or join these two nodes together. For this, we will be using an **Alpha Over** node.

3. Press *Shift + A* and search for Alpha Over. Position this node somewhere between the **Render Layers** nodes and the **Composite** node. Do not connect it to any line yet.

    The **Alpha Over** node has two image inputs. The bottom image input will be placed over or above the top image input. This can be slightly confusing at first, so let's see how it works. We want to composite our **character** over the **shadow**. So, we need to connect the **Shadow** View Layer to the top image input and the **Character** View Layer to the bottom image input to get the correct result.

4. Connect the image output from the **Shadow Render Layers** node to the top image input of the **Alpha Over** node.

5. Connect the image output from the **Character Render Layers** node to the bottom image input of the **Alpha Over** node. This will place our character above the shadow.

6. Connect the image output of the **Alpha Over** node to the **Reroute** connector, as illustrated in the following screenshot:

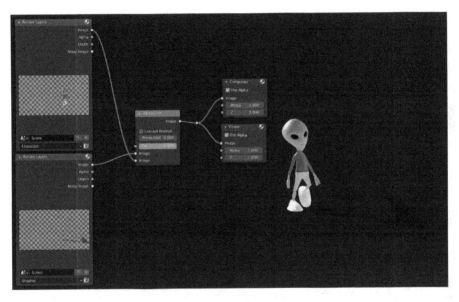

Figure 13.46 – Our character is now rendered over its shadow

Let's load our live-action image sequence and composite our character onto it.

7. Press *Shift + A* and search for the **Image Sequence** node.

8. Browse to the folder containing the live-action image sequence.

9. Press *A* to select all images in the sequence and click **Import Image Sequence**.

10. Position this node above the **Character Render Layers** node.

You can make adjustments to the image sequence on this node, such as the number of frames or the frame offset, but we will leave everything as default.

11. Create another **Alpha Over** node and position it to the right of the current **Alpha Over** node. You can also duplicate the current **Alpha Over** node by selecting it and pressing *Shift + D*.

12. Connect the first **Alpha Over** node's image output to the bottom image input of the second **Alpha Over** node. This might sound complicated, but remember that we want to place our character and his shadow *over* the live-action footage.

Please see the following reference screenshot to ensure that you are connecting the two **Alpha Over** nodes correctly:

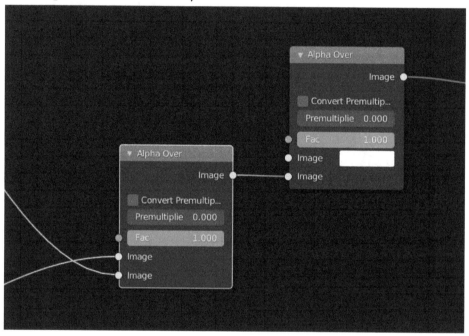

Figure 13.47 – Connecting the two Alpha Over nodes together

13. Connect the image output of the **Image Sequence** node to the top image input of the second **Alpha Over** node. This will place the live-action footage behind our character and shadow, which is exactly what we want. You can see how this should look here:

Figure 13.48 – Our character and shadows are now composited over the live-action footage

See the following reference screenshot of the node tree:

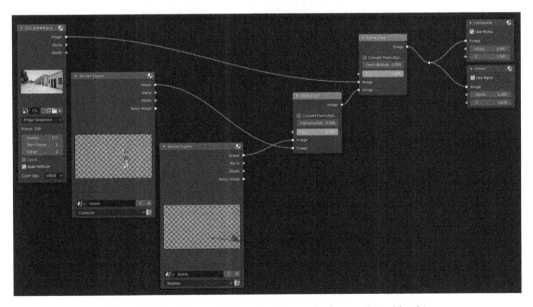

Figure 13.49 – Your node tree should now look something like this

Color grading the live-action footage

We now have full, individual control of each layer—the live-action footage, our character, and his shadow. Let's see how we can color grade the live-action footage without affecting the rest of the render layers. Proceed as follows:

1. Create a new **RGB Curves** node and position it on the line connecting the **Image Sequence** node and the second **Alpha Over** node.

2. Make a slight S-Curve using the **RGB Curves** node to add some contrast to the live-action footage without affecting the character or the shadow layers, as shown in the following screenshot:

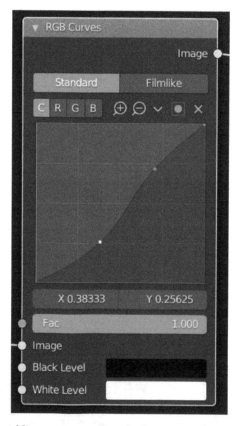

Figure 13.50 – Adding contrast to a render layer using the RGB Curves node

Notice here how the contrast of the live-action footage has increased without affecting the character:

Figure 13.51 – The RGB Curves node can add contrast to an image

3. Select the **RGB Curves** node and press *M* to toggle the node on and off to see how it affects our composition.

    Let's see how we can adjust the exposure of our character. Currently, he is a bit bright for the live-action footage.

4. Create a new **Exposure** node and place it on the line connecting the **Character Render Layers** node to the first **Alpha Over** node.

5. Adjust the **Exposure** value and see how it affects the exposure of the character in the scene. I find that a value of -0.9 works well. Experiment until you are happy with the composition. Here's what my scene now looks like:

Figure 13.52 – Adjusting the exposure of the character using the Exposure node

Next, we can match our character's saturation with the saturation of the live-action footage.

6. Create a new **Hue Saturation Value** node and place it on the line between the **Exposure** node and the **Alpha Over** node.

7. Adjust the **Saturation** value and see how it only affects the saturation of the character. I find that a value of 0.9 matches our scene better. Experiment until you are happy with the results. Here's what my scene now looks like:

Figure 13.53 – Adjusting the saturation of the character until you are happy with the results

Let's see how we can make adjustments to the shadow. We can increase or decrease its intensity, and we can even blur the shadow without affecting any of the other layers in our scene. To increase the shadow's intensity, we need to adjust its alpha value.

To do this, we need to separate the **red-green-blue-alpha** (**RGBA**) channels and make an adjustment to the alpha channel only before combining the RGBA channels again. Sounds complicated, but it's actually quite easy.

8. Create a new **Separate RGBA** node and place it on the line between the **Shadow Render Layers** node and the **Alpha Over** node.

9. Create a new **Combine RGBA** node and place it on the line between the **Separate RGBA** node and the **Alpha Over** node.

10. Connect the RGBA channels between the **Separate RGBA** node and the **Combine RGBA** node, as shown in the following screenshot:

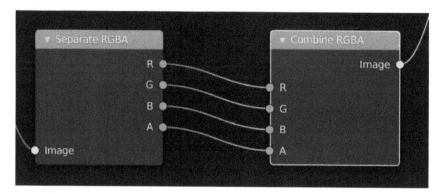

Figure 13.54 – Connecting the RGBA channels between the two nodes

You won't see any difference yet as we still need to modify the value of the alpha channel to adjust the shadow's intensity. To do this, we're going to use a **Math** node and multiply the alpha value with the custom value we set.

11. Create a new **Math** node and place it on the line connecting the **A** output with the **A** input.

12. Set the operator of the **Math** node to **Multiply**, as shown in the following screenshot:

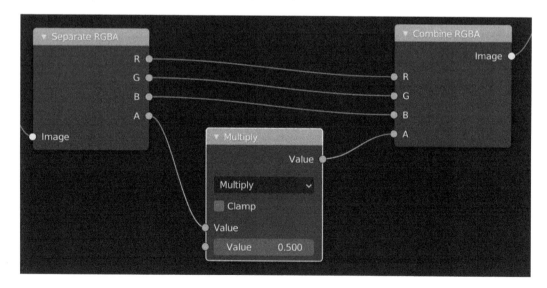

Figure 13.55 – The Math node now controls the shadow's intensity

You will notice the shadow is now slightly less intense because we are multiplying the shadow's alpha value by 0.5, making it less opaque. If we set the **Value** parameter to 1, we should see the shadow's original intensity. Increasing the **Value** parameter to anything above 1 will make the shadows more opaque or darker.

I find that a value of 1.5 works well. Experiment until you are happy with the shadow intensity. You can also tick the **Clamp** value if your shadows are overlapping each other. This will ensure the shadows are consistent in their opacity.

Try to match the look of the shadow to the following reference screenshot:

Figure 13.56 – The shadows are now slightly darker

Great! Our character and live-action footage are looking good, but let's see how we can make the shadows a bit more realistic.

Blurring shadows

We can also blur shadows without affecting the background. Let's do that now. Remember to save your project! Proceed as follows:

1. Create a new **Blur** node and place it on the line between the **Combine RGBA** node and the **Alpha Over** node, as illustrated in the following screenshot:

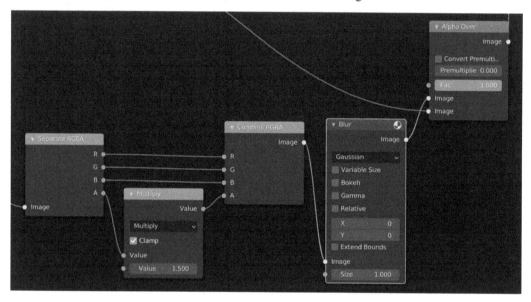

Figure 13.57 – Placing the Blur node after the Combine RGBA node

2. On the **Blur** node, set the **X** and **Y** values to 15, as illustrated in the following screenshot. This is the amount of blur we're adding horizontally and vertically. Feel free to experiment with the other values to see how it affects the image:

Figure 13.58 – The Blur node

Notice how the shadow of our character is blurred. Adjust the **X** and **Y** values until you are happy with the results. This is what my scene now looks like:

Figure 13.59 – Creating a soft shadow by using the Blur node

See the following reference screenshot of the node tree:

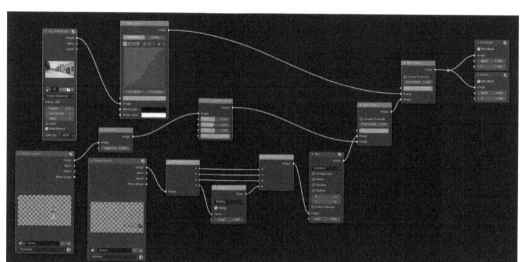

Figure 13.60 – Your node tree should now look something like this

We can also make use of the **Ambient Occlusion** render pass to control shadow areas in our scene, such as contact shadows. We can use this pass to make these shadows darker or lighter.

Notice in the following screenshot how the **Ambient Occlusion** pass is a grayscale image. We can use these pixel values to make adjustments to the overall shadows in our scene:

Figure 13.61 – The Ambient Occlusion render pass can be used to highlight shadows

Let's do that now, as follows:

1. Create a new **Render Layers** node and position it close to the second **Alpha Over** node in our node tree.

2. Click the drop-down menu at the bottom of the **Render Layers** node and select the **All** View Layer from the list. We want to use the **Ambient Occlusion (AO)** pass from the scene (**All**) View Layer.

    Next, we will need a **Mix** node to overlay the **Ambient Occlusion** pass on top of our exciting image.

3. Create a new **Mix** node and position it on the line to the right of the second **Alpha Over** node. You will notice the backdrop turns white. This is because by default, the **Mix** node has values of white, and the lower value will be overlayed over the top value. This is similar to the **Alpha Over** node. You can see an illustration of this in the following screenshot:

Figure 13.62 – The Mix node

4. Connect the **AO** output on the **Render Layers** node to the bottom image input on the **Mix** node.

5. Change the **Mix** node parameter from **Mix** to **Multiply**. This will use **Multiply** as the blending mode.

6. Now, connect the **Alpha** output of the **Render Layers** node to the **Fac** input on the **Mix** node, as shown in the following screenshot:

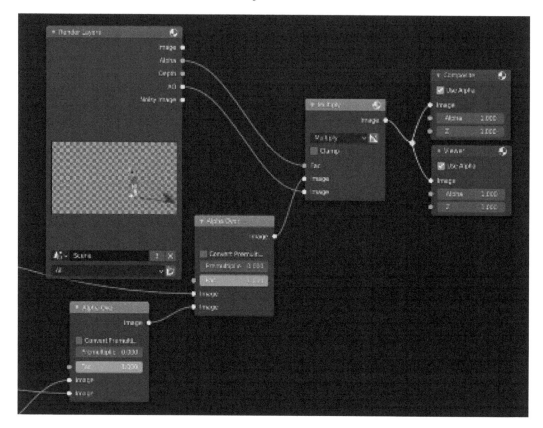

Figure 13.63 – Overlaying the AO render pass over our image

See how the shadows in the scene, such as the contact shadows, are now more visible. This might give the desired effect, but let's see how we can adjust the intensity of this AO overlay.

7. Create a new **Math** node and position it on the line between the **Alpha** output of the **Render Layers** node and the **Fac** input on the **Mix** node. This will allow us to control the alpha value of the AO pass.

8. Change the function of the **Math** node to **Multiply** and set the value to 0.5. This will set the intensity of the AO pass to 50%, which might look more realistic. Experiment with this value until you are happy with the results. Here's what your node tree should look like now:

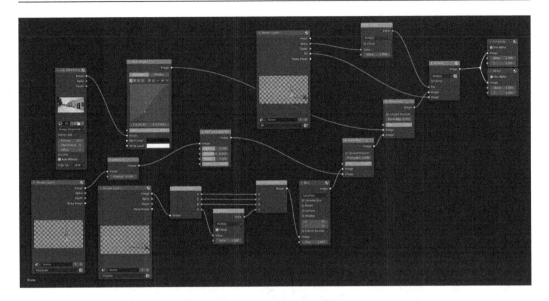

Figure 13.64 – Your node tree should now look something like this

Compositing is all about experimenting with different nodes and values to adjust the look and feel of your final render. There is so much you can do with compositing to change the feel—or even emotion—of a scene.

Color grading our image

Let's see how we can color grade our image, adding lens distortion as well as a vignette to make our final image a bit more dramatic. Please save your project now, then follow these next steps:

1. Create a new **Color Balance** node and position it on the line, to the right of the **Mix** node. We want to affect our final composite.

    Now, I could write a whole book on color balance and color grading, so I am not even going to try and explain too much on this subject. All you have to know for now is that you can make color adjustments to the darker parts, the mid-range parts, as well as the bright or highlights of an image.

Use the color wheels to adjust color, and the vertical sliders to adjust the brightness. Let's add some blue tones to the shadows and orange to the highlights of our composite. Try to match the following reference screenshot. Feel free to experiment here:

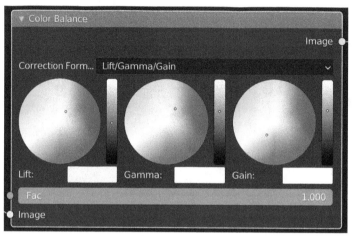

Figure 13.65 – The Color Balance node is used for color grading/correcting

2. With the **Color Balance** node selected, press *M* to toggle the node on and off. See the difference that a little color grading can do! This is what my scene now looks like:

Figure 13.66 – Color grading our image using the Color Balance node

3. Add a **Lens Distortion** node and position it on the line, to the right of the **Color Balance** node. This node can add some lens imperfections to our image, which can make it more realistic-looking.

4. Set both the **Distort** and **Dispersion** values to 0.01, which will give a very slight lens distortion and color separation effect. Experiment and see how it affects the image.

5. Enable **Fit** to resize the image to fit the frame, as illustrated in the following screenshot:

Figure 13.67 – The Lens Distortion node

And lastly, let's create a vignette effect to darken the edges of our final render. This makes the image more dramatic or can focus the viewer's attention on an area of the frame.

6. Create a new **Alpha Over** node and position it on the line, to the right of the **Lens Distortion** node.

7. On the **Alpha Over** node, change the bottom image color from white to black, as illustrated in the following screenshot:

Figure 13.68 – The Alpha Over node

The backdrop image will now turn black. This is because we are overlaying a black solid color over our composite with this **Alpha Over** node. Let's build our vignette.

8. Create a new **Ellipse Mask** node and place it below the **Alpha Over** node.

9. Connect the **Mask** output of the **Ellipse Mask** node to the **Fac** input of the **Alpha Over** node.

We are now using the **Ellipse Mask** node to control how we overlay the black solid color over our composite, as illustrated in the following screenshot. You should see a black ellipse on the backdrop image:

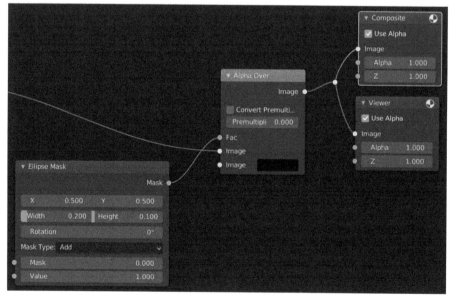

Figure 13.69 – Using the Ellipse Mask node as the factor value

10. On the **Ellipse Mask** node, increase both the **Width** and **Height** values until the mask touches the edge of the image on the image, as shown in the following screenshot:

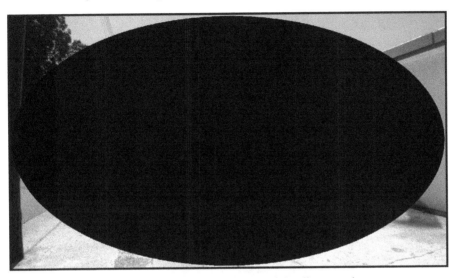

Figure 13.70 – Increasing the size of the ellipse mask

11. Create an **Invert** node and place it on the line, between the **Ellipse Mask** node and the **Alpha Over** node. Notice the mask has inverted! My scene now looks like this:

Figure 13.71 – The mask is now inverted

12. Create a new **Blur** node and place it on the line, between the **Invert** node and the **Alpha Over** node, as illustrated in the following screenshot:

Figure 13.72 – The Blur node

Set both the **X** and **Y** values to 2 0 0 to blur the mask so that we have a nice and soft vignette effect. Experiment with this value, as well as the **Ellipse Mask** size, to get a look you are happy with. Here's my scene now:

Figure 13.73 – The Blur node softens the ellipse mask

13. Create a new **Math** node and position it on the line, between the **Blur** node and the **Alpha Over** node.

14. Set the **Math** node's function to **Multiply**.

We can now control the intensity of the vignette by adjusting the **Multiply** value. 1 will give us a 100% opaque vignette, while 0 will give us no vignette.

15. Set the **Multiply** value to 0.5 for a nice vignette effect. Experiment with this value and see what works for your render. Here's my scene now:

Figure 13.74 – Our final composite

Compositing can be extremely powerful, and we have only scratched the surface of what is possible. Try experimenting with the nodes that we didn't discuss in this chapter and see how they affect the image. Read up on render passes and see how you can use many other passes to affect certain aspects of the image, such as reflections and direct or indirect lighting.

Also, refer to the Blender manual to see which new nodes are available in the version of Blender that you are using. And most importantly, have fun creating your masterpiece!

The following screenshot shows the final compositing node tree:

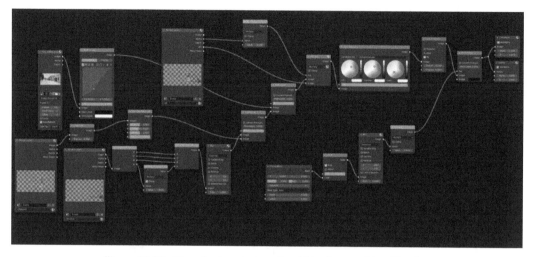

Figure 13.75 – Your final node tree should look something like this

Summary

Congratulations! You have now successfully composited your cartoon character into a live-action shot using different nodes to make adjustments to our final image. This workflow is extremely powerful, as you can imagine, giving you full control over different areas of your scene to create the final look and feel of your shot. You can even do basic color grading right inside of Blender!

In the next and final chapter, we will render our final video. Please save your project now.

14
The Final Render

In the final chapter, we're going to render our final animation! Now that we have completed the compositing stage, we can render our animation as an image sequence. Then, we're going to create an MP4 video from the image sequence for final delivery or for uploading to our favorite social media website. It's important to have a good overall understanding of the different render settings as this can both increase the quality of your final render and reduce the render time.

In this chapter, we will cover the following topics:

- Understanding the render settings
- Rendering an animation as an image sequence
- Converting the image sequence into an MP4 video

Let's get started!

Understanding the render settings

In this section, we will open our Compositing Blender project from *Chapter 13, Compositing the Alien Cartoon Character onto the Live Action Footage*, and configure the final render settings so that we can render or save the final animation to individual image files. Each frame of our animation will be rendered as an image file. Let's get started:

1. Open the Blender project that you saved in *Chapter 13, Compositing the Alien Cartoon Character onto the Live Action Footage*.

2. Click the **Layout** tab at the top of the interface to switch to the **Layout** workspace.

3. Click the **Render Properties** tab to the right of 3D Viewport to view the render settings.

    Blender has two main render engines – **Cycles** and **Eevee**. We will make use of the Cycles render engine for our final render as Cycles is Blender's unbiased, realistic render engine.

4. Under the **Render Properties** panel, set **Render Engine** to **Cycles**.

5. If you have a dedicated GPU (graphics card), set **Device** to **GPU Compute**. This will utilize your GPU for faster renders.

6. Expand **Sampling** and set the **Render Sample** count to 128.

    The amount of render samples directly relates to the final quality of your render. The more samples you use, the cleaner your final image will be and it will have less noise. However, more samples means longer render times. Experiment with different sample amounts and see what results you get. There is a fine balance between sample count, quality, and speed. I usually use a sample count of between 128 and 512.

7. Check the box next to **Adaptive Sampling** to reduce the render time by automatically reducing samples for certain pixels, based on their estimated noise levels.

8. Expand **Denoising** and check the box next to **Render** to enable denoising on your final render.

    Blender has an amazing denoising algorithm that can produce super clean renders. The denoiser filters the rendered image using information (known as **feature passes**) to remove noise while preserving details as best as possible. Blender comes with three different denoisers – **Non-Local Means** (**NLM**), OpenImageDenoise, and Optix.

    NLM is the slowest option and requires a high sample count and is mostly used for still renders. OpenImageDenoise is great if you are using the CPU for rendering or a non-NVidia GPU. Optix is the fastest denoiser but requires a compatible NVidia GPU.

9. Click the drop-down menu next to **Render** (under **Denoising**) and select the denoiser best suited for your hardware. Choose **OpenImageDenoise** if you don't have an NVidia GPU or choose **Optix** if you have a compatible NVidia GPU.

10. Set **Input Passes** to **Color + Albedo**. This will help preserve finer details when you're denoising but will take slightly longer to denoise than choosing **Color** alone:

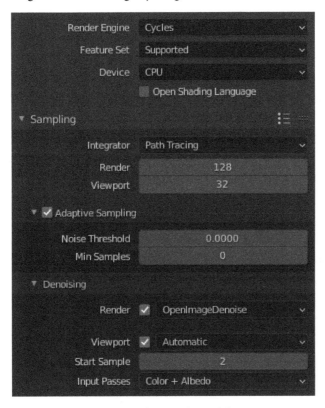

Figure 14.1 – Render samples and denoising

11. Expand **Light Paths** and then expand **Max Bounces**.

    The **Max Bounces** section lets us specify the number of light bounces in our scene. More light bounces will result in better-looking indirect lighting but will also increase the render time. Let's look at this section in more detail:

    •   **Total**: The maximum number of light bounces in your scene. I usually leave this as the default value of 12 but feel free to experiment with lower values. A value of 0 will result in direct lighting only.

- **Diffuse**: The maximum number of diffuse light bounces. I usually use a default value of 4 but again, feel free to experiment with different values and see how it affects your final render.

- **Glossy**: The maximum number of glossy light bounces. The default value of 4 should be good but experiment with different values.

- **Transparency**: The maximum number of transparency light bounces. The default value of 8 should be good but experiment with different values to see how it affects the final render.

- **Transmission**: The maximum number of transmission bounces. The default value of 12 should be good, but feel free to experiment with different values to see how it affects the final render.

- **Volume**: The maximum number of volume scattering bounces. The default value of 0 should be good, but feel free to experiment with different values to see how it affects the final render.

These can be seen in the following screenshot:

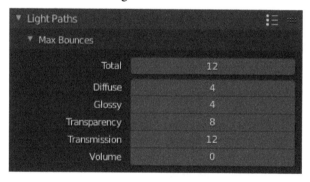

Figure 14.2 – Max Bounces render settings

You can also enable **Motion Blur** in **Render settings**, which will produce a realistic motion blur for moving objects and cameras in your scene.

Enabling Motion Blur

Let's learn how to enable **Motion Blur**:

1. In the **Render Properties** panel, scroll down until you see **Motion Blur**.
2. Expand the **Motion Blur** section.
3. Check the box next to **Motion Blur** to enable it in your renders.

4. The **Shutter** parameter determines the amount of motion blur in the render – a bigger value will produce more motion blur while a smaller value will produce less motion blur. A **Shutter** value of 0.5 will produce a natural-looking motion blur, but experiment with this value and see how it affects your render:

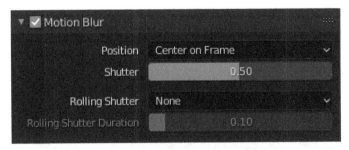

Figure 14.3 – Enable Motion Blur

5. Next, expand the **Film** section under the **Render Properties** panel.

6. Check **Transparent** to hide the HDRI from the render:

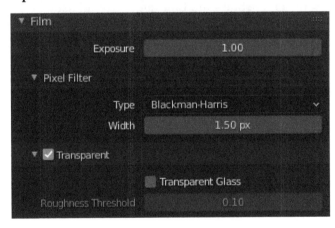

Figure 14.4 – Enabling Transparent to hide the HDRI in the scene

Next, we need to set our render's **Resolution, Frame Duration, Output Path**, and **File Format**. Let's do this now.

7. Click the **Output Properties** tab to the right of 3D Viewport.

8. Expand **Dimensions**.

9. Here, you can set the render resolution. We're going to render at a standard HD resolution of 1,080 px. Set the **X** parameter to `1920` and the **Y** parameter to `1080`.

The output resolution depends on the final destination of your render. If you require a 1:1 or square video, you can use a resolution of 1080 x 1080. If you need a vertical video, you can use a resolution of 1080 x 1920. Google is your friend if you need a specific aspect ratio or resolution for a specific device:

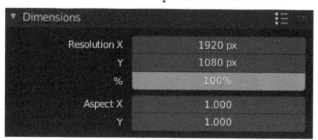

Figure 14.5 – Setting the resolution to 1080 px

10. Next, we can set the **Frame Start** and **End** values. My animation has a total of **125** frames, so I will set my **Frame Start** value to `1` and the **End** value to `125`. Match these frame numbers to the duration of your animation:

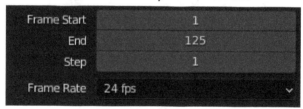

Figure 14.6 – Setting the Frame Start and End values

We don't have to set the **Frame Rate** value because we're exporting an image sequence. The **Frame Rate** value is only required when you're exporting to a video file format.

11. Expand the **Output** section. This is where we can specify the folder where the image sequence will be saved.

12. Click the **Folder** icon under the **Output** section.

13. Browse to a folder where you want to save the image sequence and click **Accept**.

14. Set **File Format** to **PNG**. This is usually a good format to use as an image sequence.

15. Set the **Color** parameter to **RGB** as we do not require an Alpha channel for our final render.

16. You can set **Color Depth** to 8 bit, which should be good enough for most renders. Experiment with a 16-bit value if required.

17. Set the **Compression** value to `15%`. This will produce a slightly smaller PNG file with a compression of 15%:

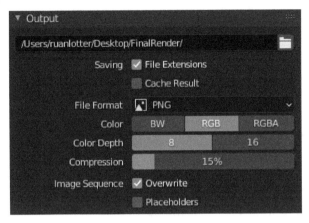

Figure 14.7 – The render Output parameters

Great – with that, we have configured the render and output settings! In the next section, we will render the image sequence to the folder we have specified. Please save your project now.

Rendering an animation as an image sequence

We are now ready to start rendering our animation, including the compositing, to a PNG image sequence. Let's do this now:

1. Click the **Render** drop-down menu at the top of the interface.

2. Select **Render Animation** from the drop-down menu to begin the render process:

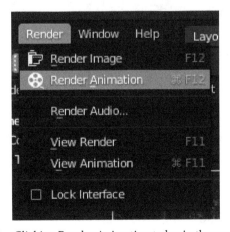

Figure 14.8 – Clicking Render Animation to begin the render process

The rendering process can take quite some time, depending on your hardware. Making use of a GPU will drastically decrease your render time. Each frame will be rendered as a PNG sill image.

In the next section, we will convert the image sequence into an MP4 video file.

Converting the image sequence into an MP4 video

In this section, we will take the image sequence and convert it to an MP4 video file format for easy sharing. Let's get started:

1. Open a brand-new Blender project.

2. Click the + symbol at the top of the interface, to the right of the workspace tabs:

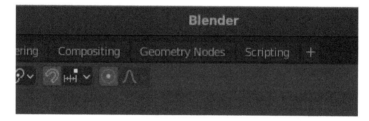

Figure 14.9 – The + symbol next to the workspace tabs

3. Select **Video Editing** from the drop-down menu. This will open the **Video Editing** workspace:

Figure 14.10 – Switching to the Video Editing workspace

The **Video Editing** workspace can be used for any type of video editing. We are going to use it to combine all the PNG images that we have rendered into a single MP4 video file.

4.   Hover your mouse cursor over the timeline area and press *Shift + A* to open the **Add** menu.

5.   Select **Image/Sequence** from the **Add** menu to import the image sequence.

6.   Browse to the folder containing the PNG image sequence that we have rendered.

7.   Press *A* to select all the PNG images in the folder. Then, click **Add Image Strip** to import the sequence:

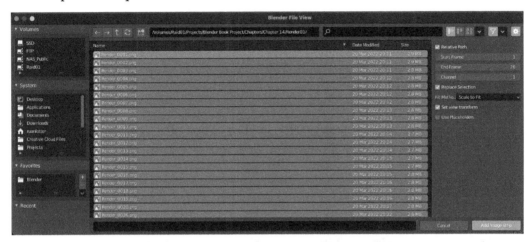

Figure 14.11 – Importing the PNG image sequence

The imported image sequence will now appear as a clip on the timeline! Press *Spacebar* to play the video:

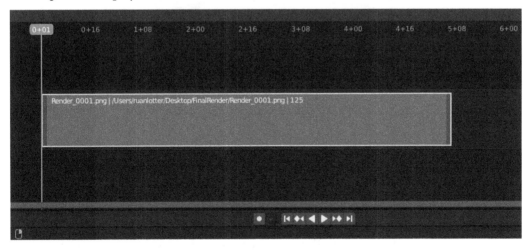

Figure 14.12 – The image sequence clip in the timeline

Next, let's set our video output settings. Here, we need to specify the resolution, frame range, and frame rate for our MP4 video.

1. Click the **Output Properties** tab to the right of the main video **Preview** – this panel might be open already.

2. Under **Dimensions**, you can set the resolution of the video. Let's render a 1080 px MP4 file – set the **X** parameter to 1920 and the **Y** parameter to 1080:

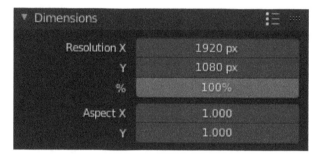

Figure 14.13 – Setting the output resolution of the video file

3. Set the **Frame Start** parameter to 1 and the **End** parameter to the total number of frames in your sequence. I am using a value of 125.

4. Now, we can set the **Frame Rate** property of the video. Feel free to use any required frame rate – I'm going to match the frame rate of the live-action footage. I know that I set the camera to 24 FPS, so I will use a frame rate of 24 for the final video:

Figure 14.14 – Setting the frame range and frame rate

5. Click the folder icon under the **Output** section.

6. Browse to a folder where you want to save the MP4 video.

7. Give your video a name. Then, click **Accept**.

8. Click the drop-down menu next to **File Format** and select **FFmpeg Video** from the list.

9. Expand the **Encoding** section. This is where we will set the video codec settings.

10. Set the **Container** parameter to **MPEG-4**.

11. Under **Video**, set **Video Codec** to **H.264**.

12. Set **Output Quality** to **High Quality**.

13. Now, we are ready to render our final animation – please save your project now:

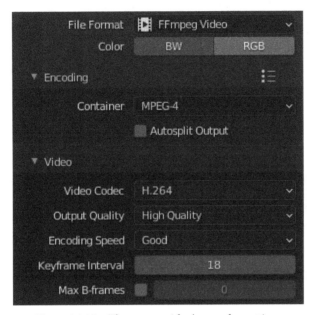

Figure 14.15 – The output video's encoder settings

14. Click the **Render** drop-down menu at the top of the interface and select **Render Animation** from the list.

Congratulations! With that, you have rendered your final animation as an MP4 file that you can easily share with friends and family or upload to your favorite social media sites or apps.

Summary

In this chapter, you successfully modeled, rigged, and animated a cartoon character. You tracked a live-action shot and composited your animated character onto live-action footage. Finally, you rendered your animation as a high-quality PNG image sequence and converted it into an MP4 file that you can easily share. By doing this, you have learned all the basics of an extremely powerful workflow that you can use to create anything that you can imagine!

Remember, the world of 3D is massive, so you may not be interested in all the different aspects of it. If that is true for you, then find something you like and that you enjoy doing, then improve and practice that specific skill. This all depends on your end goal. If you are trying to secure a job position at a big studio, then it might be wise to become an expert in one specific field, such as a 3D Modeler, Texture Artist, Rigging Artist, Matchmover/ Camera Tracker, or a Compositor, to mention a few.

But if you plan to run a studio, become a 3D freelance artist, or even a VFX supervisor, then it might be better to get a good overview and basic understanding of the whole process. Play around with the different aspects of 3D such as animation, rigging, texturing, lighting, physics, particles, camera tracking, and rendering to get a good understanding of the overall process.

This will assist you when you're communicating with artists if you choose to become a VFX supervisor, or it will give you the ability to create amazing projects all on your own. The 3D world is your UV unwrapped and perfectly textured oyster. Use your new skills wisely and, most importantly, have massive amounts of fun converting your ideas into VFX masterpieces.

Never stop creating!

Index

W

walk cycle animation
  about 273, 274, 350, 351
  inverted keyframes, creating 282, 283
  key pose number four,
    setting up 280, 281
  key pose number one,
    setting up 274-277
  key pose number three,
    setting up 279, 280
  key pose number two, setting up 278
  looping 283, 284
weight tool 368

`Packt.com`

Subscribe to our online digital library for full access to over 7,000 books and videos, as well as industry leading tools to help you plan your personal development and advance your career. For more information, please visit our website.

Why subscribe?

- Spend less time learning and more time coding with practical eBooks and Videos from over 4,000 industry professionals

- Improve your learning with Skill Plans built especially for you

- Get a free eBook or video every month

- Fully searchable for easy access to vital information

- Copy and paste, print, and bookmark content

Did you know that Packt offers eBook versions of every book published, with PDF and ePub files available? You can upgrade to the eBook version at `packt.com` and as a print book customer, you are entitled to a discount on the eBook copy. Get in touch with us at `customercare@packtpub.com` for more details.

At `www.packt.com`, you can also read a collection of free technical articles, sign up for a range of free newsletters, and receive exclusive discounts and offers on Packt books and eBooks.

Other Books You May Enjoy

If you enjoyed this book, you may be interested in these other books by Packt:

Blender 3D By Example - Second Edition

Oscar Baechler , Xury Greer

ISBN: 978-1-78961-256-1

- Explore core 3D modeling tools in Blender such as extrude, bevel, and loop cut
- Understand Blender's Outliner hierarchy, collections, and modifiers
- Find solutions to common problems in modeling 3D characters and designs
- Implement lighting and probes to liven up an architectural scene using EEVEE
- Produce a final rendered image complete with lighting and post-processing effects

Sculpting the Blender Way

Xury Greer

ISBN: 978-1-80107-387-5

- Configure your graphics tablet for use in 3D sculpting
- Set up Blender's user interface for sculpting
- Understand the core sculpting workflows
- Get the hang of using Blender's basic sculpting brushes
- Customize brushes for more advanced workflows

Packt is searching for authors like you

If you're interested in becoming an author for Packt, please visit `authors.packtpub.com` and apply today. We have worked with thousands of developers and tech professionals, just like you, to help them share their insight with the global tech community. You can make a general application, apply for a specific hot topic that we
are recruiting an author for, or submit your own idea.

Share Your Thoughts

Now you've finished *Taking Blender to the Next Level*, we'd love to hear your thoughts! Scan the QR code below to go straight to the Amazon review page for this book and share your feedback or leave a review on the site that you purchased it from.

https://www.amazon.in/review/create-review/error?asin=1803233567&

Your review is important to us and the tech community and will help us make sure we're delivering excellent quality content.

CPSIA information can be obtained
at www.ICGtesting.com
Printed in the USA
LVHW061349180623
750101LV00002B/60